Terrence McNally

Collected Plays: Volume II

Mr. McNally is an extraordinary playwright.
His plays are witty, compassionate and always written
with a stunning love of the theatre.

—WENDY WASSERSTEIN

The original American voice in theatre is as rare as any
endangered specie. Here, more resonantly than ever,
is McNally, with all the wit, the imagination,
the blistering insight that have made him one of the truly
irresistible theatrical forces in recent years.
How wonderful to be around while he is writing!

—JACK O'BRIEN

Smith and Kraus *Books For Actors*

CONTEMPORARY PLAYWRIGHTS SERIES

If you require pre-publication information about upcoming Smith and Kraus books, you may receive our semi-annual catalogue, free of charge, by sending your name and address to *Smith and Kraus Catalogue, P.O. Box 127, One Main Street, Lyme, NH 03768. Or call us at (800) 895-4331, fax (603) 795-4427.* **Smith and Kraus** *Books For Actors*

Terrence McNally

Collected Plays: Volume II

Contemporary Playwrights Series

SK
A Smith and Kraus Book

A Smith and Kraus Book
Published by Smith and Kraus, Inc.

Copyright © 1996 by Terrence McNally
All rights reserved

Manufactured in the United States of America
Cover and Text Design by Julia Hill

First Edition: May 1996
10 9 8 7 6 5 4 3 2 1

Library of Congress Cataloguing-in-Publication Data

McNally, Terrence.
Terrence McNally: Collected Plays Volume Two,
Original Uncut Versions / Terrence McNally.
p. cm. --(Contemporary Playwrights Series)
ISBN 1-57525-061-6 (paper) 1-57525-093-4 (cloth)
I. Title. II. Series.
PS3563.A323T47   1996
812'.54--dc20   94--10070
CIP

To John Tillinger, again.

Contents

Biography

Terrence McNally has written two new plays for the 1994-95 New York season. *Love! Valour! Passion!* opened this fall to critical acclaim at the Manhattan Theatre Club, and transferred to the Walter Kerr Theatre in January. His newest play, *Master Class* starring Zoe Caldwell as Maria Callas, premiered at the Philadelphia Theatre Company in March, and will move to the Mark Taper Forum in Los Angeles later this spring. *A Perfect Ganesh* had an extended run at the Manhattan Theatre Club during the spring and summer of 1993 and the film rights were acquired by Merchant Ivory for whom Mr. McNally is writing the screenplay. Other recent plays are *Lips Together, Teeth Apart,* which played to packed houses for over a year at Manhattan Theatre Club and off-Broadway's Lucille Lortel Theatre and has been produced in a record-breaking number of resident professional theatres throughout the country, and *The Lisbon Traviata,* which also had an extended run in New York and a tour in California. His earlier play, *Frankie and Johnny in the Clair de Lune* has also enjoyed great success in New York, followed by productions throughout the United States, foreign countries, and London's West End. Mr. McNally wrote the screen adaptation starring Al Pacino and Michelle Pfeiffer. He also wrote the book for the musical adaptation of Puig's Kiss of the Spiderwoman (score by Kander and Ebb) which, directed by Harold Prince, is currently on Broadway, ran in London's West End, and for which Mr. McNally won the 1993 Tony Award for Best book of a Musical. His previous stage works include: *It's Only a Play* (a revival of which was recently mounted at Los Angeles' Doolittle Theatre); *Bad Habits*; the book for *The Rink* (music and lyrics by Kander and Ebb); *The Ritz*, which he also adapted for the screen; *Where Has Tommy Flowers Gone?*; *And Things That Go Bump In The Night*; *Hope In Faith, Hope In Charity*; *Next*; *Whiskey*; and *Prelude and Leibestod*. He has written a number of scripts for television including *Andre's Mother* for American Playhouse for which he won the 1990 Emmy Award for Best Writing in a Miniseries or Special. During his career, Mr. McNally has received two Guggenheim Fellowships, a Rockefeller Grant, a Lucille Lortel Award, a citation from the American Academy of Arts and Letters, and has won the Hull-Warriner Award for *Bad Habits* in 1974, for *Frankie and Johnny in the Clair de Lune* in 1987 and for *The Lisbon Traviata* in 1989. A member of the Dramatists Guild Council since 1970, Mr. McNally has been vice-president since 1981.

And Things That Go Bump in the Night

For my father and mother

From ghoulies and ghosties
Long leggitie beasties
And things that go bump in the night
Good Lord deliver us!
—*14th Century Scottish Folk Prayer*

AND THINGS THAT GO BUMP IN THE NIGHT by Terrence McNally was performed on February 4, 5, 6, 7, 1964, at the Tyrone Guthrie Theatre, Minneapolis, under the auspices of the Office For Advanced Drama Research. It was directed by Lawrence Kornfeld. Set by Dahl Delu. Costumes by Sally Ross Dinsmore. Lighting by Richard Borgen.

Fa	Alvah Stanley
Grandfa	Ferdi Hoffman
Sigfrid	Robert Drivas
Lakme	Lois Unger
Ruby	Leueen MacGrath
Clarence	Joseph Chaikin

The Broadway production presented by Theodore Mann and Joseph E. Levine in association with Katzka-Berne Productions opened on April 26, 1965, at the Royale Theatre, New York City. It was directed by Michael Cacoyannis. Set by Ed Wittstein. Costumes by Noel Taylor. Lighting by Jules Fisher.

Fa	Clifton James
Grandfa	Ferdi Hoffman
Sigfrid	Robert Drivas
Lakme	Susan Anspach
Ruby	Eileen Heckart
Clarence	Marco St. John

THE CHARACTERS

FA: short, overweight and almost bald. He is in his middle fifties.

RUBY: his wife. Somewhat older but a good deal more youthful looking. She is larger, too.

SIGFRID: their son. Twenty-one years old. Blonde and good-looking.

LAKME: their daughter. Thirteen years old. She is wiry and tough, rather like a rooster.

GRANDFA: very, very old. But the eyes are quick and bright.

CLARENCE: early twenties, thinnish, irregular features.

THE SETTING

The time is present. A living room. Two doors. The one, Stage Left, leads to the bathroom. The other, Stage Right, leads to the various bedrooms. In the rear stage wall there are two openings: an archway with iron stairs leading to the rooms above and a windowed alcove. The tops of the steps are not visible, so that someone coming down the stairs is heard before he is seen. Through the windows of the alcove we see a photographed mural of the nighttime skyline of a large city. Facing this mural are two large chairs. Whoever sits in them is invisible to the audience.

There is an electric spinet piano against the Stage Left wall. Near it is a low table with an intercom system and a tape recorder. The other furnishings in the room—various sofas, chairs, small tables, and so forth—are stark and modern.

The lighting is white: a brilliant, blinding white which is of a uniform intensity throughout the room. There are no shadows or semitones.

ACT ONE

At Rise: The stage is empty. Absolute silence. Pitch dark. After a moment the red light on top of the intercom goes on and we begin to hear the terrible grunting and groaning noises of a person just waking up from a long and deep sleep. The sounds must be amplified to an almost unendurable volume. The theatre should reverberate. The sounds continue. Then, after a yawn of agonizing dimensions, we hear:

RUBY'S VOICE: *(A pronouncement.)* I'm up. *(Another huge yawn.)* Well almost. What time is it? *(A sound of glass breaking.)* …goddamn bottles…*(A long groan.)* Gran dio! Well I'm awake but I may not get out of bed. I might just stay here and read…or something. Mmm, I think I will. *Lakme, carina, il mio cafe …subito, subito…io moro. (A pause; the lights begin to come up—slowly, slowly, slowly.)* Is everyone out there?…the four of you? …my four…my four *what?*…are you? …that's nice…I like it when the four of you are out there… it comforts me…*yes! (A pause.)* The coffee, child. *Presto, pres— (She breaks into a cough, recovers herself, then continues in a more seductive voice.)* Sigfrid, come in here and give Ruby a nice rub on the back… hmm? You can come too, Lakme… when you bring the coffee…only please, *please* don't bounce on the mattress. *(A pause: lights coming up.)* What's it like out tonight, Sigfrid? ...*il fait beau...aupres de ma blonde ou non?* ...hmm?...*la lune*...that crazy old *lune*...what about her?...*(A pause.)*...*beaucoup d'etoiles?*...*(A pause.)*... the big dipper, Lakme! *Is* there a big dipper?...Your mummy's the big dipper! *(Her laughter fades into silence. A pause.)* I don't like this little game you're playing, children. I think we can stop now. I know you're out there. *(A pause; the lights are up to half.)* Grandfa! The chocolate-covered maraschinos you so dote on. You may have one. No, two! For being such a nice Grandfa. They're in the credenza...a blue box... Grandfa?...you're working on your *novel*...aren't you, Grandfa? ...your novel about *us*...your piece of *fiction* ...yes! ...sweet, sweet Grandfa... it's all *lies*, Grandfa, your book is all *lies. (A pause.)* I'm not amused by this. I warn you...all of you...there will be retributions. I said I am *not* amused...Answer! *(A pause; lights coming up.)* Ciao, Fa, *Ciao! Come stai?* That's Italian for "Hi, Fa, hi! How are you?"...Well? ...I had a dream, Fa. Yes! And guess who I dreamed of? Us. Really! We were ice-skating and the ice was pink...a beautiful, beautiful pink. And you kept falling down...oh, I laughed!...your pills, Fa...after every meal, he said...you didn't forget to take them, did you?...Fa?...*(A pause.)* So don't take them! Have your goddamn little heart attack! Fall on the floor dead! Go ahead! Die! Die laughing!...the four of you...you think it's so funny! Well I do, too!...miserable little...I know you're out there. So you can just stop pretending you're not. This doesn't frighten—If I ever thought you'd really left me alone in this terrible house I'd...I don't know what I'd do. Kill myself. I suppose you'd like that! *(A final pause; the lights are at full brilliance now; and then the terrified outburst.)* I WON'T BE ALONE IN THIS HOUSE!... SOMEONE...SOMEONE, COME IN HERE!! *(Footsteps are heard coming down the iron stairs.)* Who's that?... on the stair...who?...CHILDREN! ...make them behave, Fa. Make them tell me who it is...FA! *(Fa appears on the stairs. We see only the top of his head, as he holds the paper he is reading in front of his nose. He continues down into the room.)* WHO'S OUT THERE! ...PLEASE! ...SOMEONE! ...TELL ME! ...WHO? ...WHO? *(Without looking up from his newspaper, Fa has switched off the intercom. The room returns to an utter stillness. Fa goes to his chair in the alcove, the one with its back to the audience, and sits. Not once have we seen his face.)*

FA: *(After reading in silence for several beats.)* Tech, tech, tech! *(A pause.)* Mmm! *(A pause; he burps. Another pause; he sighs heavily. The silence again. Then a great banging sound from the top of the stairs. It is Grandfa's wheelchair bouncing down the stairs. It lands with a thud at the bottom. Fa does not look around; his nose remains buried in the paper.)* Now just hold your horses, Grandfa. I'll be done in a minute. *(He continues reading.)*...mmm...did you see this? Fifteen thousand dead in... Nitanganyabba?...wherever the hell that is. We tried to move those Africans out of those grass huts...told them to go underground...but do you think they'd listen to Uncle Sam? Not on your life! Fifteen thousand of 'em ...just like that! *(More footsteps are heard at the top of the stairs.)* And another twelve in New Delhi. At least we know where *that* is. Always had a stable government...those Indians. Seems some riot got started during a protest march...communist agitators, the papers says, and I don't doubt it...students probably...young people!...all twelve thousand trampled each other to death. You know, you should take more of an interest in world affairs, Grandfa. It's fascinating what goes on these days. *(Grandfa, surly and scowling, is seen on the stairs.)* They'll probably throw all the bodies in that holy river they got over there...what's its name ...the Grange!...and just let 'em float out to sea. Hell, it's cheaper than digging all those holes, isn't it? And you can't be much more underdeveloped than those Indians already are, can you now?

GRANDFA: *(Plopping himself down in the wheelchair.)* I found 'em. And guess where the little monster put 'em? Guess!

FA: *(Always reading.)*...mmm...this is interesting...

GRANDFA: The cookie jar!

FA: The government says it's moving west.

GRANDFA: *(Poking around in a large cloth bag he carries with him.)* The cookie jar, mind you! Not in the freezer again...not like last time...oh no, not her...but the cookie jar!

FA: Listen to this. "A definite westerly movement in its—"...and then inside a little parenthesis it says "the Dread, *sic*," The Dread! That's a good one for it...the Dread!...let's see now...ah, yes... " 'westerly movement in its motion is clearly discernible,' a high-ranking government spokesman who declined to reveal his identity told Washington reporters today, 'Alas,' the anonymous spokesman added."

GRANDFA: *(Who has produced a long strip of black knitting from inside the bag.)* My teeth in a goddamn cookie jar!

FA: Alas, he added! How do you like that?...So it's headed west, is it?

GRANDFA: *(Knitting furiously.)* Oh, am I ever glad this is my last night in this house. You don't *know* how glad I am.

FA: They've outlawed female circumcision in the Gabon Republic ...too risky.

GRANDFA: No one knows how glad I am!

FA: They uncovered a nest of nudists right outside of Bloomington...it was integrated.

GRANDFA: *I* don't even know how glad I am.

FA: The new Miss Universe is a Labrador girl...she edged out Miss Nigeria...it says Miss Nigeria put up quite a stink...that was ungracious of her...*(After a pause.)*...which way *is* west?

GRANDFA: We are.

FA: Are you sure?

GRANDFA: We *are* the west, much good that ever did us.

FA: *(Flat.)* Oh.

GRANDFA: *(He can't get over it.)* Eighty-five dollar teeth in a goddamn cookie jar! *(An appeal to someone.)* Gods!

FA: *(Folding the paper, handing it to Grandfa.)* Well, at least the Chinese have forged ahead in the Olympics. That's some consolation. *(He lights a cigar; great clouds of smoke rise over the chair.)*

GRANDFA: If that were my child...my *children*, I should say...the two of 'em...I'd...*(A growl.)*...ooh!

FA: *(Pondering.)* ...moving west, hunh?

GRANDFA: I wouldn't let that bother me. Not with this contraption. *(He indicates the room with a wave of his hand.)* Not with that fence out there. How many million volts is it?

FA: *(Speaking over a huge yawn.)* Three thousand, Grandfa, only three thousand. What time are they coming for you?

GRANDFA: Early. As soon the streets are open. This infernal curfew...I could've gone tonight.

FA: *(With another yawn.)* We'll miss you.

GRANDFA: I won't. Should've done this years ago. Only I thought *you* had to commit *me*. Didn't know I could do it myself. *(Slight pause.)* Well maybe you...a little bit...miss, I mean. Blood's blood. *(He looks up from his knitting.)* Dozing off on me, hunh?

FA: Just a little snooze, Grandfa. A little after-dinner snooze.

GRANDFA: Don't tell me about your little snoozes. Last all night. Days sometimes...weeks!...months! Don't see what dinner's got to do with it. Seems to me you're *always* snoozing. Certainly don't expect you up when I go in the morning...probably the last time we'll see each other for a while then...maybe never...guess this is good-bye...I don't suppose you want to kiss me. *(The first snore from Fa.)* SON!

FA: *(Immediately responding, but groggy.)* I'm listening, Grandfa.

GRANDFA: I said...*(An old gentleman's embarrassment.)* I said I didn't expect you wanted to kiss me.

FA: Now Grandfa!

GRANDFA: I didn't think so. *(A slight pause.)* It's been done before, you know.

FA: *(Sleep overtaking him again.)* Yes, Grandfa.

GRANDFA: It's a sign of affection...a kiss is. And stop calling me that! That's *their* name for me.

FA: *(Even sleepier.)* We'll drive up every Sunday that it's nice.

GRANDFA: Well don't!

FA: ...every Sunday...just like Ruby said...

GRANDFA: You won't find me!

FA: ...every Sunday that it's nice...

GRANDFA: I'll hide! I'll hide in a thicket!

FA: *(Going fast now.)* ...we'll find you...

GRANDFA: You think...you think!

FA: *(Lapsing into sleep.)* ...we'll find you...Grandfa...oh yes!...we'll...

(The snoring begins: an even, rhythmic drone. Grandfa sits a moment. He is sad. Then he goes slowly over to Fa and puts his hand on Fa's shoulder. He looks at Fa. He does not move. There is a stillness. Then:)

GRANDFA: *(A gentle moan, a benediction, a forgiveness.)* Oh. *(Now he moves away from Fa. He clears his eyes with his fist...for there has been a tear or two. His eyes chance to fall on the paper in his lap. He reads a moment, almost against his will, then throws the paper from him with a little cry. He looks back once at Fa and then, with a sudden shudder.)* Oh these are terrible times to be old in!

(More noise at the top of the stairs. Voices, footsteps, and then Sigfrid bounds into the room. He wears a heavy-knit navy blue sweater with a large white "Y" on the front. He carries a football.)

SIGFRID: *(Acting out the following with great enthusiasm.)* "Fifteen seconds to go and listen to that crowd roar!...will they do it?...there's the snap!...and it's Sigfrid...the all-American Sigfrid fading back ...he spots his receiver ...the fabulous Grandfa's in the clear...it's going to be a long throw, fans!...WILL HE DO IT??"

(Sigfrid throws the ball across the room. It hits Grandfa in the stomach with a thud. Sigfrid assumes an attitude of immense disappointment.)

Aaaaw. We could've had 'em, Grandfa. Some school try that was. Where's your oomph? You all out of oomph?

(Grandfa charges wildly at him with his chair.)

SIGFRID: *(Easily eludes him.)* Atta boy! That's the spirit.

GRANDFA: *(More sad than angry.)* If I had a gun...

SIGFRID: ...you'd shoot yourself! Okay, I'm sorry. Peace?

(No real truce is established. Grandfa only moves away. Lakme is heard at the top of the stairs. Her entrance is announced by the sound of a small child bawling her head off.)

Enter one crocodile...tearful.

(Lakme appears: her face a study in childish misery. She sobs, howls and in general carries on like there is no tomorrow. It is almost convincing. Her dress is tomboyish and appropriate for a thirteen-year-old. She might wear her hair in pigtails. She carries an array of photographic equipment: cameras, cases, and so forth. Lakme is howling like a banshee, yet perfectly capable of stopping should it be to her advantage.)

SIGFRID: *(With mock cheerfulness.)* Hello there, little one! What seems to be the trouble? You pick another fight with that German shepherd down the road? *(Lakme increases her howling.)*

Poor little Lakme. All forsook and chewed on. Comfort her, Grandfa.

LAKME: *(In heaving breaths between sobs.)* Gran...Grandfa!...Grandfa, Sigfrid tackled me!...hard!

SIGFRID: *(Mocking.)* Not true, not true.

LAKME: He *did!* Look! *(She hunts for and finds a tiny cut on her knee.)* See?...see? *(Grandfa snaps his teeth at her—three times. Lakme uses her normal voice; it is an ugly one.)*

Where did you find those?...hunh? Sigfrid, did you—?

SIGFRID: *(Absolving himself with a gesture and then pointing to her injured knee.)* That was quite a recovery...even for you.

LAKME: *(Tough.)* Oh yeah? *(She begins howling again...though not quite so effectively as before...and limps her way over to Fa. Again the congested voice.)* Fa!...Sigfrid...Wake *up!*

FA: *(A moment of groggy consciousness.)* ...moving west, hunh?... *(He is asleep again.)*

LAKME: *(Furiously shaking him.)* How are you going to have that heart attack if you sleep all the time?...Hunh?...LIAR!!

(Sigfrid has been enjoying this enormously. He bursts into laughter now; a full, open laugh. Lakme turns on him.) Well it *hurt!*

SIGFRID: *(Explaining to Grandfa.)* It was nearly an hour ago. She said "ouch"...that's all. And not one whimper all the way home. Then the moment we walk through the door upstairs...this!

LAKME: *(The anger dissipated into a general sulkiness.)* Well you certainly don't expect me to waste my tears on *you!* A lot you care...stinky! *(She sits and examines the cut on her knee.)*

SIGFRID: *(So patiently.)* Grandfa, you haven't turned your hearing aid off again, have you? *(He checks the mechanism in Grandfa's vest pocket.)* Unh-hunh! We be a naughty Grandfa. *(Then, while fiddling with the mechanism, with a trace of baby talk:)* We put this wire here...and that wire there...and we jiggle this little knobby-poo ...and now we all well again ...yes! ...now we can *hear* ...goodie!...now we can hear Sigfrid tell us not to do those bad-type things anymore...cause Ruby frets when we do our little no-goods...cause Sigfrid frets...and Lakme...cause *everybody* frets when Grandfa does his no-goods. *(He puts the hearing aid mechanism back in Grandfa's pocket.)* And now we be a nice Grandfa... now we be an obedient Grandfa...now we be a quiet Grandfa. And we sit in our nice little corners...*(Indeed, he has maneuvered Grandfa and his chair to a tight little corner, Stage Right.)*...and we knit quietly away at our nice little...*(He holds up Grandfa's knitting a moment.)*... shrouds?...and we write our nice little *novels...*

GRANDFA: *Chronicle!*

SIGFRID: …and no one even knows we're alive. Yes!

GRANDFA: *(Steely-eyed; making it a noun.)* Abominable!

SIGFRID: *(Not at all unpleasantly.)* Oh you foul-mouthed old Shakespearean you! Shame on you. Not even a decent iambic. *(Coming back over to Lakme.)* How now, scab?

LAKME: There *will* be one! And I have a dance recital coming up next week…two solos! It'll look terrible.

SIGFRID: Then you'd better tippy-tap-toe your way into Ruby's bedroom and let her kiss it. *That*'ll make it go away.

LAKME: *(Flaring.)* I don't tap dance! We do modern…acrobatic modern.

SIGFRID: All right, then acrobat-modern your way in there…*slither.*

LAKME: *(Rolling down her pants leg.)* You're such a cheat, Sigfrid. You say we're going to play touch football and then as soon as I get the ball you change it to tackle.

SIGFRID: And what about that stiff-arm? You practically gouged my eye out.

LAKME: That was different. That was a tactic. *(The little lady bit now.)* Besides, if I were a twenty-one-year-old…boy? hah!…

SIGFRID: *(He means this.)* Watch it, Baby Snooks!

LAKME: *(Continuing.)* …I'd certainly be embarrassed to be seen playing football in a public park with a thirteen-year-old child.

SIGFRID: Oh you would?

LAKME: Yes! And when the thirteen-year-old child just happens to be a thirteen-year-old *girl!*…

SIGFRID: A *what?*

LAKME: …his own little *sister,* in fact…well, that's just about the worst thing I ever heard of. And then hurling her to the turf like that…a vicious *tackle!*

SIGFRID: *(Suddenly on the defensive for the first time.)* Now look, you little dwarf, you *tripped.*

LAKME: *(Amazed that he could have taken her seriously.)* I know that, stupid. Of course I did. Honestly, Sigfrid, you can be so *dense* sometimes. You know what a little liar I am.
(Sigfrid sulks.)
Wow! Aren't you getting touchy all of a sudden.

SIGFRID: *(Still put off.)* What time is it?

LAKME: *(Shrugging.)* Probably time to wake her. Gee, Sigfrid, I was only kidding. You've got about as much of a sense of humor as that thing in the park…what's-his-name. What a puss on that one! A lousy catch, too.

SIGFRID: *(He has turned on the intercom and now speaks into it.)* Ruby?… Wake-up time. *(Then to Lakme.)* There's some jokes I don't like.

LAKME: *(With great affection.)* You're such a dope. *(She gets up to join him at the intercom and makes a final reference to her injured knee.)* I don't mind getting 'em here so much…I mean the principle behind the thing…it's just the *ploys* you use. This really hurts. *(She joins him at the intercom and puts one arm affectionately around his waist.)*

SIGFRID: *(Again into the intercom.)* Hey Ruby!…wake-up time! *(Then to Lakme.)* I can't help it. It's just my nature. I'm very…

LAKME: *(Anticipating him, so that they say the word together.)*…ployful! *(They laugh and jostle each other like the very best of friends…which, of course, they very often are.)*

RUBY'S VOICE: *(On the intercom; it is very small, very frightened.)* Sigfrid?…is it you, Sigfrid?

SIGFRID: No, Karl Marx and Trotsky! Who do you think?

LAKME: Batman and Robin!

RUBY'S VOICE: *(With some relief.)* Lakme!

SIGFRID: *(The little game over.)* Come on, Ruby, hustle it.

LAKME: Get up to "get up." Wait'll you see him, Ruby! The *game.*

RUBY'S VOICE: *(Firm now, the rage mounting.)* You miserable little…vipers!… pythons!…*asps!*

SIGFRID: *(Himself annoyed now.)* Hey, now can it, snake-woman, and just get up! Christ! You ask us to wake you and then—

RUBY'S VOICE: *(Hell hath no fury.)* I *AM* UP!—you bastards!—you utter, utter bastards!—you think you're pretty *funny,* don't you?—
(Sigfrid and Lakme have been exchanging perplexed glances since the outburst.)

SIGFRID: Ruby!

RUBY'S VOICE: …had our little kicks for the evening, didn't we? …hunh?…we showed *her* what kinds of games we can play…we had ourselves one big fat *laugh!* HAH!

SIGFRID: *(Who has been trying to get a word in.)* Ruby, what—?

RUBY'S VOICE: *(Colder now, more under control.)* If you ever do that again I will take you upstairs and push you off the roof…the four of you!

LAKME: Do what? She's flipped, Sigfrid. She's finally flipped.

RUBY'S VOICE: *(Exploding again.)* HOW *DARE* YOU PRETEND YOU'RE NOT OUT THERE!…HOW *DARE* YOU!!

SIGFRID: We didn't. I mean we weren't.

RUBY'S VOICE: *(Much, much calmer.)* …such bastardy…such unspeakable bastardy…*(A final groan of rage and despair.)* Ooooh!

LAKME: She must have had one of her dreams again. Were you down here, Grandfa? *(Grandfa, as usual, only glowers and goes on knitting.)*

SIGFRID: *(With his oh-so-weary, patient tone.)* I'll be right in there, Ruby.

RUBY'S VOICE: Don't. Besides, the door's locked…*and* bolted.

SIGFRID: Then will you just calm down and let me explain?

RUBY'S VOICE: Scorpion!

SIGFRID: Are you?…are you calm now?

RUBY'S VOICE: *(In complete control now; imperial tones; relishing every moment of the exchange. After all, she is being made up to.)* Considerably…and don't patronize.

SIGFRID: All right, now tell me what happened. Was it one of your dreams again?

RUBY'S VOICE: *(A deliberate sulk.)* No.

SIGFRID: You're sure…you're sure it wasn't one of your nightmares?

RUBY'S VOICE: *(Peevish.)* Yes I'm sure! and the word's *cauchemar.*

SIGFRID: Then you must—

RUBY'S VOICE: *(Regal.)* Say it!

SIGFRID: *(Anything to accommodate.)* Cauchemar.

RUBY'S VOICE: *(Wincing at the pronunciation.)* Mon *dieu!* Lakme!

LAKME: *(With great care and love for every syllable.)* Cauchemar.

RUBY'S VOICE: *(After a slight pause for consideration.)* Bravo! Is Sigfrid blushing? I should hope so.

LAKME: *(So in love with herself.)* Cauchemar.

SIGFRID: *(His turn to explode now.)* Damn it, Ruby! If you're not interested in this—!

RUBY'S VOICE: *(Curt.)* I am *extremely* interested.

LAKME: *(Delirious.)* Cauche— *(Sigfrid slugs her.)*

RUBY'S VOICE: *(After a slight pause.)* What happened?

LAKME: *(Not in a whine.)* Sigfrid hit me.

RUBY'S VOICE: *(Matter-of-fact.)* Hit him back.

(Lakme does so. Sigfrid doesn't respond. They are used to this ritual.)

LAKME: I did.

RUBY'S VOICE: *(Continuing where she left off.)* I am extremely interested as to why…*why* with all the care, love and protection I have lavished on you…*why* with all the lovely and nice things I have given you…this house, to mention only one…*why* with your fabulous good looks, your locks so fine and golden, your firm, trim *beautiful* body…which I always encouraged you to nurture…*why* with so *much*…with so *many* goodies in your little hopper…*why* *(With an abrupt change of tone.)*…you turned out to be such a miserable son of a bitch. *(Short pause.)*

GRANDFA: *(To his private world-at-large.)* I could answer that. *(But he doesn't.)*

SIGFRID: *(He's had it.)* Christ!

LAKME: *(Virtue triumphant.)* That puts your little light under a basket!

RUBY'S VOICE: *(Gently remonstrating.)* Bushel, dear, *bushel!*

LAKME: *(Discovering a delightful new word.)* Bushel-basket! *(Then making it an expletive to hurl at Sigfrid.)* Bushel-basket!

RUBY'S VOICE: *(Stopping Lakme cold.)* And that goes for you, too! *(Pause.)* You're *both* sons of bitches. *(Pause.)* You're all *four* sons of bitches. Can you imagine what those fifteen minutes were like for me? Can you possibly conceive the *terror* of them? Of thinking you're alone in this fearful, hideous house?

Utterly, completely *alone?* And then hearing footsteps…on the stairs…and no answer…no answer at all? Can your pea-sized little hearts even *begin* to understand what an experience like that does to a person? …Can they? *(Pause.)* I *quivered!*…yes!…for fifteen minutes…I quivered like a fern!…not knowing *who* was out there…*what* was out there…it could have been *anything!* Fifteen minutes of unspeakable terror!…and you people…you smug, hurtful, hateful *monsters!*…making me think that I was alone…that it had finally *happened* even! Yes! I was that terrified…pretending you weren't there when I most needed you. Oh you must be very pleased with yourselves. *(Her emotions are spent; the recall of the terror has been a complete one; she is silent now.)*

SIGFRID: *(With a sad sigh.)* Ruby, Ruby, Ruby. You *will* jump to conclusions, won't you? and scare yourself half to death. If it's happened once, it's happened a hundred times. *(His tones is extremely gentle, as if he were talking to a child.)* What *really* happened?…you called and no one answered?

RUBY'S VOICE: *(A little girl nursing her wounds.)* Yes.

SIGFRID: So you *assumed* we were trying to frighten you? By pretending not to be here?

RUBY'S VOICE: You might have been.

SIGFRID: Oh, *Ruby!*

RUBY'S VOICE: We all play tricks on each other…don't we?

LAKME: But not like *that.* Never tricks like *that.*

SIGFRID: Did you really think we'd go that far? That we'd make *jokes* about it?

RUBY'S VOICE: *(A plea for understanding.)* I get so frightened when I'm alone…

SIGFRID: *(Cutting in.)* But you weren't *alone!* *(A pause.)*

RUBY'S VOICE: *(A trifle disappointed.)* I wasn't?

SIGFRID: No! You woke up early, that's all. No one had come down yet.

LAKME: Sigfrid and I were here in plenty of time for wake-up. We all were.

SIGFRID: If you were upstairs maybe there'd be some *reason*…well *no,* not even then. Christ, Ruby, it's a good thirty minutes 'til curfew.

LAKME: Sigfrid and I were on the *streets* up until ten minutes ago, and we're not all gone to pieces. *(A pause; no response from Ruby.)*

SIGFRID: Ruby…?

RUBY'S VOICE: The four of you are out there, you said. What about Grandfa? I don't hear Grandfa. Is he working on his novel?

SIGFRID: He's knitting.

LAKME: Say something to her, Grandfa.

GRANDFA: *(Obligingly, loud and clear.)* Harpy! And stop calling it that! It's a *chronicle.* I'm writing a *chronicle!*

RUBY'S VOICE: *(More cheerful by the moment; sing-song.)* Hello, Grandfa! It's a piece of fiction, Grandfa. You're writing a novel, Grandfa. And Fa! How's Fa? Is he…?

LAKME: No. Just sleeping.

RUBY'S VOICE: I wasn't going to say that.

LAKME: Well he might just as well be.

SIGFRID: Ruby!

RUBY'S VOICE: I'm coming! Did you find someone?

SIGFRID: (Weary, patient; but getting her out of there.) Yes, Ruby.

RUBY'S VOICE: Male or female? and *do* say male.

LAKME: (Sibilating.) Oh, yes! *Very* male. Very *definitely* male.

RUBY'S VOICE: Oh. It's going to be one of *those* nights.

SIGFRID: (Endless patience.) That's right, Ruby. One of *those* nights.

RUBY'S VOICE: I don't approve, of course, but *la vie n'est pas en rose.*

LAKME: We had a little trouble with him. He kept thinking better of it.

RUBY'S VOICE: But he's *coming*, Sigfrid? You're *sure* of it?

SIGFRID: Yes, Ruby, he'll be here.

LAKME: He'd *better* be. Can you imagine it alone down here? Just the four of us? Yikes!

RUBY'S VOICE: Oh it's going to be a lovely, lovely evening! I can feel it in my… what, Sigfrid?

SIGFRID: (Still playing along with her.) Fangs, Ruby, you can feel it in your fangs.

RUBY'S VOICE: Yes! Yes, I do.

SIGFRID: (Finally impatient, but not unpleasant.) It *might* be if you'd just get out here.

RUBY'S VOICE: (In a tiny dither now.) I'll *be* there!…don't fuss at me…I'm struggling with this damn peignoir…all these pearl buttons. If you're so impatient turn on the recorder. I taped another Message to the World this morning…probably my last…it's rather a summation.

LAKME: (Rushing to the tape recorder: paroxysms of joy.) Another Message to the World, Ruby?

RUBY'S VOICE: I'd call it definitive…the very last word. See what you think. *I* certainly can't imagine anything else to say on the matter. It's a closed book now, as far as I'm concerned.

SIGFRID: (Good naturedly; joining Lakme by the tape recorder.) You're such a pope, Ruby. You and your encyclicals. What's this one called?

RUBY'S VOICE: (So grand.) The Way We Live!

(The red light on the intercom goes off, as Lakme sets the tape reels to spinning.)

RUBY'S RECORDED VOICE: (A private voice, such as one uses when alone; yet with a full range of color and nuance.) The Way We Live. Message to the World number 812.

(Short pause; Sigfrid and Lakme have settled themselves on the floor.)

The Way We Live…and perhaps this is regrettable…it would seem is open to some question. *(Short pause.) Some* question. Open to question, that is, if certain nameless people were to have their say…to *protest*, as it were.

(Sigfrid and Lakme glare suspiciously at Grandfa, who glares right back at them.)

And by that I mean *you*…yes, *you!*

(Now Sigfrid and Lakme glare at each other with suspicion.)

A fuller explication then has been demanded and shall be given. *Explication,* my unseen accusers, and I know you, not exculpation. *(Short pause.)* The way we live is compounded of *love*…love which neither nurtures the receiver nor lays fallow the sender but will suffice for each…of *hate*…and more of it than we can often cope with…yes!…and of a numbing, *crushing* indifference…an indifference which kills… slowly, finally, *totally!* and for which our cruelty (and pain now is our only reminder that we yet live)…for which the cruelty we do unto each other is but a temporary antidote…*(Short pause: then in a frightened timid, funny little voice.) C'est triste…n'est-ce pas?* (Another *short pause and a change of tone.)* God…gods…some*one*…some*thing*…what*ever:* things done or not done and then called good or bad; the price of eggs even!…these *things* men speak of, attain to, do battle for…the way we live does not involve us with them. They are the concerns…no, *were!…were* the concerns of peoples, nations…yea individuals…who thought they were to prevail. We shall *not* prevail…so be it. We shall *not* endure…but who was ever meant to? And we shall *not* inherit the earth…it has already disinherited us.

(Ruby enters the room through the door Stage Right. Sigfrid and Lakme turn and are about to greet her when she motions them with her hand to keep silence. She goes toward them and, with one hand on each of their heads, she joins them as they listen.)

The way we live is a result…a response…an *oblivion* to ourselves, each other…and what is out there. If we are without faith, we find our way in the darkness…it is light enough. If we are without hope, we turn to our despair…it has its own consolations. And if we are without charity, we suckle the bitter root of its absence…wherefrom we shall draw the sustenance to destroy you. *(And this is the saddest part.)* Go…seek not to know us…to understand…the compassion of it will exhaust you and there is so little strength left us now…so little. *(Short pause; then, very quickly, in an everyday tone.)* Spoken by me this December morning. Unwitnessed, unheard, alone.

(A word now about Ruby's appearance. It is a spectacular disappointment. Oh, the peignoir she wears is fancy enough and there are many rings on her fingers and expensive slippers on her feet. But Ruby herself will disappoint you. Her face is without make-up and seems almost anonymous. The intense lighting in the room, you see, washes the "character" out of her face, so that it is impossible to tell

very much about her except that she is no longer young. As for her hair, well she might as well be bald, for she wears one of those large elastic cloth bands women use to pull the hair back from their face before applying make-up. The appearance of her entire face, in fact, is best suggested by this word bald. *Or* plucked clean. *Or* erased. *The gaudy rings only draw attention to the unvarnished fingernails, some of which are bitten to the quick. And the few toes which peep out through an opening in front of the slippers are not especially clean. So this, for the time being, is Ruby. Immediately after the conclusion of Ruby's long speech on the tape recorder, there is a good moment of silence. Then:)*

FA: *(Waking momentarily.)* Good-bye, Grandfa…Come and kiss me, Grandfa.

GRANDFA: *(Fa's had his chance.)* I'm knitting.

FA: …poor Miss Nigeria…

GRANDFA: Knitting and listening to this harridan spout balderdash. You never hear such— *(But Fa is already asleep again.)* Balderdash, Ruby!…pure balderdash! *(Neither Ruby, Lakme nor Sigfrid have moved since the conclusion of the tape. Now Ruby, making something of a moment of it, switches off the machine.)*

RUBY: *(Chanting almost.)* Ecco la testimonia d'una traviata…una testimonia nera.

LAKME: *(Flopping over backwards on the floor; quite overcome by, though not really understanding, all she has just heard.)* Nero? nerissimo!…wow!
(Sigfrid has remained silent and brooding to one side.)

GRANDFA: *(Continuing to grouse away in his corner.)* Message to the World, she calls it. That's no message…it's garbage, *that's* what it is…*pig* food!

LAKME: *(Trying to reconstruct a certain phrase.)* "And if we are without faith…we shall suckle…?"…is that right, Ruby?…"suckle"…?

GRANDFA: Yes, that's right. *Suckle!* Suckle your way like pigs!

LAKME: "…suckle our bitter root in the darkness…?"

RUBY: *(Completing it.)* …it has its own absence."

LAKME: Absence?

RUBY: *(Getting it right now, a little irritable.)* Consolations. It has its own *consolations.*

LAKME: Which has? Our bitter root or our darkness?

RUBY: Well *something* like that! How should I know?

LAKME: You *said* it!

RUBY: That was this morning…hours ago…*centuries.*

LAKME: *(A little mollified.)* That part about destroying you. That's the part I liked best.

RUBY: You would. *(Then, pressing her hands to her temples.)* Suddenly I have a headache. Ruby's evening vapors.

LAKME: *(They all love these little word games.)* You mean vespers. Ruby's evening *vespers.*

GRANDFA: *(He does, too.)* No, *vipers!* She means *vipers!* Evening *vipers!* The three of them.

RUBY: I mean *vapors!* *(Sinking into one of the armchairs.)* Prestos, cara, presto.

LAKME: Wait'll you see this fink we got coming over here tonight! One of those demonstrators!

RUBY: *Va! Fuggi!*

LAKME: *(Running on.)* Finks! They're all finks. They're not going to change anything. Not with signs!

RUBY: *Fuggi*, damn it, *fuggi!*

LAKME: *(Stopped cold.)* Fuggi?

RUBY: From *fuggire:* to make haste...to pick up our little feet and vanish...to *scram!*

LAKME: *(Still puzzling.)* Fuggi—? *(Now she's got it.)* Oh.

RUBY: Yeah, *oh!* Piccola nitwit.

LAKME: *(Nice and prissy.)* I'm sorry, Ruby, but we can't *all* of us be such opera queens. I mean some of us are *normal.* Some of us speak *English* when we want something. Some of us—

RUBY: *(Stern, but a little amused in spite of it.)* Will you get in there and get that coffee?

LAKME: *(On her way out, but wanting to prolong it, so she sings.)* "Mi chiamano Lakme, ma il perche, non so."

RUBY: *(Very strong.)* Va!

LAKME: *(In a charming little voice.)* Vo. *(She fairly twinkles through the door, Stage Right, and is gone.)*

RUBY: *(After thinking it over a moment.)* I am *not* an opera queen. Sigfrid, you don't think I'm an opera queen, do you?

(Sigfrid turns away from her.)

God knows I'm *some* sort of queen, but not *that. (Then, feeling a little chill.)* Where's that draft coming from? Sigfrid, you didn't leave the door open? *(She turns to him, really turns to him for the first time since her entrance, and immediately bursts into a wild gale of laughter.)* Sigfrid!...look at you!...that outfit!...that *costume!*...I *never!*...Where on *earth!*...You're *outlandish* in that sweater! *(Then, singing hilariously.)* "Boola boola, boola boola, bool—"

(Sigfrid, furious, hurls a cushion to the floor, then moves away to another part of the room. Ruby pauses, then mockingly.)

Oh, a little more than kin and less than kind, are we this evening, I see.

GRANDFA: *(Moving forward, ready to do battle.)* Leave Shakespeare out of this! Abuse the language in your own words, woman...and my God how you abuse it!...but not in his...not in Shakespeare's.

RUBY: *(Acknowledging this.)* Grandfa! Sweetest old thing on two wheels! How old! Will you never tell us! Two hundred?...three hundred?...four?

GRANDFA: It's criminal how you abuse the gift of speech, woman, *criminal!*

RUBY: *(Effusive.)* Each day could be...*should* be...your very last...but it never is. Keeping us in such suspense! Sly, sly Grandfa.

GRANDFA: *(Determined to be heard.)* CREATURES LIKE YOU SHOULD HAVE THE VERY *TONGUES* CUT OUT OF THEIR HEADS!

RUBY: *(Stopping her ears.)* Grandfa! Don't shout at us like that. We're not the deaf ones; *you* are.

GRANDFA: Well you *should.* Right out of your heads with a big rusty knife.

RUBY: *(Saccharine.)* Yes, dear. We all heard you. Grandfa thinks I abuse the gift of speech, Sigfrid. He thinks I should have the very tongue cut out of my head with a big rusty knife. He thinks I'm a creature.

GRANDFA: *(Rumbling on.)* Message to the World! I never *heard* such contamination.

RUBY: We can't *all* be your beloved Shakespeare, Grandfa.

GRANDFA: I'll say!

RUBY: *(A little less playful here.)* I meant it when I said it.

GRANDFA: So did he!

RUBY: Forsooth!

GRANDFA: And it didn't come out garbage! It was poetry. It *sang!*

RUBY: With a hey-nonny-nonny and a ho!

GRANDFA: Shakespeare *respected* words! And you know why? Because Shakespeare respected *people!*...human beings...*men!* But *you*...this family!...

RUBY: How you prate, uncle, how you will prate!

GRANDFA: Message to the World! It would've turned my stomach if that meal I had to cook for myself hadn't already turned it.

RUBY: And how nice for you that it was your last one.

GRANDFA: Last what? Meal? You're damn right it was...nice for me.

RUBY: And *won't* you be happy up there on that little farm? All you old retired actors...all you old Shakespeareans...lolling around all day...in wheelchairs...being *pushed!*...just lolling around and mewling sonnets at each other all day long? Mewling sonnets over social tea biscuits and a drop of sherry? Won't that be *fun?* And doing real live theatricals for the Sunday visitors? Grandfa as Lear! Grandfa as Macbeth! Grandfa as *Lady* Macbeth! Well why not? They did it in *his* time. They did it in *god's* time. And won't *that* be fun! Grandfa in a skirt with candle...enter deranged...*uno sonnambulo!*... and tears the house down. Oh, you'll be *very* happy up on that farm. I just *know* you will.

GRANDFA: *(A little sad now, his prospects are none too cheerful, but with a simple dignity.)* I have friends up there...*some*...old thespians like myself...there's a few of us still left...they say the food's not too bad...the care...I'll...*manage.*
(A pause. Ruby, restless as ever, moves away from Grandfa, who remains Center Stage, brooding. Silence.)

FA: *(Muttering in his sleep.)* Moving west, hunh?...so it's moving west?...

RUBY: *(With a somewhat forced gaiety.)* *What* is? What's moving west? What is Fa mumbling about? *(No one answers. Long silence. A tension is building.)* It can get so *silent* down here!…so *dead!* I ask you: Are we the only people in the world or are we not? Hmm? Sometimes I think we are. I really do. *(Another pause. More silence. More tension.)* When is this person coming, Sigfrid? Not soon?…not *now?* I mean just look at us. We haven't even begun to get ready…any of us!

(He does not answer; pause, silence, tension.)

Sulky boy. *(The silence is deafening.)* Lakme! *(Short pause.)* If somebody doesn't say something, if somebody doesn't say something soon…

(Suddenly she stops short. What has happened is that Grandfa has made a funny sound. It might have been merely a sigh. But then again, it may have been the signal for a seizure. Anyway, Grandfa has not moved since he last spoke. He makes the funny sound again. Ruby rushes to his side. Her voice and movement now indicate apprehension, yes, but also a certain amount of relief. After all, her energies are engaged.)

Grandfa!…What's the matter, Grandfa!

(Grandfa doesn't respond.)

It's Grandfa, Sigfrid, it's Grand—!

GRANDFA: *(Cutting her off, suddenly alert.)* What are you howling about, woman?

RUBY: Oh!

GRANDFA: What are you howling about now?

RUBY: I thought you were—

GRANDFA: *(Warding off her attentions.)* Keep your distance! Don't need you fiddling at me. Thought I was—*I* know! Didn't you? Well I *wasn't!*

RUBY: *(A little icy now.)* I *thought* you were. It alarmed me.

GRANDFA: *Hoped!* you mean, don't you? Hoped!

RUBY: All right, Grandfa, all right.

GRANDFA: You want to know what I *was* doing?

RUBY: Not especially.

GRANDFA: I was *thinking!*

RUBY: How nice for you, Grandfa, how very nice for you. Grandfa was only *thinking,* Sigfrid!

GRANDFA: That's right, *thinking!*

RUBY: I *said* how very nice for you.

GRANDFA: Thinking it over. *Everything!*…you…me…us…*everything! That* ought to put the fear of God in you, woman, not that you ever believed in Him!

RUBY: *(A little sorry she got into this.)* You just put everything you're thinking about in that little book you're writing, Grandfa. Scribble it in your little novel.

GRANDFA: *(She has touched a sore point.)* Chronicle! It's not a novel. It's a *chronicle.*

RUBY: Chronicles record the *truth,* Grandfa. Your book is full of *lies.* Therefore, your book is a *novel.*

GRANDFA: "Time Was: A *Chronicle.*" A book of *facts*…historical *facts!*

RUBY: Not *facts*, Grandfa. *Lies!* Unhistorical non-facts! Nonsense!

GRANDFA: *(Never relinquishing the offensive.)* Facts about *you*…the *truth!*

RUBY: *(Her last defensive.)* That's *wonderful*, Grandfa. You go right *on* with your little novel. You go right on deluding yourself. Don't waste a *minute!* There's so little *time* left!

GRANDFA: *(Not to be stopped.)* I *will!* Old people *remember*, you know. They remember *everything!* That's their function…to *remember!*

RUBY: *(Retreating now.)* Lakme!…Where *is* that child?

GRANDFA: *(Pursuing.)* Only young people don't *like* that!…they don't *like* to remember…they're *afraid!*…afraid of the *truth*…facts *frighten* them… *memory* frightens them …*old people* frighten them!!

RUBY: *(With more than a little desperation.)* Isn't it wonderful, Sigfrid? …at his age…so *spry!*

SIGFRID: *(Turning on her with a rage that has been building inside him ever since the tape recorder episode.)* LEAVE HIM ALONE, RUBY! JUST *ONCE*, LEAVE PEOPLE ALONE!!

(Ruby is quite taken aback and for the moment absolutely speechless.)

GRANDFA: Don't you stand up for me! I don't need your help!

SIGFRID: CHRIST, RUBY, *CHRIST!*

(Sigfrid's explosion has produced a tense, angry silence. Even Grandfa is willing to withdraw for the moment and he goes back to his corner. From inside his knitting bag he will soon produce a small book, his chronicle. From time to time during the following he will write in it. But only after much deliberation. Sigfrid has moved away from Ruby who stands watching him, her own anger mounting. Then, after a long pause:)

RUBY: *(With a repressed and terrible fury.)* That wasn't called for, Sigfrid. That wasn't called for at *all.*

(Sigfrid doesn't answer.)

And I *told* you to take off that ridiculous sweater. You're *home* now. The camouflage is no longer necessary!

LAKME'S VOICE: *(A sudden intrusion on the intercom.)* Hey, opera queen! Black?

RUBY: What?

LAKME'S VOICE: Your coffee. How do you want it? Black?

RUBY: No, *blue!*

LAKME'S VOICE: Well *sometimes* you take a little brandy in it.

RUBY: *(Always glowering at Sigfrid, her eyes never off him.)* Brandy never changed the color of anything…except maybe my teeth. *(Then, directly to him.)* That was disloyal, Sigfrid. That was a *betrayal.*

LAKME'S VOICE: So that's how you want it?

RUBY: *Yes*, that's how I want it! *(Then, again to Sigfrid.)* I don't *like* betrayals. I don't *need* betrayals. I *won't have* betrayals!

LAKME'S VOICE: *(More confused than ever.)* With *brandy?* You want it with *brandy?*

RUBY: YES, I WANT IT WITH BRANDY!

LAKME'S VOICE: *(The little snot.)* I'm sorry, Ruby, but we haven't studied "Tanking up Mommy" yet. That's a *high school* course. Elementary school children aren't supposed to *know* about things like that.

RUBY: *(The rage always directed at Sigfrid.)* Well they *should!*

Lakme' Voice: Take it up with the PTA. Parent Termites Association, if they let you in.

RUBY: *(Directly to Sigfrid again.)* *Some* people we don't humiliate each other in front of. Those are the *rules* ...the way things are *done!* ...and I think you'd just better *stick* to them.

LAKME'S VOICE: *(Another sally.)* Parent Tarantulas!

(Ruby snaps off the intercom. The room is silent. She paces again: tense, irritable. Then:)

RUBY: There *is* a draft. *Did* someone leave that door open or didn't they?

(Again no one answers; then, going to Sigfrid and taking his lowered face in her hands, utterly without guile or a trace of anger.)

Hey, I love you, prince. *(She kisses him on the forehead.)* No matter what I say...although I meant it...I do love you.

SIGFRID: *(Anguished, trying to explain to her.)* You went too far this time, Ruby. Your Message went too far.

RUBY: *(A local caress; stroking his brow.)* "Love which neither nurtures the receiver nor lays fallow the sender but will suffice for each."

SIGFRID: You *said* it, Ruby. This time you *said* it.

RUBY: *(Always soothing him.)* What, Sigfrid, what did Ruby say?

SIGFRID: How it is! You *acknowledged* it...the way we live. You can't do that, Ruby. You'll wreck it...the set-up...*everything*. It all falls apart then.

RUBY: *(Oblivious to the real cause of Sigfrid's anguish, she continues to stroke and soothe him.)* Sshh, *caro*, sshh!

SIGFRID: *(Deliberately, wanting her to understand this.)* There is a line, Ruby...I thought you knew about it, but I guess not...a *line*...a line about *that* thin between making a go of it anymore or not. And it's not easy, Ruby. *God* no! A line that holds everything together for us down here in this stinking basement. And that's what it is: a stinking hole in the ground...a goddamn *prison!*...no matter *how* much we'd like to pretend that it isn't. A *line*...and that's *all* it is but it's the only thing left us between...what?...*that thing out there*...*each other?* It's our *life*line, Ruby...what we hold on to. *Paper-thin*, I know that...*transparent*, you just saw right through it...but it's *there* and, oh *Christ*, how very much we need it. So *please*, please Ruby, don't ever play hop-

RUBY: *(Almost a murmur.)* How beautiful he is…

SIGFRID: *(He has tried to reach her.)* Ruby!

RUBY: …how very beautiful.

SIGFRID: *(Defeated, an edge creeping into his voice now.)* Don't you *understand,* Ruby? Don't you understand *anything?*

RUBY: A prince! My son is a *prince!*

SIGFRID: Or maybe you just don't *listen.* Maybe you don't listen so you won't have to trouble yourself. So you can *prattle!*

RUBY: *(Making light.)* Oh, Sigfrid!

SIGFRID: You *do,* Ruby. You've started to *prattle! Listen* to yourself. Listen to *some-one* for a change.

RUBY: *(Attempting to defend herself now.)* Grandfa and I were only—

SIGFRID: Grandfa has nothing to do with it! Are you *deaf?* Didn't you *hear* what I just said? Don't you listen to *anyone?*

RUBY: Sigfrid, when you get like this—

SIGFRID: And *you! How* do *you* get? You rattle off a goddamn Message like that and then come sailing in here like the Queen of Sheba!

RUBY: *(Desperately trying to take control of the situation.) That's* who I am. The Queen of Sheba!

SIGFRID: *(Not letting her: grabbing her wrist maybe; hard, in her ear.)* The *Message!* You went over the *line* with your goddamn Message!

RUBY: *(Writhing.)* It was…I didn't *mean* to, Sigfrid!

SIGFRID: *(Merciless.)* It won't *work* for us down here that way, Ruby! It *can't!* It's not *strong* enough! *We're* not strong enough! And you *accepted* it. You gave *in* to it! THAT *IS* HOW WE LIVE!

RUBY: *(Breaking.)* I was alone, Sigfrid! …*alone!*…the *strain* sometimes …the *strain!*

SIGFRID: Don't tell me about the—!

(He breaks off as Lakme enters with the coffee.)

LAKME: *(Brightly.)* Eccomi!

RUBY: *(Low, to Sigfrid.)* The *strain!*

LAKME: *(Taking a look over Grandfa's shoulder as she passes him.)* "Message to the—?" Hey, now Grandfa's started one! That ought to be something.

(She gives the coffee to Ruby, who has come back to her chair.)

Here, slurp. *(Then, suddenly flinging her arms around Ruby's neck and kissing her on the cheek.)* Oh how much I love my Ruby! Nobody loves their Ruby as much as I love mine.

RUBY: *(Responding warmly, almost desperately.)* And my Lakme! How I love my lit-tle Lakme! *(Then, hugging Lakme close to her bosom, with her eyes directly on Sigfrid.) Both* my children…such beautiful children…so *strong*…so…*right.*

LAKME: *(Seeking and finding a little girl's comfort in Ruby's arms.)* That was a sad Message to the World, wasn't it? The saddest one you ever made. They're not usually so…sad.

RUBY: *(Holding Lakme close, but really an appeal to Sigfrid.)* But not to frighten you…no!…never that.

LAKME: But I *do* get so frightened sometimes, Ruby…when I wake up and I haven't left a light on and my room is dark…I get so frightened!

RUBY: *(In a soft voice, almost to herself.)* We all do, Lakme. We all do.

LAKME: Imagine things…terrible things!…and I hear them, too!… noises… noises I don't know about…and I *see* them sometimes!… forms!…shadows!…everything buzzing!…swirling!

RUBY: Yes, Lakme…yes.

LAKME: Is that why, Ruby? Is that why you made the Message?

RUBY: *(Not a direct answer because it is Sigfrid she is trying to reach.)* In the morning …early …when you're sleeping…the four of you …and I'm alone…sitting here…thinking…waiting for it to end …the night …another night and it has not yet happened …*then* …when it's quiet …no sounds…no sounds at all…I try to …*understand*…understand what has happened to us… why…and sometimes I have premonitions… tremors…not heart tremors… nothing like that…but *soul* tremors… tremors of the *soul*…when the very *earth* seems to rise up…hover a moment, suspended… somehow suspended…and then fall back. *(And this directly to him.)* Sigfrid knows these moments, too.

LAKME: *(In answer to this.)* Yes! When I was little and the wind blew and there was thunder.

RUBY: *(With a soft smile.)* Yes, when you were little and the wind blew and there was thunder. And Sigfrid! Especially Sigfrid. How he howled when the shutters banged and the thunder clapped!

LAKME: But it's not that way now…not anymore…not when we're together.

RUBY: Remember, Sigfrid? Remember those nights? The howling, the hiding under the bed, the— *(Sigfrid bolts to his feet and goes out the door Stage Right, banging it behind him.)* It was the *strain*, Sigfrid!

LAKME: What's the matter with *him*? Everybody's so moody in this family.

RUBY: *(Getting up, moving away from Lakme and with a note of irritation in her voice.)* That door *is* open.

LAKME: *(Exasperated.)* Oh *no*, Ruby! Not you, too, now.

RUBY: Go upstairs and close it.

LAKME: Just because Sigfrid's in a lousy mood, *you* don't have to—

RUBY: *(Making herself understood.)* Someone's left that door open!

LAKME: *(Relieved, she thought Ruby was in a bad mood.)* Oh *that*. Well of course it is.

RUBY: Then go upstairs and close it.

LAKME: *(Peevish; it's a ridiculous request.)* But *why?* It's not even time yet. Wait 'til curfew.

RUBY: I don't care what time it is. I don't like that door left open.

LAKME: Ruby!

RUBY: *Anytime!*

LAKME: *(A quarrel is building.)* Well it *is*. It's open *lots*. We just don't bother to tell you. You can get so hysterical over *nothing*, Ruby.

RUBY: This isn't nothing!

LAKME: Usually it's open right up until the last minute. You only *think* it's closed.

RUBY: Thank you. I hadn't known that. I'll take care of it *myself* from now on.

LAKME: *That'll* be the day.

RUBY: *(Lakme has scored a point.)* I'm asking you to go up there and close it.

LAKME: It's not *time*, yet, Ruby! How are we ever going to get any fresh air down here if we keep that door closed all the time? Answer *that!* We'd all suffocate if we left it up to you.

RUBY: *(As her desire becomes more insistent, her tone of voice becomes more desperate.)* I don't want that door left open.

LAKME: *(The voice getting meaner; victory is sweet.)* People need *air*, Ruby. They have to *breathe*. *Some* people, that is. *Normal* people. I don't *know* about opera queens. I don't know what they use for oxygen. Arias, probably. Love duets!

RUBY: *Please!*

LAKME: *(Giving no respite.)* Of course we could cut little gills in our necks and then flood this place and live like fish. I suppose *then* you'd be happy. All of us turned into a bunch of *fishes! (A pause; then:)*

RUBY: *(Evenly.)* It's simply that I feel safer when I know that door is closed…that's all I meant…that I would feel *safer*.

LAKME: But it can't *happen* until after curfew!

RUBY: They *think*.

LAKME: Well it can't.

RUBY: They *think*.

LAKME: Well it can't.

RUBY: They only *think!*

LAKME: *(Stubborn, but on less firm ground.)* They're almost *certain*. It's never happened yet. With all the millions of people killed *after* curfew, you'd think one…just one, after all these years…would've gotten it *before* if it was *ever* going to happen then. *(Short pause.)* Besides, even when it *does* happen—…I mean, *if* it ever happens…how do we know it won't come right through that door and down those stairs? Right *through!* How do we *know?*

RUBY: Because the government—

LAKME: *(Furious at herself, the situation, and the tears welling up within her.)* The government! What do *they* know? What does anyone *know?* *(Short pause; then, in a sudden outburst of rage:)* What about last week, Ruby? Remember *that* little incident? You turned the fence on at noon! At *noon!* If that dog hadn't put his leg up against it to *pee,* Sigfrid and I would've *both* gotten it! You were afraid, so you turned the fence on at *noon* and nearly *killed* us! You've gotten so afraid, Ruby, you'll *make* it happen! You'll *kill* us, you're so frightened!

RUBY: *(Who has regained her composure, but with some effort.)* Are you going to go upstairs and close that door or not?

LAKME: *(Wild defiance.)* NO!

RUBY: I see.

LAKME: Why don't you go up there and do it yourself, Ruby? Or are you too *scared* to go back up once you've come down?

RUBY: *(An indefinite threat.)* All right, Miss Lakme, *all* right!

LAKME: *(Moving in for the kill now.)* You *are* too scared, aren't you? Hunh? *Aren't* you?

RUBY: I think you're going to regret this little interview.

LAKME: Oh *am* I now?

RUBY: Yes, *are* you now!

LAKME: Do tell! Do tell!

RUBY: I *tell!* I *tell!*

LAKME: You don't say!

RUBY: I *say!* I *say* all right—! *(Disgusted she cuts herself off when she realizes she has allowed the argument to degenerate into childish bitchiness. Then, turning in her chair, she addresses Grandfa, her only escape.)* What time are they coming for you, Grandfa?

LAKME: *(At once, realizing she has lost the advantage and determined to pursue the argument to the finish.)* How? *How* am I going to regret it? You going to have Fa *spank* me? Then first you'll have to *wake* him and I doubt even *you* could wake Fa up.

RUBY: *(Flaring briefly.)* I've *tried.* You know how I've tried!

LAKME: *(Unrelenting.)* Or are you going to cut my allowance off? Go ahead! Buy your own booze for a change. Get *Sigfrid* to buy all those stupid movie magazines.

RUBY: *(Losing this round, too.)* They…they *help* me!

LAKME: *(Like machine-gun fire.)* How *else*? How *else* am I going to regret it? Go ahead. Tell me. Because I don't think I'm going to regret it at *all.* You're too scared to make *anyone* regret *anything.* You're even scared of *us,* I bet. *Aren't* you, Ruby, *aren't* you?

RUBY: *(Blurting an ugly, painful truth.)* Yes, if that makes you any happier, *yes!*

LAKME: *(Still not satisfied with the blood she has drawn.)* You never *do* anything, you never *go* anywhere, you haven't been out of this house in…*years,* practically!

All you do anymore is sleep in there in the daytime and then come out here and sit up all night.

RUBY: *(The anger mounting now: the confession of fear should have mollified Lakme.)* That will do, Lakme.

LAKME: And look at yourself! Have you done that lately...*looked* at yourself? You used to be beautiful. You *were* a queen...a *real* queen. But *now!* And your mind! *That's* going, too. You used to *talk*, Ruby...make *sense*...really *talk*. And people would *listen* to you...*could* listen to you. But that was *before*. Before the booze. Before the movie magazines and junk. Before all day in bed with a bottle and a copy of *Screen Stars*. Why don't you get a *real* screen star in there with you for a change? *Someone!* You haven't even had *Fa* in bed with you since...since *me* probably!

RUBY: *(Out of control.)* I SAID THAT WILL DO!

LAKME: *(Quite matter-of-factly.)* You've gone to pot, mother. That's what—
(A buzzer sounds, loud, drowning Lakme out. It is a harsh, ugly, rasping noise. Ruby chokes back a scream. Her knuckles whiten, she is holding the arms of her chair so tight. Lakme only marks time, ready to resume speaking the moment the buzzer is silent. Five seconds of this terrible sound. And then utter stillness.)

LAKME: *(At once.)* That's what I think. You've gone to pot. *(Then, getting up:)* Come on. Fifteen minutes. He'll be here. We'd better start getting ready.
(Ruby sits trembling, whimpering almost.)
That was just the warning buzzer, Ruby! It's fifteen minutes 'til curfew! That's exactly what I was talking about! *(She goes to Ruby, embraces her and continues with enormous tenderness.)* Look, Ruby, I'll close the door. I'll turn the fence on. We'll be all safe and sound again. But *after*. After curfew. Honest I will. Even *Grandfa* wants the door closed then and he's so old he might as *well* be...dead! But he still wants that door closed. Don't you, Grandfa?
(Grandfa looks up from his journal, growls at her, and then resumes writing.)
You just can't be nice to that man. *(Then, to Ruby, with a little laugh.)* Besides, goose, if we closed that door now our little guest might not think we were down here and trot right back where he came from. Or what if he ran into the fence while it was on? He'd end up like that dog...*sizzled!* That would be great...just great! An evening without someone! Just the five of us! You know what happened the last time we tried that.

RUBY: *(Very low, toneless, a private memory.)* We nearly killed each other.

LAKME: You're telling me! And we certainly don't want *that* to happen again. Now, kiss-and-make-up, Ruby.

RUBY: *(The same.)* Sigfrid actually had his hands around your throat. I almost let him.

LAKME: *(Demanding.)* Ruby! Kiss-and-make-up! Kiss-and-make—!
(Ruby slaps her sharply across the cheek.)

RUBY: Kiss-and-make-up, Lakme. Kiss-and-make-up.

(*Long pause. No one moves. Then, breaking the silence, Sigfrid's voice on the intercom.*)

SIGFRID'S VOICE: Ruby?...Ruby?

RUBY: (*In a strange, almost monotone voice which will seem all the more sinister because of its deadly calm. And all the while she talks to Sigfrid, she never once takes her eyes from Lakme.*) Yes, Sigfrid, Ruby's here.

SIGFRID'S VOICE: I'm all right now, Ruby.

RUBY: Yes, *caro*, yes.

LAKME: (*Low, her eyes locked with Ruby's.*) I knew you'd do that.

SIGFRID'S VOICE: Are *you*, Ruby? All right?

RUBY: Oh yes...yes. (*And with slow, deliberate movements...almost like a priest performing some sacred rite...she loosens the hairband. Masses of hair tumble to her shoulders. This is the beginning of Ruby's transformation.*)

LAKME: (*Low again.*) Sooner or later...I knew you would.

SIGFRID'S VOICE: I'm sorry I blew up like that. But sometimes...

RUBY: Yes...I know...

SIGFRID'S VOICE: What you said...about the strain...

RUBY: (*Combing her hair out with long, slow strokes.*) There *is* no strain...not now...in fifteen minutes there will be no strain.

SIGFRID'S VOICE: His name is Clarence.

RUBY: Clarence.

LAKME: Clarence. (*A pause.*)

RUBY: We are strong, children. In some ways we are strong.

SIGFRID'S VOICE: Clarence.

LAKME: Our guest.

RUBY: It's only *before* that we are not so strong.

LAKME: Clarence.

SIGFRID'S VOICE: Our game.

RUBY: But soon...in fifteen minutes...*then*...then we are strong.

SIGFRID'S VOICE: Clarence...our guest.

LAKME: Clarence...our game.

RUBY: Fifteen minutes and we will be strong again. (*A pause.*)

SIGFRID'S VOICE: Lakme! You'd better get ready.

LAKME: (*Getting to her feet.*) Coming. You need any help, Ruby?

RUBY: (*Always in that strange voice, as if she were talking to herself.*) And if we are without charity, we suckle the bitter root of its absence...

LAKME: Hey! That's it.

RUBY: ...wherefrom we shall draw the sustenance to destroy you. (*Short pause.*) Clarence.

LAKME: You *do* remember it.

RUBY: There's only one trouble, Sigfrid…just one. They always *stay* the night. They never leave. They always *stay.*

SIGFRID'S VOICE: I know.

RUBY: They never…go *out* there.

LAKME: *(On her way out.)* I think I know what you're talking about.

RUBY: *Why,* Sigfrid, why do we let them *stay* the night?

SIGFRID'S VOICE: You always said…

LAKME: *(At the door.)* I *think* I do. *(She is gone.)*

SIGFRID'S VOICE: …not to go too far.

RUBY: I did?

SIGFRID'S VOICE: We agreed on it. The three of us.

RUBY: I see. *(A pause.)*

SIGFRID'S VOICE: Ruby?

RUBY: Yes.

SIGFRID'S VOICE: What are you thinking?

RUBY: That we might.

SIGFRID'S VOICE: Try?

RUBY: Yes.

SIGFRID'S VOICE: I don't know.

RUBY: It's a possibility.

SIGFRID'S VOICE: Yes.

RUBY: That way we would know…for once and for all we would know.

SIGFRID'S VOICE: Yes.

RUBY: It would serve some…*purpose.*

SIGFRID'S VOICE: Yes.

RUBY: Clarence. *(A pause.)*

SIGFRID'S VOICE: We'll see, Ruby. All right? We'll *see. (Sounds of a slight scuffle are heard over the intercom.)* Dammit, Lakme!

LAKME'S VOICE: Well it's *mine!*

SIGFRID'S VOICE: Give it to me!

LAKME'S VOICE: Oh piss on you!

(The intercom snaps off. Ruby sits combing out her hair. A moment of silence. Then Grandfa begins to move in on her, slowly at first but then picking up speed.)

GRANDFA: *(Circling her chair, needling like a mosquito.)* Who's it going to be, Ruby? Who's the victim for tonight? I know what goes on in here after I go to bed. I *know.* Thank God I never had to *watch.* Thank God for *that.* I thought I'd seen plenty in my time, but *this*…what you people do.

RUBY: *(Lipsticking her mouth a brilliant red.)* There are things, Grandfa, things which you do not understand.

GRANDFA: I understand corruption…decay! I understand *that!*

RUBY: *(With studied disinterest as she continues making up.)* Do you?

GRANDFA: I can *smell* it, woman! Smell it! There's a stench in this house. A stench of putrefying *rot*. Human *rot!...people!...flesh!*

RUBY: Things which you do not understand.

GRANDFA: *(Not pausing.)* And it's all here! Written down! The truth! Everything!

RUBY: Your *novel*, Grandfa? Are you referring to your novel?

GRANDFA: It's not a novel! It's a chronicle! How it was! I wrote it down. I remembered it. The truth. "Time Was: A Chronicle."

RUBY: But your book is full of lies, Grandfa. We don't know those people. They're fictitious ...fabrications. They never existed. Chronicles are meant to tell the *truth*. No, dear, you've written a *novel*...a book of *lies*.

GRANDFA: *(Finding himself on the defensive.)* You've *made* it that way. There was a time—

RUBY: *(With great force; she has no intention of continuing this conversation.)* WAS! *(Short pause.)* There *was* a time, Grandfa...*was*. *(Another pause; Ruby puts the final touches to her make-up. The Transformation is nearly complete.)*

GRANDFA: *(After a while; very sadly.)* It wasn't meant to be this way.

RUBY: *(Rather distantly.)* Perhaps Grandfa...just *perhaps*.

GRANDFA: *(His voice growing fainter.)* Things weren't meant to be this way.

RUBY: But they *are*, caro...they *are*.

GRANDFA: *(Fainter still.)* People weren't meant to be this way.

RUBY: *(With a sad mockery in her voice.)* How, Grandfa, how were people *meant* to be?

(Grandfa scarcely tries to answer her question. Ruby takes out a large and fantastic wig and settles it on her head. Facing Grandfa fully she repeats her question with a bitterness turned more against herself than him.)

Tell us, Grandfa. tell us how people were meant to be. For we should dearly like to know.

(The wig is in place. The Transformation is complete now. The Ruby before us is utterly different from the "anonymous" woman of her entrance. What we see now is garish, hard, almost obscene. There is a pause. The silence is broken by Fa crying out in his sleep.)

FA: *(In great terror; he is having a nightmare.)* WEST!...IT'S MOVING WEST!

GRANDFA: *(Trying to answer Ruby now.)* Not like...not like you.

FA: RUN!...RUN FOR YOUR LIVES!

GRANDFA: Like...like here...*(He holds up his Chronicle.)*...as you *were*...

RUBY: *(With the same sad mockery.)* Imperfect?...weak?...afraid?

GRANDFA: *(Low, but spitting it out.)* Human, woman...*human*.

RUBY: *(The beginning of a wild laugh.)* As you *portrayed* us, Grandfa, in your funny, funny book? Your *novel*? You want us to behave like *that*?

(POW! A rubber-tipped toy dart has been fired through the Stage Right door hitting Grandfa squarely in the back of the head. The Chronicle falls from his hand.

He does not turn to see who fired the dart. He knows. Lakme bursts into the room. She is in the highest spirits, dressed in her Green Hornet costume and ready for Clarence.)

LAKME: Sic semper tyrannis! *(Then, rushing toward Grandfa, doing a little dance around him.)* The Green Hornet! Bzzzzzzz! Bzzzzzzzzz!
(Grandfa turns away from her and moves slowly towards the Stage Right door.)

RUBY: *(Calling after him at the end of a laughing jag.)* Why is it, Grandfa, why is it that you can be so quiet at times…like a mouse…a knitting mouse…and at other times so noisy? Why is that?

LAKME: Hey, Grandfa! Aren't you going to chase me? Come on, try to run me down! *(Then, to Ruby, truly perplexed.)* What's the matter with *him*?

RUBY: Your Grandfa is suffering from an acute attack of how-it-was.

LAKME: Oh, he's off on *that* tack again! *(Then, stooping and retrieving the Chronicle.)* Hey, Bede! You dropped your Chronicle, Bede! *(Then, again to Ruby.)* The Venerable Bede. I know about him from school. He wrote chronicles, too.

RUBY: But your Grandfa is a novelist. The oldest first novelist in captivity.

LAKME: *(Annoyed: she wants to finish this.)* Please, Ruby, *please*. And you know why he was venerable? Because he was old…just like Grandfa. That's the only reason he was venerable.

RUBY: That's a very good reason.

LAKME: *(Bitchy.)* Well of course I wouldn't know about that…*age*. Besides, what's so venerable about being old? Just a lot of blue veins on your legs and gums. That's all old is. Hell, that's no accomplishment.

RUBY: Lakme!

LAKME: *(Mincing.)* Cripes, that's no accomplishment. *(Short pause.)* Ruby, are you venerable?

RUBY: Taci, fanciulla, taci!

LAKME: *(Clapping both hands over her mouth.)* Umph!
(It might be remembered at this point that everyone, including Sigfrid, who now enters through the Stage Right door, is in the sunniest of dispositions. Joy, for the moment, is abounding.)

SIGFRID: *(He is dressed entirely in black; he calls over his shoulder to Grandfa who has already exited through the same door.)* Cheer up, Grandfa. It's your last night here. *(Then, to the others.)* I spied a tear on Grandfa's cheeklet. One large, goopy tear. Right here.

RUBY: Who would have thought the old man to have so much salt in him?
(Sigfrid has joined Ruby while Lakme, to one side, begins to thumb through Grandfa's Chronicle.)

LAKME: *(Reading from the Chronicle.)* "Message to the World." That's all he wrote: "Message to the World." And then it's blank.

SIGFRID: How do I look?

RUBY: Like hell. Look how you stick out there. You used to have such a firm stomach, Sigfrid. I'd never seen such firmness. Whatever happened to it? You're all soft around there now.

SIGFRID: *(Glumly regarding his waistline; maybe there is a hint, just a hint, of flabbiness.)* Well...your bazooms have dropped.

RUBY: Well of course they have! There's no one I especially want to keep them *up* for. And that's the only thing that keeps them up there: will-power!...sheer concentration. So naturally they're drooping from the lack of it. They're probably piqued. Well wouldn't you feel neglected? *(She addresses her bosom.)* Isn't that what you're doing down there...sulking?...isn't it?
(Sigfrid, still concerned with the real or imaginary bulk at his waistline, has begun a set of strenuous sit-ups. Lakme continues with the Chronicle.)

LAKME: *(It doesn't make any sense to her.)* "There is a *line*, Ruby...a line about *that* thin." What is this stuff? *(She turns to another place in the Chronicle.)*

RUBY: What about *me*? How do *I* look? Apart from my fallen grapes, that is.

SIGFRID: *(Always exercising.)* You look...

RUBY: *Attention!*

SIGFRID: ...Rubyesque. Why don't you go put your costume on?

RUBY: I thought you told me it was going to be one of *those* nights.

SIGFRID: It is.

RUBY: Considering how *long* it's going to be before you need me...considering the hour *wait* while you two play Boy Scouts...considering what's going to *happen* as soon as he gets here...considering all *that*, I don't see what the rush is.

SIGFRID: Well while you're *waiting*, sweetheart—

RUBY: *(Perfectly aware she is interrupting.)* Sigfrid, it just occurred to me! Whenever it's a girl, you introduce her to me before you go in there, and when it's a boy you don't want him to meet me until *after*. Why is that?

SIGFRID: It's the way things are *done*, Ruby.

RUBY: Oh?

SIGFRID: It's a heterosexual society we live in.

RUBY: Preposterous!

SIGFRID: I'm sorry, Ruby, but it *is*.

RUBY: Well—then I don't see the connection between before and after. *(Short pause.)* Oh yes I do. Oh *yes* I do!

SIGFRID: As I was saying, *madre*...while you're in your little boudoir *getting-up*...while you're in there *considering* the agonizing *wait*...why don't you consider slipping into that *walkure* outfit. You know, the one with the cast iron boobies and the winged helmet.

RUBY: *(Correcting.)* Wingèd. And thank you all the same.

SIGFRID: Ruby! You look so feminine in steel.

RUBY: No! It *chafes.*

SIGFRID: *(The last sit-up.)* Suit yourself.

RUBY: Oh! I *will!* I *always* do.

    (Sigfrid gets up, paces a moment.)

LAKME: *(Looking up from the Chronicle.)* Hey, Sigfrid! This part's all about you. He even wrote down some of those poems you used to write. *(She delves into the Chronicle again with renewed interest.)*

RUBY: I don't think he's coming, Sigfrid. I think our little guest has stood you-know-who up.

SIGFRID: He'll *be* here, Ruby.

RUBY: You're *sure?*

SIGFRID: I *know.*

LAKME: "Sigfrid is a sickly child, prone to respiratory ailments. Sometimes his face and little hands turn an alarming blue. Ruby is heartsick." Did you used to be *blue,* Sigfrid? I didn't know that. *(No one responds; she continues reading.)*

RUBY: But *when?* According to *my* watch—

SIGFRID: *(Checking his own.)* Christ! Why didn't you tell me it was so late?

RUBY: The warning buzzer, Sigfrid…nearly fifteen minutes…I can't imagine you didn't hear it.

SIGFRID: *(Getting into a foul mood; maybe Clarence isn't coming.)* Dammit, Clarence.

RUBY: *(Her resignation is calculated to annoy him.)* Well…I think you'd just better run upstairs and lock up for the night. Turn the fence on. It's obvious he's not coming.

SIGFRID: I said he'll *be* here and he *will!*

RUBY: Two minutes, Sigfrid, two minutes 'til curfew.

    (A pause; Sigfrid paces, the inner tension rising. Ruby watches with some amusement.)

LAKME: *(Again a voice in the silence.)* "We read Shakespeare together in the late afternoon. Sigfrid's enthusiasm is boundless. He has the makings of poet. A poet's soul." *You,* Sigfrid, a *soul?* Hah!

RUBY: *(Deliberately provoking.)* Who is this person, Sigfrid? Who is this person who isn't coming?

SIGFRID: His name is Clarence.

RUBY: I *know* what his name is. What I'm asking you is something *about* him. Some nights there is a *link.* Is there a *link* with Clarence?

SIGFRID: *(Impatient, always looking at his watch.)* The incident about the slide.

RUBY: *That* Clarence?

SIGFRID: *That* Clarence.

RUBY: *(Smiling strangely.)* Well…in that case…what we said…what we said about letting them *stay* the night…assuming they ever *come*…

SIGFRID: *(Curt.)* No.

RUBY: *(Starting to laugh.)* …instead of going *out* there?…

SIGFRID: *No* I said.

RUBY: *(Her laughter mounting.)* Why, Sigfrid…murder?…would it be murder?

SIGFRID: *(Moving away from her, about to explode, literally counting the seconds till curfew.)* Come on, Clarence, come *on!*

LAKME: *(Approaching to show him something in the Chronicle.)* Sigfrid—

SIGFRID: *(Pushing her away from him.)* Shut up, Lakme!

LAKME: *(Indignant.)* What did I do?

SIGFRID: Jesus, Clarence, *Jesus!*

LAKME: *(Loud and mean; fixing Sigfrid's wagon.)* You want to hear some poetry everybody? You want to hear some of Sigfrid's *poetry?*

SIGFRID: *(Immediately aware of what she is up to.)* Cut it, Lakme!

LAKME: *(Fearless.)* We'd forgotten, Sigfrid. We'd forgotten what a poetic *genius* you were!

SIGFRID: I said *cut* it!

LAKME: *(Reading.)* "A sky, a blue sky, the eagle soars."

SIGFRID: *(Going after her.)* Give that to me.

LAKME: *(Dodging him.)* "High soars, high soars the eagle." What kind of sores, Shakespeare? Big pussy ones?

SIGFRID: GIVE ME THAT BOOK!

LAKME: "Can I soar? Can I soar, too?" Suits us, Shelley. Take a big flying leap right off the roof!

SIGFRID: You goddamn little bitch!

LAKME: You were some poet, Sigfrid. Some poet! I mean this stuff is a real eyesore. A real "I soar." You were a *Shelley!* You *are* a—!

(His hands on her throat. Sharp silence.)

RUBY: *(She has been in a private reverie during the quarrel and is coming out of it now. There is still a smile on her lips.)* Murder, Sigfrid? Would it be—? *(She turns, aware of the silence; then, at once:)* Sigfrid!

(Short silence, no one moves, the doorbell sounds.)

Allons, mes enfants, il faut commencer.

(Short silence, again no one moves, again the doorbell sounds.) Il faut commencer! *(Sigfrid slowly takes his hands from Lakme's throat. An ugly moment of silence between them.)*

SIGFRID: *(Terrifying.)* Don't you ever…*ever*…EVER! do that again.

LAKME: *(A threat.)* That *hurt,* Sigfrid, that really *hurt.*

(The doorbell again, insistent this time.)

RUBY: *(Cutting them apart with her voice.)* The *door,* Sigfrid! The *game* is at the door!

SIGFRID: Get the camera ready.

LAKME: I'll *kill* him!

SIGFRID: *(About to go upstairs.)* And Ruby, do it *right* this time.

RUBY: *(Again with the same strange, cruel mockery.)* Murder, Sigfrid? Would it be murder?

(Sigfrid has disappeared up the stairs. Ruby and Lakme are on their way out. The curfew buzzer sounds again; this time louder than before. Ruby and Lakme freeze. Ruby covers her ears with her hands. Five seconds of this terrible noise. Then the silence. Ruby moves quickly toward the Stage Right door.)

LAKME: *(Following.)* I'll *kill* him!

(Ruby is out.)

Ruby? What's the matter, Ruby?

(Now Lakme is gone, too. The stage is empty. No sounds, nothing moves. Then, from upstairs, the sound of an enormous iron door slamming shut. Reverberations. Then silence again. Footsteps are heard and a moment later Clarence is seen coming down the stairs. He carries a large placard, the type that pickets carry, which reads: "There Is Something Out There.")

CLARENCE: *(With a nervous laugh.)* Whew! That was close. The bus...*(His voice trails off as he realizes he is alone on the stairs. Then, turning, he calls back up.)* Sigfrid?... *(As he turns, we can read the other side of his placard: "We shall prevail." The curtain is beginning to fall.)* Gee, it's nice down here...very nice. *(Clarence is into the room. Sigfrid is heard on the stairs. And now the curtain is down.)*

END OF ACT ONE

ACT TWO

At Rise: The room is the same. As before, the lighting is white and brilliant. Clarence's placard, the "There is Something Out There" side facing us, rests against the wall near the Stage Left door. Clarence is alone in the room. He wears a woman's dress, stockings (fallen to the ankles), and shoes. But there is no mistaking him. We are perfectly aware it is a male in the wrong attire. We only wonder how he got there. His uneasiness in this strange and empty room is immediately apparent. His movements are tense and fidgety. He wanders. A long silence. And then a loud snortle from Fa in his chair. Clarence stiffens, retreats a little, pauses. Another snortle. Clarence is edging towards the chair. He is there. He looks down at Fa, hesitates, bites his lip and then throws caution to the winds.

CLARENCE: I'm Clarence. *(No response.)* My name is Clarence.

FA: *(Giggling foolishly.)* Hello, Miss Nigeria!...hello there!

CLARENCE: No, *Clarence.*

FA: Bye-bye, Grandfa!...come and kiss me, Grandfa!

CLARENCE: Sir?

FA: *(Almost a mumble.)* West...moving west...unh...*(Fa lapses into a deep sleep. Snoring sounds.)*

CLARENCE: *(After a while; thoroughly miserable.)* Oh this is dreadful...*Sigfrid!*
(And at once Grandfa comes through the Stage Right door. He has a suitcase.)

GRANDFA: *(A parody of senility.)* Well well well. Looky here.

CLARENCE: Good evening.

GRANDFA: Fa! Wake up! Fa! We got company. Something of Sigfrid's. Something Sigfrid dragged home.

CLARENCE: I'm Clarence. My name is Clarence.

GRANDFA: Who?

CLARENCE: Clarence.

GRANDFA: You sure?

CLARENCE: Sir?

GRANDFA: Nice name.

CLARENCE: Thank you. *(Pause.)* It's English.

GRANDFA: What's that? You're English.

CLARENCE: No, my *name. Clarence* is English.

GRANDFA: And you? What are you? Or shouldn't I ask that question?
(He laughs wildly. Clarence manages a weak smile.)
You're the guest.

CLARENCE: Sir?

GRANDFA: The guest. You.

CLARENCE: Well I'm *a* guest. I don't know if I'm *the* guest.

GRANDFA: You are.

CLARENCE: I'm a friend. A friend of Sigfrid's.

GRANDFA: Ah yes, Sigfrid. Fine lad, fine lad.

CLARENCE: Yes, isn't he?

GRANDFA: Lakme, too.

CLARENCE: Lakme?

GRANDFA: His sister. Fine lad, fine lad.

CLARENCE: Fine *lad?*

GRANDFA: And let's not forget Ruby. Fine lad, fine lad.

CLARENCE: Ruby?

GRANDFA: Their mother. Fine lads, all of 'em. You, too. Fine, fine, lads and laddies.

CLARENCE: *(Taking the suitcase and setting it down.)* Here, let me take that for you.

GRANDFA: Thank you, thank you kindly.

CLARENCE: You're taking a trip?

GRANDFA: Off to the looneybin, first thing in the morning.

CLARENCE: The *where?*

GRANDFA: The looneybin. Bin for loons. I'm a loon.

CLARENCE: You're joking, of course.

GRANDFA: I don't know. I suppose that's why I'm a loon.

(*He laughs his wild laugh again. Clarence moves away from him, ever so slightly.*)

CLARENCE: Gee, it's nice down here.

GRANDFA: We like it. It's nice and homey.

CLARENCE: That's what's so wonderful about it. It doesn't look at all like a basement. It's so…so cheerful.

GRANDFA: Well, we've tried to brighten it up some. A little blood, a little spleen.

CLARENCE: (*Trying for firmer ground.*) I guess you're Sigfrid's grandfather.

GRANDFA: (*Enormously funny.*) Who'd you think I was? His grandmother?

CLARENCE: (*Laughing, too.*) Well not *really!*

GRANDFA: Oh, you're a droll one, you are.

CLARENCE: (*Reckless.*) Of course you might've been his *aunt!* (*The laughter is raucous, slightly hysterical.*)

GRANDFA: Or his auntie! (*Then, quickly, straight-faced.*) Nice dress you got there.

CLARENCE: (*Snapping to.*) Sir?

GRANDFA: Eh? Sorry, I don't hear too well.

CLARENCE: I suppose you're wondering why I have this dress on.

GRANDFA: (*Breezy.*) Oh no! No no!

CLARENCE: Well you see—

GRANDFA: Happens all the time around here. It's a regular little Junior League Sweden. If you're not one thing, you're the t'other.

CLARENCE: Sir?

GRANDFA: You don't hear so well yourself. (*Short pause.*) Florence.

CLARENCE: Sir? (*Then, correcting himself.*) I beg your pardon?

GRANDFA: Florence.

CLARENCE: No, Clarence.

GRANDFA: Funny name for a young man.

CLARENCE: Clarence?

GRANDFA: No, *Florence. Florence* is a funny name for a young man.

CLARENCE: Yes!…Yes it is. (*A pause.*) I'm *Clarence. My* name is—

GRANDFA: (*Crabbed.*) I *know* what your name is. I was *saying* that *Florence* is a funny name for a young man. If your name were *Florence*, it would be funny.

CLARENCE: Yes…I suppose it would…Florence…*my!*

GRANDFA: (*Sweetly.*) Nice frock, Clarence.

CLARENCE: Sir?

GRANDFA: (*Thundering.*) I SAID: NICE FROCK, CLARENCE!

CLARENCE: Oh.

GRANDFA: I haven't *seen* such a nice *frock* in a *long* time.

CLARENCE: Thank you.

GRANDFA: *(The goading becoming more obvious.)* Sort of a...*Florentine* design.

CLARENCE: Yes. *(Then, aghast.)* Oh, but it's not *mine.*

GRANDFA: Finally!

CLARENCE: Sir?

GRANDFA: Nothing!

CLARENCE: I can't find mine.

GRANDFA: You lost it?

CLARENCE: Just vanished.

GRANDFA: You actually lost it?

CLARENCE: Poof!

GRANDFA: You actually managed to lose your *frock?*

CLARENCE: No, my *clothes.*

GRANDFA: *(Deadpan.)* Oh.

CLARENCE: I lost my *clothes.*

GRANDFA: *(Daylight dawning.)* Ah! You lost your *clothes.*

CLARENCE: This is all I could find.

GRANDFA: Now I understand.

CLARENCE: I don't wear a frock...*dress!*

GRANDFA: Unless, of course, you've lost your *clothes. Then* you wear a frock.

CLARENCE: Well I certainly hope you don't think I came *over* here like this. A boy in a *dress!* That would be a sight!

GRANDFA: Oh yes! indeed it would...*is,* in fact.

CLARENCE: It's the craziest thing. Everything I had on when I got here...gone!...just like that. I can't understand it. I've looked everywhere.

GRANDFA: It's a careless generation, the younger one.

CLARENCE: My socks even.

GRANDFA: Well, you know the old saying: sooner or later we all end up in our rightful clothes.

CLARENCE: No, I never heard that one.

GRANDFA: Well you trust in it. When all else fails, boy, trust in the old sayings and they'll never let you down.

CLARENCE: *(With a smile and a shrug.)* Well you certainly can't say I'm not a good sport about it. Most men would...*(His voice trails off; he moves across the room.)*

GRANDFA: *(With a sadness now.)* Yes...they would...most men.
(Grandfa seems about to leave the room. Clarence with his back to him, continues:)

CLARENCE: *(With a relaxed genuineness we have not seen yet.)* Talk about giving the Movement a bad name! We've got a major demonstration in the morning. I'm a squadron secretary; I'll be leading an entire platoon. That's all we need at a time like this: a squadron secretary in a dress! There's enough opposition to us as it is.

(Grandfa is listening to Clarence.)

Why people should be against anyone trying to make this a better world, I'll never know. But they *are*. We've actually been *hooted*. Physically attacked sometimes. It's awful when that happens.

GRANDFA: *(A sad realization. Softly. Almost to himself.)* You don't know what's going to happen, do you?

CLARENCE: *(Without pause.)* But *someone's* got to care about it...the world... and I'm willing to be one of them. Especially *now!* Sure it's out there and sure it gets a little closer every day and sure it's probably going to win out in the end...but so what? We've *still* got to oppose it. And so what if we fail? We've got to *try*. That's the only justification for being alive any more...*trying*.

GRANDFA: *(Without pause.)* Why they brought you here and you don't even know?

CLARENCE: You may think this is crazy...and lots of people do...but I don't believe in despair. No matter what happens...and a lot has...I can't, I won't, *don't* believe in despair. It's not something you can believe *in*...despair. It's a deadend. It'll choke you to death.

GRANDFA: Poor baby, poor baby.

CLARENCE: But I don't believe in...what?...joy?...happiness?...I don't believe in them either. I can't. I just can't. It's the *struggle* I believe in ...the endeavor ...the struggle from one to the other. People trying to be better than they really are. No, I don't mean that ...People trying to *change* things. Yes! People trying to change things. I hate not being able to change things. It's like man's perfectability...who cares about that? It's his *im*perfectability that matters. I suppose that's why I don't think about God very often. He's not very interesting. *(Short pause; then, turning to Grandfa with a smile.)* Am I making any sense to you? Probably not.

GRANDFA: *(Just looking at Clarence.)* You poor, poor baby.

CLARENCE: And I probably shouldn't get so up in arms about it...the Movement.

GRANDFA: *(Directly to him.)* You weren't talking about the movement, Clarence.

CLARENCE: Oh I was! I probably talk too much about it. It's just that it's sort of a passion with me. Sometimes I wonder what I'd do without it. Stop boring people half to death, I suppose! *(He laughs, wanders a little, checking his watch.)*

GRANDFA: You're the movement, Clarence. You. You are.

CLARENCE: *(Again ignoring a remark he'd rather not deal with.)* Gee, I wish Sigfrid would come back. He went to get his mother. What did you say her name was? Ruby? I hate introductions.

GRANDFA: *(A weary sigh.)* Go home, missy...please...go home.

CLARENCE: *(Awkward.)* It was such a coincidence...running into each other like that this afternoon. We hadn't seen each other since the sixth grade. That's… *(He is counting the years up on his fingers.)*

GRANDFA: While there's time…pick up your skirts and run along home.

CLARENCE: *(Unable to prolong it.)* I beg your pardon?

GRANDFA: You heard me…maybe you didn't want to…but you did.

CLARENCE: I…no, no I didn't…something about home?

GRANDFA: *(Flat.)* That's right. Something about home.

CLARENCE: Well? Well *what?*

GRANDFA: You *like* bringing out the worst in them? Is that it?

CLARENCE: Well if you don't speak up, if I can't even *hear* you, I don't see how I'm supposed to *converse* with you.

GRANDFA: Do you know *why* you were brought here?

CLARENCE: Sigfrid and I—

GRANDFA: *Sigfrid! Sigfrid* is why you were brought here. And Sigfrid is why you came.

CLARENCE: Well of course he is! We're old friends.

GRANDFA: Sigfrid doesn't have any friends. He has victims…*mice.* Mice for the cats to play with. They'll rip your guts out. The imperfectability of man! That's their food. They'll devour you. Run, boy, I say run for your life. Get up those stairs and run.

CLARENCE: *(A little peevish.)* I honestly don't know what you're talking about.

GRANDFA: I'm talking about what will happen to you if you stay here. He's already put you in a dress. And God knows what happened in the other room. I'm sure it wasn't very pretty. But that was only a beginning. It's your *soul* they're after now and they won't sleep tonight until they've had at it. Had at it *good!* Your *soul.* And that hurt doesn't heal so easy. I know. I live here.

CLARENCE: *(Edgy.)* I don't know what you're talking about.

GRANDFA: *(Full voice.)* I'm talking about *you.* Who you are! I *know* who you are. *What!* So do they. AND THEY WILL REVILE YOU FOR IT. That is their *function.* They'll make you *belong* in that dress. They'll make you what you already *are.* They'll make you want to *die.*

CLARENCE: *(Ugly.)* I DON'T KNOW WHAT YOU'RE TALKING ABOUT!!! *(A silence.)*

GRANDFA: *(Gently.)* God help you, Clarence, God help you.
(The quiet is shattered by the horn fanfare announcing Norma's entrance from Bellini's opera. There is no specific source for the music. It is very loud. It will continue.)

CLARENCE: *(Distracted.)* What?…music …the music …where? …why? …Sir!
(Grandfa is headed for the door: slowly, slowly.)
Wait! Where is everyone?…what's going to happen?…this music …I didn't know what you were talking about …I didn't know …please, stay!

(Grandfa is gone.)
I didn't...know...
(He is alone. The music builds. At the first beat of the orchestral verse of the chorus, Lakme comes skipping into the room. She wears her Green Hornet dress and cape. As she skips about the room in time to the music, she scatters rose petals from a tiny basket. Clarence watches, stupefied, unable to speak at first. Then:)
Who...?

LAKME: *(At once, always skipping.)* Lakme...the Bell Song one...Delibes. Ruby used to sing it. You didn't know our mother was an opera queen? An *ex*-opera queen? Sigfrid didn't tell you?
(Clarence looks with a jaw agape.)
A *real* old friend.

CLARENCE: *(Strangled.)* What?

LAKME: *(A cheerful explanation.)* The intercom. You and Grandfa. And isn't *he* the old pro? Pro for *prober.*

CLARENCE: What's happening?

LAKME: Ruby. It's her entrance. *(Then, quickly, as an afterthought.)* Oh! and you knew. You knew what he was talking about. Grandfa.
(And before Clarence can get out even a muffled reply to this, the volume of the music goes up several decibels and a chorus begins singing the second verse of Norma's entrance music. Lakme, always dancing, joins in at once.)

VOCAL CHORUS: *Norma viene: le cinge la chioma*
La verbena ai misteri sacrata;
In sua man come luna falcata
L'aurea falce diffonde splendor.
Ella viene; e la stella di Roma
Sbigottita si copre di un velo;
Irminsul corre i campi del cielo
Qual cometa foriera d'orror.
(And, just as Lakme entered on the first beat of the orchestral verse, Sigfrid has entered on the first beat of the vocal selection. He still wears his black shirt and slacks. But now he carries an enormous sabre. He holds it out in front of him with great reverence, as if it were a sacred object. His expression and movements are solemn, trancelike. He walks a slow circle around the room, taking no notice of Clarence who, as soon as he entered, has been questioning him.)

CLARENCE: Where have you been? Sigfrid. Where? And will you please tell me what's going on? You tell someone to wait for you and then...*this.* Sigfrid?

SIGFRID: *(With a terrible, controlled fury.)* Ruby! Her entrance!

CLARENCE: *(After he has recovered from this.)* I...I don't understand.

LAKME: *(Helpful.)* You'd better sing. She won't like it if you don't.

CLARENCE: I...

SIGFRID: *(The same voice.)* Sing!

(Clarence, rather foolishly, tries to join in. The music is coming to another climax.)

Down.

(Sigfrid and Lakme kneel, facing the Stage Right door.)

Down!

(Clarence kneels, too. The horn fanfare sounds again and Ruby makes her long-awaited entrance. It and she are spectacular. She is wearing an elaborate, flowing white dress, rather suggestive of a nineteenth-century wedding dress. There is a splash of blood across the bodice and part of the skirt. She moves majestically to a spot Center Stage and stands there, motionless, until the music ends. Clarence, Sigfrid and Lakme are almost prone on the floor, their heads bowed, they are not looking at her.)

RUBY: *(After a pause, with an imperial gesture, Norma's opening recitative:)* "Sedizioso vo—" *(She stops singing on the vowel "O" and yawns hugely, not bothering to cover her mouth. Then she stretches, very slowly and yawns again. Ruby acts affectedly, and she knows it.)* La Ruby non canterá stanotte.

SIGFRID AND LAKME: *(Together, exaggerated cadences.)* Che peccato!

RUBY: È troppo stanca.

SIGFRID AND LAKME: Maledetto.

RUBY: È troppo vecchia.

SIGFRID AND LAKME: Poverina.

RUBY: *(Sitting.)* Buona sera a tutti!

SIGFRID: *(Low, to Clarence.)* Isn't she terrific? Didn't I tell you?

RUBY: Mi sento male. Mi sento noiosa. Mi sento many things. But most of all *mi sento* blue.

SIGFRID: *(Low, to Clarence.)* One in a million.

LAKME: One in *ten* million.

RUBY: *(Arms outstretched.)* Abbraciami, tesori, abbraciami.

SIGFRID: *(Excusing himself to Clarence.)* She wants to embrace us.

LAKME: No, she wants *us* to embrace *her*. There's a difference.

RUBY: *(Taking Lakme and Sigfrid into her arms.)* Ah, mes enfants. Mes veritables enfants. Comme je suis heureuse. Et comme je ne suis pas heureuse. Mais ce soir…peut-être…je— *("Seeing" Clarence, she breaks off.)* Who is that, please?

LAKME: That? Oh that's Maria Malibran.

RUBY: Maria Malibran, you little dwarf, *the* Maria Malibran…the very *great* Maria Malibran…is neither a snippit nor a waif. That one *is*. Furthermore, she is quite dead and has been for some time now. Sigfrid, who is this?

SIGFRID: Qui?

RUBY: *(Pointing.)* That. That person.

SIGFRID: *(Terse whisper.)* L'invité.

RUBY: Ah! Our guest! *(To Clarence.) Nous vous avons attendé, cheri.*

CLARENCE: *(From across the room.)* Hello. I'm—

RUBY: *(Brightly.)* We'll be with you in a moment, dear.

LAKME: *Il s'appelle Clarence.*

RUBY: Hmm, I thought as much. Where did you find this one?

LAKME: *À la demonstration. Clarence porte des affiches.*

RUBY: *(Amused.) Davvero,* Sigfrid?

LAKME: They're old friends. They went to school together. Up to the sixth grade.

SIGFRID: *(Low, not for Clarence's ear.)* The slide. The incident on the slide.

RUBY: *(Scrutinizing Clarence.) Piccolo naso…*

LAKME: *(Translating for Clarence.)* She says you've got a small nose.

RUBY: *…mento debole…*

SIGFRID: Weak chin.

RUBY: *…orecchi grandi…*

LAKME: Big ears.

RUBY: *…pallido…troppo pallido…*

SIGFRID: And you're pale. Much too pale.

RUBY: *Ma la vestita è carino…molta carina.*

LAKME: *(To Ruby.)* It should be. It's yours. *(To Clarence.)* But your dress is sweet. Very sweet.

RUBY: And what a perfectly atrocious body!

LAKME: Sigfrid knows that, Ruby.

RUBY: I wouldn't have thought he was your type at all. Never in my life.

SIGFRID: It was the best I could do.

RUBY: It's the bottom of the barrel, Sigfrid. The veritable bottom of the barrel. This is hardly worth the effort.

SIGFRID: You try it next time, you think it's so easy. You try finding someone.

RUBY: To think your standards have fallen so low. I'm deeply shocked. It mustn't have been very pleasant for you.

LAKME: As he said, it was the best he could do.

RUBY: *(With a sign of finality.) Ebbene, comminciamo la commedia.*

LAKME: *(Yelling to Clarence.)* Hey! You!

RUBY: Not that way, Lakme. Properly very properly. Sigfrid, he's your friend.

SIGFRID: Just…

RUBY: Yes, darling?

(He only looks at her. She smiles up at him. Then Sigfrid goes over to Clarence, takes him by the arm and leads him back to Ruby. There should be a suggestion of royalty granting an interview during the next scene.)

SIGFRID: Clarence, I'd like you to meet my mother. Ruby, this is Clarence.

RUBY: *Enchantée.*

CLARENCE: *Enchanté.*

RUBY: I beg your pardon?

CLARENCE: *(Who doesn't speak French or Italian or anything.)* Enchanté?

(Ruby shifts in her chair.)

Please don't get up!

RUBY: *(Settling back.)* Oh I won't. I wasn't, in fact. But you sit down. Here…on the hassock. *(Clarence sits at her feet.)*

You've met our little Lakme? Our own *piccola cosa nostra?* Why yes, of course you have.

CLARENCE: No, I don't think so.

LAKME: Yes he did. In the park this afternoon. He played football with us. *Attempted* to play football with us. He's pretty stinky at it.

CLARENCE: Was that you?

RUBY: Lakme's twelve. Aren't you, sweetheart?

LAKME: *(Peeved.)* Thir*teen*, Ruby.

RUBY: Well how am I supposed to know?

LAKME: *(Beginning a long one.)* Thirteen years old and total monster.

RUBY: *That* we know.

LAKME: Will you let me finish this? Will you let me do it right this time?

RUBY: You haven't said hello to Clarence. You're not being polite.

LAKME: *(Brusque.)* Hello, Clarence. Now may I?

RUBY: *Avanti, avanti.*

LAKME: *(Finding her place.)* …years old and total monster. Have been for some time. I'm bright…extremely bright. Close to genius, in fact. I know everything a thirteen-year-old girl isn't supposed to know. Even ninety-three-year-old girls aren't supposed to know what I know. I know so much they don't know what to do with me. "They" meaning everyone. Everyone outside this house. Ruby and Sigfrid are different. At least they hate me.

(Appropriate comments from Ruby and Sigfrid.)

I have talents. I must have. Only I don't know what they are yet. So I play the piano. Bach, mostly, but sometimes Mozart. My favorite thing in the world is the Green Hornet. He makes people tell the truth and goes "Bzzz, bzzz" at them until they do. I do love the Green Hornet. My unfavorite thing is…well, lots of things…finks being in the vanguard. Fink! My favorite color is white…because it's blank. Time of day: night…blanker. Time of year: winter…blanker blanker. Fink! Millions of tiny sprouts of golden hair on my legs and arms. In the sun they glisten. Breasts moving along nicely. Not much bigger than a scoop in a nickel cone right now. Eyes and teeth: sharp and healthy. Fink! Other favorites: book, The Iliad; poem: "The Rubaiyat"… yeah, "The Rubaiyat"; movie: none; ocean: the Dead Sea; tree: tulip; flower: pansy…the flower variety; dress: the one with strawberries I wear on Fridays; painter: none…well maybe Leonardo; color: black; person: me. Fink!

(She finishes with a flourish; Sigfrid and Ruby express their approval.)

RUBY: *Brava, Lakme, brava!*

SIGFRID: Hey, you've made a few changes in it.

LAKME: *(So pleased with herself.)* Unh-hunh! *(Then, to Clarence.)* Yeah?

CLARENCE: I thought you were a…a boy. The way you were dressed. Sigfrid's little brother or something.

LAKME: I *could* say something about appearances being deceiving, but I won't. *If you know what I mean.*

SIGFRID: Clarence had quite a little tête-à-tête with Grandfa, Ruby.

RUBY: Yes, I heard them.

CLARENCE: …heard?…

RUBY: The intercom. Poor Grandfa. Look, children, over there. His little bag's all packed. We're putting him in an asylum tomorrow.

CLARENCE: Yes, so he told me.

SIGFRID: Grandfa is insane.

CLARENCE: Yes, he told me that, too.

RUBY: He's written a novel.

CLARENCE: Oh. *(Pause.)* Is that what makes him insane?

(Ruby nods her head.)

Oh. *(Pause.)* How does that make him insane?

LAKME: He thinks it's the truth.

CLARENCE: Oh. *(Pause.)* Well, lots of famous writers cracked up right toward the end. *(A joke.)* Sometimes before!

LAKME: *(Tight-lipped.)* Grandfa isn't famous.

SIGFRID: *(Tight-lipped.)* Grandfa isn't a writer.

RUBY: *(Tight-lipped.)* Grandfa is insane.

CLARENCE: Oh. *(Pause.)* Still, it's sad putting old people away. I don't believe in it unless it's absolutely necessary. My grand—

RUBY: It was, Clarence, in this case it was. Nevertheless, that's a lovely sentiment. Extremely lovely. You have our support.

(An extremely loud snortle from Fa.)

Oh, Fa! I do wish he'd go somewhere else to make those dreadful noises. He can be such a water buffalo about it.

CLARENCE: Is that…?

RUBY: That's our Fa. Rip Van Winkle with a bad heart. Fa won't be with us much longer, we're afraid.

LAKME: *(Skeptical.)* Afraid? Hah!

RUBY: It's imminent. We've been expecting the worse for quite some time now.

CLARENCE: That's awful.

RUBY: Yes, I suppose it is. But you see, Clarence, Fa has not been affectionate with us. He's slept, while we have…how shall I say it?…not slept. It's been a hard row to hoe without our *babbino*, but we've managed.

SIGFRID: *Triumphed*, Ruby. *Triumphed* is a better word.

RUBY: *(Arms outspread to Lakme and Sigfrid again.)* Abbraciami ancora, tesori, abbraciami! *(She holds them close.)* Aren't they wonderful, Clarence? Aren't my babies wonderful?

CLARENCE: They're…very nice.

RUBY: You use words so judiciously, Clarence. So judiciously. *(Then, in another tone.)* Halloween?

CLARENCE: *(Not catching the implication.)* Please?

SIGFRID: *(Moving away from Ruby, the efficient host bit.)* Drinks! I completely forgot. Ruby? What are you having?

RUBY: Cognac, a little cognac, darling. *(Then, directly to Clarence.)* Je ne pouvais pas exister sans le cognac.

CLARENCE: Yes.

SIGFRID: Lakme?

LAKME: A martini, stupid, what do you think? *(Then, to Clarence.)* You should have seen your face when I first came in here. Stupefication!

SIGFRID: Clarence? *(And before Clarence can answer.)* You're not uncomfortable? Sitting on the floor?

CLARENCE: No, I'm fine, just fine.

SIGFRID: Let's see, does that get everyone? All-righty. And a pernod for me. *(He works at the bar.)*

LAKME: *(Who has been considering all this.)* Stupefaction. I can *say* stupefaction. I *prefer* stupefication. It's more stupefacient than stupefaction…stupefication, is. Stupid!

RUBY: That will do, Lakme. I should think that will do for quite a while now.

LAKME: I'm being *nice*. Aren't I? Aren't I being nice?

CLARENCE: *(To Ruby.)* My little sister—

RUBY: *(Beaming.)* It's such a relief to see Sigfrid bring someone nice home for a change. We've had some of the most awful people here. Right where you're sitting. Riffraff! And if there's one thing I won't have in my basement, it's riffraff. Trash is all right…and Sigfrid's brought home enough of it…but I draw the line at riffraff…Well, do you blame me?

CLARENCE: It's not very pleasant.

RUBY: I wish you could have seen the girl he brought home with him last week. A belly dancer. An Arab belly dancer.

SIGFRID: She was amazing.

RUBY: I'm glad you thought so. The hair, Clarence. Horrible black hair. Everywhere. And the skin. Oily, oily.

SIGFRID: Olive, Ruby, an Arab's skin is olive.

RUBY: I call it *oily*. Now if that had been a *real* stone in her navel…

SIGFRID: Well Clarence isn't riffraff, Ruby.

RUBY: *(To Clarence, sharing an enormous joke.)* Just *trash? (Everyone laughs; Clarence manages a smile.)* You don't say much, do you?

SIGFRID: *(Coming forward with the drinks, passing them around.)* Clarence is shy, Ruby. Clarence has a father who used to beat him as a child. Clarence has a mother—

CLARENCE: Sigfrid!

SIGFRID: Relax, sweetheart. It's no skin off *your* nose. You told me and now I'm telling them.

CLARENCE: That was…different.

SIGFRID: Not really. *(Continuing.)* …a mother who smothered him with affection. She still does, in truth. And Clarence works in the public library. It is not difficult, therefore, to *explain* why Clarence is shy. It is not difficult to explain *Clarence*. There are reasons for him. *(Toasting.) Skol,* Clarence.

RUBY: *Skol,* Clarence.

LAKME: *Skol,* Clarence.

CLARENCE: *(Instinctively raising his hand to drink.) Skol.*
    (They drink to him.)

RUBY: *(Reflectively.)* There's something about you, Clarence…I can't quite put my finger on it…something about you that makes me think it's Halloween.

SIGFRID: It's the dress, Ruby.

RUBY: Mmm, I suppose it is.

SIGFRID: Clarence can't find his clothes. He asked if there wasn't something of yours he might put on.

CLARENCE: No!

RUBY: Well it *is* a bit damp down here this evening. You were afraid he might catch cold. I don't mind, do I?

CLARENCE: That's not true.

RUBY: *(Running on.)* Mind? Of course I don't mind. One thing life has taught me…and perhaps this is *all* it has taught me…is never to mind anything. Since I stopped minding, which was not so many years ago, I have…on occasion…been amused. And I suppose being amused is the closest thing left us to grace. *(Then, directly to Clarence, with all her charm.)* Don't you think so, Clarence?

CLARENCE: Mrs.…

RUBY: Ruby. The name is Ruby.

CLARENCE: That's not true about…I didn't ask to…

RUBY: To *what*, dear?

CLARENCE: This…this dress.

RUBY: *(Placating.)* Sigfrid's only joking…*maybe* he's only joking…either way; I know that. Besides…hmm?
    (Lakme is whispering into Ruby's ear. Ruby laughs and nods her head affirma-

tively several times. Meanwhile, Sigfrid joins Clarence on the hassock, putting one arm affectionately around his shoulder.)

SIGFRID: Ruby's a good sport. We all are. So you be one, too. Just... relax.

CLARENCE: *(A whisper.)* That was a lie.

SIGFRID: *(Good-natured.)* Oh, grump, grump, grump.

CLARENCE: Well it *was*. It was embarrassing.

SIGFRID: *(Logically.)* How can it be a lie when it's not true in the first place?...hunh?

RUBY: *(Back to Clarence and Sigfrid.)* I'm sorry. You were saying...?

SIGFRID: *(Sweetly.)* Clarence was just accusing me of telling a lie and I was explaining to him that it's not a lie unless it's true.

RUBY: Why of course! *Tout le monde* knows *that*. There's no point to be a lie if it's not true. *(As before.)* Don't you think so, Clarence?

(Lakme is at the rear of the room.)

SIGFRID: What's she up to?

RUBY: Lakme thought our little guest might enjoy a little music. Little guest, little music. One of the records, dear.

CLARENCE: Mrs....Ruby. It's just not true.

SIGFRID: Sshh. You're going to like this.

RUBY: *(Rising to the occasion. A command performance.)* I had a career in grand opera, you know. I was a diva...a prima donna...quite one of the best. "La Regina dell'Opera": me! The Queen of Opera. Or as the children so idiomatically put it: I was an opera queen. That's idiomatic *and* literal both!... Well, to press on: I was beautiful then and there was music in my voice...beautiful, beautiful music. I could sing anything...and I often did. There was no role too high, too low, or too in-between. And on stage...ah! on stage...and you must believe this, I was beautiful...so very, very beautiful.

SIGFRID: *(Whispered.)* That's Ruby's Lucy Lammermoor Mad Scene Dress. See the blood? She's just killed her husband.

RUBY: Lucy Lammermoor, Beatrice di Tenda, Elvira in Puritani, Amina...ah! such very good friends we were! How I loved them! How I was loved *as* them!

SIGFRID: *(Whispered.)* Ruby specialized in mad scenes. "La Luna dell'Opera."

RUBY: And now they are both gone: the beauty and the music...dearly departed ornaments of my being. They are but shadows now ...happy or unhappy shades I do not know. The one, frozen for a single terrifying instant snatched from eternity, my eternity, in a red Moroccan leather album of yellowing photographs...hundreds upon hundreds of them. The other, my voice...my beautiful voice...echoed endlessly on the eroded grooves of a spinning black disk...just this one. *Ascolta.*

(The music starts now. Instantly her mood lightens and her speech tempo becomes faster. The recording played should be that of an incredibly awful soprano singing

an elaborate coloratura aria. Florence Foster Jenkin's recording of the Queen of the Night aria is suggested. The actress should "play" with the music at all times during the following speech mouthing certain phrases of music, pausing in her speech to listen to certain passages, conducting a little. Sigfrid and Lakme alternate between rapt attention and trying to keep a straight face. Clarence is flabbergasted.) Aaaah! Wolfgang Amadeus! *Bravo, mei figli bravi...*the unhappy mother, the enraged Queen of the Night, swears vengeance and vows to deliver Pamina from her captor's hands ...Vengeance! ...This phrase: lovely, lovely...I sang this once in Moscow...at the Bolshoi...in Russian, no less...those dreadful thick vowels...

CLARENCE: *(In a whisper.)* Who's—?

(Sigfrid fiercely motions him to be silent.)

RUBY: After the performance I was delivered to my hotel in a troika drawn by several thousand delirious students who then proceeded to serenade me with folk songs from the streets beneath my windows...I sat alone on my balcony...it was a warm evening, warm for Moscow...alone and weeping... weeping and toasting them with vodka...they sang until dawn...when the Kremlin's domes first were flecked with the morning sun's gold...Here! The cadenza! Marvelous!...Once in Milano...after my debut at the Scala in a revival of "Gianna D'Arco"...revived for *me, ça va sans dire...*the manager, the manager of Scala said to me: "Ruby, *tu hai la voce delle anime di Purgatorio*"...which means, roughly translated: "Ruby, you sing with the voice of the souls in Purgatory"...well, *something* like that. You see, he'd heard the *pain* in my voice...and not only the joy. It was the exquisite mingling of the two that so enthralled him... This part, now. I would rush about the stage brandishing this enormous dagger. One critic said it was an awesome moment...Oh, the memory of those nights!...those days...the continental tours with Brunnhilde, my pekingese, and my three male secretaries...the steamer trunks stickered ten times over with those magic names: Paris, Rome, Vienna, London, Bayreuth, Peiping, Manila, Camden, New Jersey...yes, Camden, New Jersey...Athens, Napoli, Palermo ...Palermo where I first met Fa, after a Delilah at the Teatro Massimo. He'd come there to export the olives...Here! The portamento!...Oh the glory! the glory! *(Her voice trails off and she is lost in revery, listening to the music with closed eyes, her head back. The music ends. There is a pause. Then Ruby opens her eyes and leans forward toward Clarence.)* Well?

LAKME: Well?

SIGFRID: Well?

CLARENCE: I...unh...I...

SIGFRID: Tell Ruby what you thought, Clarence. Go on.

CLARENCE: I...I don't know very much about music. I really shouldn't venture to make a judgment.

SIGFRID: Oh, go ahead, venture!

LAKME: *(Sing-song.)* Nothing ventured, nothing gained.

CLARENCE: Especially opera. I don't know anything about opera. *(A weak joke.)* Wagner wrote Puccini as far as I know. *(They are not amused.)* Really...I'm not qualified.

RUBY: *(Edgy.)* That quality of the *voice*, dear. We're interested in what you think of *that*.

CLARENCE: Oh...*that*...it was wonderful, Mrs....

LAKME: Ruby. Her name is Ruby.

CLARENCE: ...just wonderful.

RUBY: Yes?

CLARENCE: What else can I...? It reminded me of...of a bird. A lark maybe. I don't know. But it certainly was wonderful. You're very talented. *(The three of them explode with laughter.)* What?...What's so funny?...Did I say something wrong?

RUBY: *(Rocking with laughter.)* He's so pathetically polite.

SIGFRID: *(The same.)* You're very talented, Ruby!

RUBY: And so patronizing.

LAKME: A bird. You reminded him of a bird.

CLARENCE: *(The light slowly dawning.)* Oh...I see...that wasn't you!

LAKME: Do tell!

CLARENCE: *(Joining in the laughter himself.)* No wonder!...well I'm glad it wasn't...ha ha...that was the worst thing I ever heard in my life...ha ha ha...it was awful...where did you find that record...who was she? *(Abruptly, the laughter ceases and they stare fiercely at Clarence.)*

RUBY: *(Sharp.)* A very dear friend.

CLARENCE: *(Caught in mid-laugh.)* Oh.

RUBY: A seventy-two-year-old lady.

LAKME: A seventy-two-year-old *Negro* lady.

SIGFRID: A seventy-two-year-old Negro *servant* from the deep Deep South.

RUBY: Seventy-two-year-old Negro lady servants from the deep Deep South who sing Mozart arias are *not* to be ridiculed. *Ever!*

LAKME: Racist! Dirty Nazi racist!

CLARENCE: *(Thoroughly chastened.)* I...I didn't know.

RUBY: You may laugh *with* us, Clarence, at yourself...but not at sweet old Aunt Jemima from the deep Deep South.

(Again they explode with laughter. Clarence sits dumbly, not knowing what to do or say or think. Ruby leans forward to pat his cheek.)

Clarence! Where's that smile! That famous smile of yours!

(Clarence doesn't react.)

Now! Together! Sing!

(She leads them in a rousing chorus of "For He's a Jolly Good Fellow." Suddenly the lights dim to half and hold there. The singing falters. Ruby is determined to finish the song, but for a moment she is the only one singing. Then Sigfrid joins in, rather limply at first, but soon belting it out with his full voice. Lakme has stopped singing altogether and moves away from the others. Even though her back is to us, we can tell from her heaving shoulders that she is fighting to hold back enormous sobs. The lights come swiftly back up to full, as Ruby and Sigfrid finish the song boisterously.)

CLARENCE: I don't know what to think of you people. One minute you're friendly, the next you're making fun of me.

SIGFRID: *(Poo-pooing.)* Oh! Don't mind us. That's our way.

CLARENCE: Fun at my expense!

RUBY: *(Looking across the room at Lakme.)* Lakme!

SIGFRID: And whose fault is that? *You* admired the singing. A cat in heat, a God-knows-what, and you admired the *singing*.

CLARENCE: Because I thought it was…I was only trying to be polite.

RUBY: Stop that, Lakme.

SIGFRID: So you made a fool of yourself? Oh baby, learn to laugh at yourself. Learn it quick. It's the only thing that makes sense anymore.

CLARENCE: I'm sorry, but I don't have a sense of humor.

SIGFRID: *(Flip.)* Neither do we. Think about that.

RUBY: Lakme, I asked you to *stop*.

SIGFRID: What's the matter with her?

RUBY: The fence. Go to your room, Lakme.

SIGFRID: *(Going to Lakme, not unkindly.)* Come on, little one, calm down now.

LAKME: *(Pulling away from him.)* Keep away from me!

SIGFRID: We're here. We're all together. Don't—

LAKME: KEEP AWAY!

SIGFRID: *(Getting angry.)* Now look, Lakme!

RUBY: Make her go to her room, Sigfrid.

LAKME: I said keep *away!*

RUBY: *(Delighted sarcasm.)* Brave little Lakme. Fearless little Lakme. Our own little St. Joan of the Underground. "Leave the door open, Ruby. It's fifteen minutes 'til—"

LAKME: Shut up, Ruby, just shut up!

RUBY: *(Delighted with herself.)* Coraggio, Lakme, coraggio!

LAKME: JUST DO WHAT YOU SAID YOU WOULD. MAKE HIM GO OUT THERE. BUT GET IT OVER WITH AND LEAVE US ALONE. JUST DO IT. *(She leaves quickly through the Stage Right door.)*

SIGFRID: *(Following.)* Lakme!

RUBY: Sigfrid! Not yet.

SIGFRID: But she'll—

RUBY: Be all right.

SIGFRID: But she won't—

RUBY: She will. Sit.

SIGFRID: But—

RUBY: SIT!

> *(He obeys.)*
> The line, Sigfrid, you said something about the line?
> *(He doesn't answer.)*

CLARENCE: *(A voice in the void.)* Is there anything the matter? *(A long pause.)* Is there?

RUBY: *(Abruptly.)* Tell us about the way you live, Clarence.

CLARENCE: Sir? I mean…*(He laughs.)* Excuse me.

RUBY: *(Not amused.)* The way you live. I want you to tell us about it.

CLARENCE: I don't understand. The way I live? Me?

SIGFRID: *(Reasonably.)* What you believe in, Clarence. A statement of principles…life principles.

CLARENCE: Like my philosophy? Is that what you mean? My philosophy of life?

RUBY: *(An edge in her voice.)* It's called the way you live.

CLARENCE: *(Amused.)* But why? I'm not even sure if I have one.

RUBY: You're alive, aren't you?

Clarence. Well, yes.

RUBY: Then you have one.

CLARENCE: Well, I suppose I do…I must…only I hadn't really thought about it.

RUBY: You gave Grandfa an earful.

CLARENCE: Please?

SIGFRID: *(Always more conciliatory than Ruby.)* Now's your opportunity, Clarence.

CLARENCE: What do you want with it? My philosophy of life?

RUBY: *(Insistent.)* It's called the way you live.

SIGFRID: We'd like to tape it.

CLARENCE: Tape it? You mean on a—? *(Sigfrid nods.)* But why would anyone want to do a thing like that? Tape someone's phi—…way he lives?

SIGFRID: Ruby collects them. All our guests do it. She's looking for the answer.

RUBY: I *have* the answer. I'm looking for corroboration. I find it consoling. Usually.

CLARENCE: *(A little intrigued with the idea.)* You mean we'll probably end up saying the very same thing? Or just about?

RUBY: *Or* just about.

> *(Sigfrid has been setting up the recorder.)*

RUBY'S RECORDED VOICE: *(Very loud.)* "…wherefrom we shall draw the sustenance to destroy you…"

RUBY: On *"record,"* dear, not on "playback."

(Sigfrid has already turned the machine off and now sets a microphone in front of Clarence.)

CLARENCE: *(To Ruby.)* That was *you*. Was that from *your…*? *(Noticing the microphone.)* Is this what I talk into? I feel like I'm on the radio. Gee, I bet I make a mess out of this. *(Sigfrid motions for silence and points to the spinning reels.)* You mean I'm on already? Heavens! I'm really not prepared, you know. *(A pause.)* Unh… unh…the way I live…no, let me start again…unh…*(He takes a deep breath.)* The way I live…The way I live is…the best I can do. I try. I mean I really try. And I think I'm improving. I think I am becoming a better human being day by day. I really do…Anyway, I'm trying. *(Then, turning to Ruby and Sigfrid.)* This is awful. I told you— *(They motion to him to continue.)* I believe in…well, lots of things. *(From this point he begins to warm to his subject.)*

It's hard to express them. They're like abstractions. *They're* not abstractions, but what there is about them that makes me believe in them is…an abstraction…sort of. People…trees…the sunshine… snow…a clear cold day in November…things like that. Beauty. Something… beautiful. *(Short pause.)* And I think it's sad that we can't enjoy these things the way we were meant to. Because of…the circumstances. No, these were not the best of times to have been born in. I should have preferred the Renaissance, when it was easier to…live, I suppose. And that's the important thing. To live. That's why we're alive. Otherwise, there's no point to it…life. *(Shorter pause.)* I love life. I suppose that's a corny statement, but I do. I know it's fashionable to be morose these days, but I frankly can't see anything to be morose *about!*…well, *some* things, but certainly not enough to talk about killing yourself or not giving a damn anymore or anything like that. Just about the last thing I'd ever do is kill myself. There aren't enough reasons to. There are just too many good things in the world not to want to be alive. Just think of all the beautiful things men have made. Music, art, literature…Shakespeare alone is a reason to be alive. How could anyone not want to be alive after there's been a Shakespeare on this earth? I can't imagine it. And even if I've never seen it real…and maybe I never will…how could anyone not want to be alive when there is a city in Italy named Florence? How could they? Just *knowing* about Florence!…what it *means* to us that it's there. That there *was* a Florence, is and will be. It…it makes the rest of this planet tolerable. Florence is *why* we're alive. It's what we're *about*. *(A pause.)*

And the things you can do! The simple things. What about them? Just to take a walk even. It can be wonderful! Or to be by the sea and feel that air on your face and see what the horizon means. You can actually *see* the curve of the earth. Just what they taught you in school and it's true. That's a wonderful thing to see for yourself. Or just to sit in a park...with the sun spilling all over you...watching the people. The other people. They're not you, and that's what's so beautiful about them. They're someone else. Sit and wonder who they are. What they ate for breakfast, what paper they're reading, where they live, what they do...who they love. And that's another reason. Everybody loves somebody...or they will...sometime in their life. *(A pause.)*

Anything that makes you want to live so bad you'd...you'd die for it... Shakespeare, Florence... someone in the park. That's what I believe in. That's all. That's the way I live.

(A silence. Sigfrid turns off the recorder.)

RUBY: Shakespeare, Florence, and someone in the park. That was nicely spoken, Clarence.

CLARENCE: Was it all right? I sort of enjoyed it once I got into it. What happens now? With the tape, I mean.

SIGFRID: We put it aside...save it...keep it for reference.

CLARENCE: Were they very similar? Yours and mine?

RUBY: Not quite, Clarence, not quite.

CLARENCE: *(Completely at home now.)* And another nice thing...I should've taped it...sometimes you run into old friends. People you haven't seen for over ten years. It's very nice when that happens. *(To Ruby.)* Only he doesn't remember anyone from that school. All the friends he had and he can't remember a single one. He didn't remember *me* until I—

SIGFRID: Just one.

CLARENCE: Who is that? Billy...unh...Billy...

SIGFRID: The kid on the slide.

CLARENCE: Oh...him.

SIGFRID: The one who fell off the slide and broke his arm...and then said he was pushed. Remember him?

CLARENCE: Only the incident. But remember Mrs. Chapin?...the fifth grade?...the one with the long neck? Old rubberneck? We used to draw her picture on the blackboard with miles and miles of neck snaking all over the place. Don't you remember her? You were her favorite. It got her. About two years ago. She must have been out after curfew. They found her in the park.

SIGFRID: Well, those bachelor ladies who prowl the parks after dark usually come to a bad end.

CLARENCE: I thought you liked Mrs. Chapin. And even if you didn't...

SIGFRID: Yes?

CLARENCE: That's not a very nice thing to say. After all, the woman's *dead*.

RUBY: *(A sudden exclamation.)* Now I know who you're talking about...this boy on the slide. Not the boy who *fell* off the slide, Sigfrid, the boy you *pushed. Then* he fell, after you'd pushed him. Yes, of course, he fell and broke his leg.

CLARENCE: Arm.

RUBY: Arm was it?

CLARENCE: I…I think it was.

RUBY: Funny, you seemed so certain a moment ago.

SIGFRID: *(Rather amused.)* I pushed him, Ruby? He didn't fall and *then* say I pushed him? I really did push him in the first place?

RUBY: Yes, *caro*, yes. And so they expelled you.

SIGFRID: Well, what do you know about that? Clarence?

CLARENCE: I'd always heard he…fell.

RUBY: And little Sigfrid was expelled. That wasn't the only reason, of course. There had been previous incidents. But all the same, you *did* own up to it. Well, after a fashion you owned up to it. In your own sweet time, you might say…after they'd *tricked* you into it. *(To Clarence directly.)* Were you at that assembly?

CLARENCE: Yes.

RUBY: Police state methods! That's what it was. Putting that injured boy upon the stage with his leg in a cast…arm, you said? Well, whatever it was …putting him up there and making the other students stand up one at a time until he could say *"Him.* He's the one who did it." Well of course Sigfrid owned up to it! Who wouldn't? With some brat's finger, accusing you, stuck in your face and that man, that principal with all the moles, shouting at you? Naturally Sigfrid said he did it. *(Short pause.)* And he *had!* (Shorter pause.) So they expelled him. *(Longer pause; she moves away from them.)*

CLARENCE: *(Breaking an awkward silence.)* What happened then, Sigfrid? After the sixth grade?

SIGFRID: *(Curt.)* Nothing.

CLARENCE: Nothing?

SIGFRID: Nothing.

CLARENCE: Well *some*thing—

SIGFRID: NOTHING.

LAKME'S VOICE: *(Suddenly, on the intercom.)* "A sky, a blue sky, the eagle soars." That's what happened, Shelley, that's what happened after the sixth grade. You wrote poetry."

SIGFRID: You goddamn little—

LAKME'S VOICE: *(Joshing.)* Oh come on, eagle, I can't find the projector.

SIGFRID: Just lay off me, dwarf girl, hunh?

LAKME'S VOICE: You can be such a poop sometimes, Sigfrid. Now will you get in here and help? I'm in the darkroom.

(The red light on the intercom goes off.)

SIGFRID: *(Getting up.)* Ruby?

CLARENCE: *(Getting up, too.)* Can I—?

SIGFRID: No.

CLARENCE: Where are you going?

SIGFRID: You'll see.

CLARENCE: Is something going to happen?

SIGFRID: You might say that. *(He is gone.)*

CLARENCE: I hate surprises. *(Then, to Ruby.)* Is that what happened? Sigfrid wrote poetry? *(No response.)* I wrote a poem once. For my mother. On her birthday. When I was little. "God bless the Lord. God bless my mother. She has good things in her oven." She's always saved it. *(Long pause.)* It was unfortunate.

RUBY: *(Irritable, facing Clarence for the first time since she last spoke.)* What was?

CLARENCE: That they expelled him. Sigfrid was very popular at that—

RUBY: Lots of things are *unfortunate*. Sitting here in his goddamn basement night after night is *unfortunate*. That thing out there is *unfortunate*. Life is *unfortunate*.

CLARENCE: The Situation. You mean the Situation.

RUBY: *(Flat.)* That's right…the Situation.

CLARENCE: *(In solemn agreement.)* It's been this way so long now…all my lifetime.

RUBY: *(Bitter.)* Twenty years, isn't it? Isn't that what the *textbooks* say?

CLARENCE: You know, I've never seen a sunset…and the moon only in the daytime when it's not really the moon…the way it should be the moon.

RUBY: Twenty years…two hundred…two thousand.

CLARENCE: Before the curfew, when you could go out nights, did you ever see an eclipse of the moon? I think I'd rather see an eclipse of the moon than the moon itself. From what I've read—

RUBY: Once.

CLARENCE: What was it like?

RUBY: Dark, very dark.

CLARENCE: *(Disappointed.)* Oh.

RUBY: It was in Florence.

CLARENCE: Florence! You've been in Florence!

RUBY: It was lovely…very dark and very lonely.

CLARENCE: Everything is *was* now.

RUBY: Shakespeare, Florence, and someone in the park.

CLARENCE: That's scarcely what I'd call a deathless sentiment. *(The lights suddenly dim to half.)* The lights again! Something's happening to— *(The lights come back to full.)* See how jittery I am? Something happens, a little thing like the lights, and I start …shaking, almost. Anything goes wrong and I think it's started to happen…that it's finally out there. If we only knew *when*…or if it's *ever* going to happen. It's this waiting that's so terrible…the not-knowing.

RUBY: We know it's out there. That's enough.

CLARENCE: But we don't even know what it *is*...specifically what it is. Oh, I read books, newspapers accounts, but...well I wish I could *see* it. So I could know what it is we're so afraid of. ...Not up close. I know you can't come face-to-face with it...what happens then. But from a distance: that's what I'd like. If I could be on the top of a very high mountain and look down into a valley where it was happening. I'd have a telescope and I'd scrunch down in the foliage and spy on it. Just so I could get some idea of what it was like...some inkling...even from far off. But they say all the safe hiding places are gone now. Sure you can see it...millions of people have...and they're all dead.

RUBY: Here it's safe. No one dies down here.

CLARENCE: All you can do is try to imagine it...what it's like. Do you do that? I see this cat...a big cat, but more like a monster, sitting outside a mousehole. It's out there...all the time...waiting to pounce. It's got long claws and teeth...big teeth. Except it doesn't eat you...just takes you away to someplace alone...someplace dark and cold...with no sounds. And it won't ever go away unless ...unless...I don't know what will make it go away. But if we stay here, where it's light and warm, just a little bit even, it can't get at us. It can't take us away with it to that place. But if you go out there... *(Pause.)* What do you think it is?

RUBY: I don't know.

CLARENCE: Don't you have any idea what it's like?

RUBY: Not really. I would only suggest...*suggest*...that it has something to do with the unbearable difference between the way things are...us, for example...and the way they should be...us, for example.

CLARENCE: Oh.

RUBY: Does that disappoint you?

CLARENCE: *(It does, of course.)* No. It's just that I'm so frightened of it and your idea sounds so...so intellectual. *Aren't* you frightened of it?

RUBY: If it gives you any pleasure to know this, Clarence, I am terrified beyond belief and, occasionally, out of my mind.

(The lights dim again, hold a moment and then come back to full strength.)

CLARENCE: What's happening? The fuses keep—

RUBY: It's not the fuses. It's those dumb stray animals wandering into the fence.

CLARENCE: You mean it's...electrified?

RUBY: We have to keep people out somehow. There are signs posted at regular intervals. Of course if Darwin were right the animals should have learned to read by now. You don't approve, I suppose?

CLARENCE: No...it's just that...well how often does it happen?

RUBY: Four or five a night. Dogs...cats...an occasional parakeet. The city picks them up the next morning along with the garbage.

CLARENCE: *(Sickened.)* That's awful…it shouldn't be like this…fences, basements, curfews…no…it shouldn't be this way.

RUBY: Well it is.

CLARENCE: That's exactly why I'm so concerned! Because it *is* this way and it must *not* be.

RUBY: That's right! You're concerned. I'd nearly forgotten.

CLARENCE: Of course I'm concerned. One *has* to care…passionately!

RUBY: *("Finding" a sock under one of the sofa cushions and holding it up rather conspicuously.)* Passion…ah yes, one must have passion …where would we be without passion? *(She has found another sock.)* Passion for Shakespeare…passion for Florence…passion for someone in the park.

CLARENCE: *(A little nervous; those are his socks.)* Don't you care? …about …? *(He gestures vaguely toward the outside.)*

RUBY: The only issue of *passionate* concern in this family…the only one any of us really care about…is who's going to get who: where, when, and how.

CLARENCE: *(The smugness beginning to creep into his voice.)* I was talking about something else. Those are social relations…personal problems …neuroses. I was talking about more universal themes …the ones that really count.

RUBY: *(Idly, examining a pair of undershorts she has found under another sofa cushion.)* Oh…and what are they?

CLARENCE: Life…survival…that thing out there…I don't know.

RUBY: *(Helpful.)* The big things?

CLARENCE: Yes.

RUBY: The major issues of our times?

CLARENCE: That's right.

RUBY: And not personal…how shall I put it?…unpleasantness?

CLARENCE: Especially not that.

RUBY: *("Convinced.")* I see. Well in that case perhaps we *should* concern ourselves…so much being at stake. Universal themes at our back door and we're worried about ourselves! Heavens!

CLARENCE: *(Confidentially, to an ally.)* People think too much about themselves these days. They encourage their neuroses. They coddle them, if you ask me.

RUBY: Well we'll certainly put a stop to *that.*

Clarence. I hope I'm not sounding smug or anything.

RUBY: You? Smug? Clarence!

CLARENCE: I have that tendency.

RUBY: But how exactly does one go about it? Being concerned, I mean. What does one *do*, for example?

CLARENCE: It's more a question of being than doing actually.

RUBY: You must do *something.*

CLARENCE: Well, I *read*…I've been in a few demonstrations…I wrote a letter to—

RUBY: I asked you what you were *doing*.

CLARENCE: Well…don't you see…it's more a question of allowing myself to become involved…recognizing my responsibility to the issues at large. Commitment! That's the important thing: to be committed.

RUBY: I don't understand. Committed to what? An asylum, like Grandfa?

CLARENCE: No! Something large.

RUBY: Elephants are large. Are you committed to elephants?

CLARENCE: You know what I'm talking about. Something larger than myself…something…I don't know…*purer!*…a cause, an ideal …something outside of me…away from the littleness inside …nowadays people are all hunched over their navels when they have the stars to reach for!

RUBY: Had.

CLARENCE: I beg your pardon?

RUBY: *Had* the stars to reach for.

CLARENCE: *(Sadly.)* Yes, *had*.

RUBY: "Everything is *was* now." Those are your words. *(Short pause.)* Well, if that's all you're doing I suppose it's better than nothing. I suppose it's better than us.

CLARENCE: Maybe I'm not as aggressive as I'd like to be…outgoing…I'm more introspective.

RUBY: But committed.

CLARENCE: I try to be.

RUBY: Dedicated…no distractions.

CLARENCE: Well sure. You can't worry about these things twenty-four hours a day.

RUBY: *(The coup de grâce.)* I shouldn't think so. I mean there you were: marching around town all afternoon in this nippy weather…waving your little sign…the wind trying to pull it out of your hands. Marching and waving that sign and being committed and all. That's what I call a big day. You need a distraction after an afternoon like that. No wonder you toddled over to the curb when you saw that good-looking son of mine giving your little sign the once-over. No matter how committed you are, you certainly don't pass up a good-looking distraction like Sigfrid without at least inquiring. After all, he might be committed, too! No harm in asking. "Hello there. I'm looking for something larger than myself. What about you?" asks the commitment. …I know this scene well…The distraction smiles but does not answer. They never do. "Oh dear," fidgets the commitment, "I *do* wish he wouldn't stare at my little sign like that." The other marchers, with whom the commitment had begun the parade, marchers, of a somewhat different commitment, perhaps, are moving along now. Soon they will be out of sight. "Are you a commitment or a distraction?" pleads the boy with sign. "Are you one of us or not? I must know." The distraction only smiles, beckons with his head and begins to move away. "But I'm committed! I can't go with you!" he cries after the departing form. What to do? What to do? And as he stands there, soon to be alone...his feet numb with cold...watching the commitments march up the street one way and the distraction walk slowly down it the other...he remembers those immortal words of Clarentius, the saddest commitment of them all: "You can't worry about these things twenty-four hours a day." Hey! Distraction! Wait for me! *(She whistles with two fingers in her mouth, then breaks into laughter and prods Clarence in the ribs.)* Wasn't it that way, Clarence? Wasn't it?

CLARENCE: *(Turning away.)* I don't know what you're talking about.

RUBY: That boy of mine may be a lousy commitment but he's one hell of a distraction!

CLARENCE: I'm sure I wouldn't know.

RUBY: Oh you wouldn't, would you?

CLARENCE: No I wouldn't!

RUBY: *(Fast and tough.)* Look, sweetheart, you check the guilt baggage at the front door when you come into this house. It's not like outside down here. We don't play games...well, that's not true exactly...but we don't play *those* kinds of games. We deal with what's *left* us...not what we'd like to *add* to the mythology. It's a subtraction process and if the answer is zero that's okay, too. Now you just be a sweet little distraction and simmer down.

CLARENCE: I'm not a distraction!

RUBY: You're just someone who happened in off the street, all committed up for Halloween? Is that it?

CLARENCE: NO!

RUBY: *(Making him look on her face.)* "And someone in the park!" That's your commitment, Clarence. Not Shakespeare, not Florence, not what's out there, but someone in the park! And that someone happened to be Sigfrid!

CLARENCE: *(Broken now.)* I...I didn't come here for that.

RUBY: But Sigfrid wanted it that way. So you let him.

CLARENCE: I didn't want him to.

RUBY: But you let him. Oh Clarence...Clarence, Clarence, Clarence.

CLARENCE'S RECORDED VOICE: *(A mocking echo.)* Oh Sigfrid...Sigfrid, Sigfrid, Sigfrid.

RUBY: I beg your pardon?

(He neither answers nor looks at her. Sigfrid and Lakme enter through the Stage Right door. He carries a slide projector; she, a movie screen.)

LAKME: Here we are. Ready to go.

SIGFRID: Did you two have a nice talk while we were gone? Did Clarence try to convert you to the cause, Ruby?

RUBY: Sshh! The Clarence is temporarily out of commitment.

SIGFRID: Aaaaaw!

CLARENCE: I'd like to go home, please.

SIGFRID: But love-blessing! Lakme's produced an entertainment…a sight and sound entertainment…especially for you.

CLARENCE: I'd like to go home.

RUBY: *Pounce!* Remember, Clarence?…that mean old pussycat?

SIGFRID: What old pussycat?

RUBY: You're an old pussycat.

SIGFRID: *(He and Lakme are busy setting up.)* Do you know what Clarence did, Ruby? He told his father I was a girl. Me. Can you imagine it? And he told his mother he was coming over to see a boy. Such double-think!

RUBY: Oh I see! His daddy lets him sleep with girls and his mummy lets him sleep with boys. They're a very conventional pair, your parents.

CLARENCE: *(Strong, for him.)* Stop it!

RUBY: That's right, Clarence. Tell us off.

CLARENCE: *(Standing.)* I'd like my clothes, please. My *own* clothes.

SIGFRID: But, buttercup, you're in them.

CLARENCE: WHERE ARE THEY?

SIGFRID: *(Mocking.)* Hoo hoo! Hoo hoo!

LAKME: *(Simultaneously.)* Arabella's in a huff. She's huffed.

SIGFRID: We're getting waspish! Oh oh oh oh!

LAKME: *(A little dance.)* Bzz…bzz…bzz!

CLARENCE: I don't have to stay here.

LAKME: Oh yes you do. *(Mock horror.)* There is something out there! Grrr!

CLARENCE: Not if I can find my clothes I don't.

LAKME: Poor lady, poor lady Godiva.

CLARENCE: Do you know where they are?

SIGFRID: Pout, pout, pout. Pretty Alice Pout.

CLARENCE: Stop that! I'm not pouting. I'm getting mad. And my name's not Alice.

SIGFRID: Sorry, Joan.

CLARENCE: *(The explosion.)* WHERE ARE MY CLOTHES!

SIGFRID: *(Ugly, ugly, ugly.)* WHERE'S YOUR SENSE OF HUMOR YOU MEAN!

LAKME: THAT'S WHAT YOU'RE LOOKING FOR!

SIGFRID: YOU CAN'T LIVE WITHOUT A SENSE OF HUMOR! NOT ANY MORE! NOT NOW!

LAKME: DOPE!

SIGFRID: SO WHERE IS IT! HUNH!

LAKME: HUNH! *(Long pause.)*

SIGFRID: *(Quietly, and with a hideous calm.)* You've also got a lousy body.

LAKME: Skin and bones.

SIGFRID: *(He means it.)* Shut up, Lakme.

CLARENCE: *(Pathetic.)* I didn't say you *hid* them.

SIGFRID: We did, of course.

CLARENCE: I didn't accuse you.

SIGFRID: Maybe you should've.

CLARENCE:…*(A sickened, moaning sound.)*…

SIGFRID: *(Almost gentle.)* You're rather a toad, aren't you?

CLARENCE: I'm…I'm just not strong. But I think things!

SIGFRID: Yes, I suppose you do.

RUBY: *(Not breaking this mood.)* Shakespeare, Florence, and someone in the park. Two are names and one's a person. Right, Clarence? …right?

CLARENCE: *(Sitting, numbed.)* Right.

(A pause. Lakme, Sigfrid, and Ruby are ready now and return to a lighter mood.)

RUBY: Lakme, what's the name of your production?

LAKME: "The Way You Live."

RUBY: The way who lives, dear?

LAKME: Him!

RUBY: Clarence! It's about you. Lakme's entertainment is about you.

LAKME: *(Finishing the arrangements.)* Okay. You ready, Sigfrid?

SIGFRID: All set.

RUBY: *(Clapping her hands.)* It's beginning, it's beginning! *Nous commençons, Clarence. Nous commençons!* Can you see all right from there?

(Sigfrid sits where he can control both the slide projector and the tape recorder. Lakme sits at the piano.)

LAKME: "The Way You Live. Clarence Fink: This is Your Life." Lights!

(All the lights in the room go off except for a dim spot on Clarence, who sits with his back to the movie screen. Not once will he look at it. Throughout the scene that follows our concentration is on Clarence live on the hassock and Clarence on the screen. The voices of Sigfrid, Lakme, and Ruby are but sounds in the dark.)

LAKME: *(Narrating over musical commentary.)* Lakme Productions bring you "The Way You Live"…an entertainment conceived, produced, and directed by Lakme Herself. Visuals and audio by Sigfrid Simp. With occasional shrieks, howls, and whoopings by Ruby Rat. Clarence Fink! This is your life!

(The picture on the screen comes sharply into focus now. We see Clarence marching along with his poster.)

There you stand, Clarence Fink. A young man of bold convictions and forthright ideals. Admired…loved…respected even by all who know you. As you march boldly into the future, wagging your sign behind you, do you remember…beneath that facade of confidence and hope… do you remember, Clarence Fink, do you remember this? Ruby!

(The slide changes to a wretched grass hut.)

RUBY: It was a miserable beginning. The palace had seen better days. The windows all were broken and the great marble floors were cracked and stained. Your mother, good queen Nefertiti, was reduced to taking in dirty linen and your pa, Old King Cole, was putting on airs.

(We see a very old, very toothless Chinese couple working in a rice paddy.)

Yet you loved them all the same. And *you*...why you were the favorite child... their pride and joy. At feeding time they always made certain you had a dab more food in your bowl than the others. Sigfrid!

(Hundreds of starving children holding empty bowls.)

SIGFRID: You were a bright child: walking at five years, talking at ten, committing nasties behind the barn...I mean hut...at fifteen. Oh, you were a precocious one. Pretty soon it was time to move on. Your horizons were unlimited. And after all, look at what happened to your brothers and sisters...all two hundred of them.

(A cemetery with hundreds of identical markets.)

The fearful chee-chee fly was rampant!

LAKME: First you said good-bye to your pa. He'd given up putting on airs and found a more spiritual occupation.

(A colored nun playing baseball.) It was a difficult parting.

CLARENCE'S RECORDED VOICE: "Are you sure it's all right in here, Sigfrid? I mean no one else will come in?"

(Clarence barely responds to the sound of his own voice. His head, shoulders only sag even more.)

LAKME: See, Ruby? Sight *and* sound.

SIGFRID: Your mother was more reluctant to see you go. You were the only child left...and the firstborn, too...and she had plans for you: Hollywood plans.

(A Shirley Temple pin-up.)

But she relented.

RUBY: That last time we saw her! Who can forget it? Misty-eyed you stood at the rear of the train, waving a lavender hanky-pank at the receding figure you had loved so well. *(A rather whorey nude with enormous breasts.)* That's *her*, Sigfrid! That Arab girl you had here last week!

SIGFRID: Olive-skinned. What did I tell you?

RUBY: Will you look at those...?

LAKME: Knockers.

RUBY: Lakme!

LAKME: Sorry.

CLARENCE'S RECORDED VOICE: "I think it's their fault. I really do. Ask any psychiatrist. Parents make their children...well, you know."

SIGFRID: What, Clarence? Make their children what?

CLARENCE'S RECORDED VOICE: ...*(An absurd giggle.)*...

SIGFRID: Oh, *that.*

LAKME: You came to the big city. It was cold and you were lonely. You drifted, spent hours at the movies, took odd jobs.

(The Radio City Rockettes.)

But nothing seemed to last.

SIGFRID: You did strange things. There was no rhythm to your life...no internal logic. You took to roller-skating, mumblety-peg, anacrostics...You were beginning to let people push you off slides...Oh, various and sundry vices... you embraced them all.

(A small boy urinating against a wall.) In short, you were a mess.

CLARENCE'S RECORDED VOICE: "Not very often...you see, I...well I'm almost a virgin."

LAKME: Categorically untrue!

CLARENCE'S RECORDED VOICE: "Really! Cross my heart and hope to die."

LAKME: Not after tonight you're not. Sigfrid took care of that. Clarence didn't even get to have his own organism, Ruby.

RUBY: Sshh! Sigfrid, where were we?

SIGFRID: In short, you were a mess.

RUBY: Ah! But salvation was just around the corner...well at the curb, actually...and you went right over to it.

(Sigfrid dressed in the collegiate sweater he wore at his first act entrance.)

RUBY: SNAP! And the poor little fishy gobbled up the big bad worm.

SIGFRID: Now that's what I call commitment.

CLARENCE'S RECORDED VOICE: "I'll probably lose my rank for leaving the parade like that. They're very strict. I'm a squadron secretary."

SIGFRID: You can be our squadron secretary, Clarence.

CLARENCE'S RECORDED VOICE: "Oh well, I'll tell them I got sick. I doubt if they'll check up on me."

(Sigfrid and Clarence talking on the street.)

LAKME: *(More agitated.)* Now this is where it gets exciting. Your heart starts to beat faster. It's the moment supreme! What you've been waiting for. Talk to him, Clarence! Pour your heart out. Tell him in your very own words!

CLARENCE'S RECORDED VOICE: "Is there a hanger?...This is my best pair of slacks."

SIGFRID: Is that all you said to me? At a time like that! Clarence.

CLARENCE'S RECORDED VOICE: "Oooooooom, these sheets are cold! Brrrrr!"

RUBY: That's better. Go on, go on.

(Clarence and Sigfrid outside a house.)

Fa! We simply must have the hedges trimmed. Look at them.

SIGFRID: That's a rotten picture of me, Lakme.

CLARENCE'S RECORDED VOICE: "I always leave my socks on...well, if it's going to bother you."

LAKME: Clarence wanted to wear his socks to bed.

RUBY: I can hear that, dear. Sshh.

SIGFRID: I think it's uncouth to wear one's socks to bed.

RUBY: Well *you!*

(Clarence by a bed, unbuttoning his shirt.)

LAKME: This is the beginning of the sexy part. I used an F15 lens.

(From this point the slides are shown more rapidly. The "slide" directions that follow are merely an indication of where we generally are in the sequence.)

CLARENCE'S RECORDED VOICE: "Gee, I'm glad we ran into each other. It's been a long time…six years after grade school…then college…it's been over ten years…and I still recognized you the instant I saw you…"

(Clarence with his shirt off.)

RUBY: *(Awed by the sight.)* Oooooooo!

SIGFRID: Aren't those pectorals something, Ruby? Pret-ty snazzy.

RUBY: These are wonderful pictures, Lakme, just wonderful.

LAKME: Thanks.

CLARENCE'S RECORDED VOICE: "Sigfrid, do you ever get lonely? I mean for someone more than just a friend…"

RUBY: You mean someone in the park, dear.

SIGFRID: He means me.

CLARENCE'S RECORDED VOICE: "Someone you can really be with…I do…"

(Clarence taking off his pants.)

"Sometimes…you may think this is silly…but sometimes…at night…I cry about being lonely…at night…when I can't sleep…and that thing is out there…I get frightened…and I cry…

(Clarence in his undershorts. Each slide is met with increasing hilarity.)

I get frightened…and I'm lonesome…and I cry…

(Sigfrid has set the tape recorder at a faster speed. Clarence's recorded voice takes on a ridiculous tone.)

Maybe I talk too much but…I don't feel safe most places…I'm nervous…I feel cold sort of…but not here…oh, no, not here…I feel safe here…it's warm…very, very warm.

(Sigfrid and Clarence in bed.)

Oh Sigfrid…Sigfrid, Sigfrid, Sigfrid."

LAKME, RUBY, AND SIGFRID: *(Mimicking in unison.)* Oh, Sigfrid Sigfrid, Sigfrid, Sigfrid.

(At this moment, which has been building up inside him ever since this sequence began, Clarence stands with an incredible look of pain and terror on his face. At the same instant, his face appears on the screen in close-up with exactly the same expression on it. The two faces should seem to overlap.)

CLARENCE: …*(An animal howl from the guts.)*…*(A brief silence and suddenly*

Clarence has bolted across the room and we hear his footsteps running up the stairs. A moment later and we hear the iron door opening. A long silence in the dark room. The only light comes from the slide of Clarence's face.)

SIGFRID: *(After a pause, tentative.)* Ruby?

RUBY: *(Calm.)* He'll be back, Sigfrid. Clarence will be back.

SIGFRID: But maybe he—

RUBY: *(Strong.)* Clarence will be back.

CLARENCE'S RECORDED VOICE: "I don't want to ever go home. I could stay heeerrre foooorrevv—"

(The tape drags to a halt; the lamp in the projector goes out. Absolute darkness now.)

SIGFRID: *(After another pause.)* Ruby?

RUBY: It's one of the animals, Sigfrid.

SIGFRID: *(A decision.)* Lakme, get the flashlight.

RUBY: The light will come back, Sigfrid. It always does.

SIGFRID: I'm going up there.

RUBY: It was one of the animals, Sigfrid!

SIGFRID: We don't know, Ruby. WE DON'T KNOW!

(He runs up the stairs, Lakme right behind him.)

RUBY: Sigfrid! Lakme! Come back here! Don't leave me alone down here! SIGFRID! LAKME! PLEASE! *(Silence, darkness.)* You miserable…you goddamn miserable… *(She has found a flashlight, turns it on and is somewhat comforted.)* I WON'T BE LEFT ALONE DOWN HERE! *(She is standing over Fa's chair.)* Fa?…Fa?…Fa!…you son of a bitch…you did it…you went ahead and did it…when?…when?…*(A hysterical laughing jag is building.)*…you son of a bitch…you really did it…without even telling us…the goddamn son of a bitch went ahead and did it…children!…children!

(The laughter builds and builds. Sigfrid appears at the top of the stairs, carrying Clarence's body. Ruby shines her flashlight on them.)

He did it…your son of a bitch Fa went ahead and did it…do you hear me?…Fa's dead…Fa's finally dead.

(The laughter, completely out of control and hysterical, continues. Sigfrid is coming slowly down the stairs with Clarence in his arms. Tableau. The lamp in the slide projector comes back on and once again we see Clarence's face. The tape recorder starts playing.)

CLARENCE'S RECORDED VOICE: "…ever and forever and forever. I don't want to ever go home…"

(Fast curtain.)

END OF ACT TWO

At Rise: The room is again the same. But now the slide of Clarence's face domi-
nates the stage. The picture is enormous, filling the entire rear wall. A person will
seem very small standing next to it. Candlelight. Black crepe…maybe. Fa is still
in his chair, the top of his head or perhaps one arm barely visible to the audience.
Ruby, Sigfrid, Lakme, and Grandfa are seated facing away from each other and
each one at the greatest possible distance from the other three. It is a formal group-
ing. After all, the final grimmest ritual is being played out now. There is a still-
ness in the room we have not heard before.

CLARENCE'S RECORDED VOICE: "…and that's another reason. Everybody loves
somebody…or they will…sometime in their life. *(A pause.)* Anything that
makes you want to live so bad you'd…you'd die for it. That's what I believe
in. That's all. That's the way I live." *(And then, with a foolish giggle in his*
voice.) Was it all right? *(A long pause; no one moves.)*

RUBY: *(Dispassionate.)* The strong has survived…the weak have not…and what is
there more to say? Those who remain…and those who do not…it is that simple. The survival of the strong. There is strength and there is weakness and
there is only they. But oh! such a din there is when they collide. Am I not
right, Clarence? There is trembling…there is clamor…there is a spasm of the
earth. There is *struggle.* And then…there is this…how it ends…the silence.
(Somewhere, in the nethermost region of the theatre, there sounds a faint, dull
thump.) This is how the world is. This. And so be it. *(A pause.)*

GRANDFA: *(Very sad, very low, and very far away.)* No.

RUBY: Lakme.

LAKME: *(Controlled, yet with some difficulty.)* The strong have survived…the weak
have not…and what is there more to say? *(Tiny pause.)* …the way his eyes
were open…just like the dogs' are…

RUBY: Those who remain…

LAKME: *(At once.)* …and those who do not…it is that… *(Change of voice.)* I never
saw dead before. *People* dead.

RUBY: Simple, Lakme. It is that simple.

LAKME: Yes! It is that simple. There is strength and there is weakness and there is
only they. But oh… *(Faltering.)* …but oh!…

SIGFRID: *(With a terrifying suddenness.)* BUT OH! SUCH A DIN THERE IS
WHEN THEY COLLIDE!

LAKME: …when they collide. *(Pause.)* I don't remember.

RUBY: *(Gently coaxing.)* There is trembling…there is clamor…there is a spasm of
the earth.

LAKME: There is struggle.

RUBY: And, then, there is this…how it ends…the silence.

LAKME: Yes. *(And again, the thump.)*

LAKME AND RUBY: *(Low in unison.)* This is how the world is. This. And so be it.

GRANDFA: *(Despairing with all the force an old man can summon.)* NOOOO-OOOOO! *(A sharp silence. Nothing stirs.)*

LAKME: *(A faint, distant voice.)* Just like the dogs' are.

RUBY: Sigfrid. *(No response.) Parle, mon beau prince, parle.*

SIGFRID: *(Low.)* I can't do it, Ruby.

RUBY: The strong have survived…the weak—

SIGFRID: I SAID I CAN'T DO IT!

(Sharp silence again. Ruby laughs softly.)

LAKME: *(After a while.)* What about Fa? Why doesn't anyone say anything about Fa? *(A pause and again the thump, ever so slightly louder.)* He's dead, too.

SIGFRID: *(It is a mixture of sadness and contempt; for Clarence, himself…everything.)* You were so…simple for us, Clarence. So simple.

RUBY: *(At once, trying to steer him back on the right track.)* The strong have survived…the weak—

SIGFRID: *(Drowning out the sound of her voice.)* You were so simple!

RUBY: *(If she must relent.)* Be careful, Sigfrid. Be very careful then.

SIGFRID: *(Never looking at or listening to her; this is actually a monologue that follows.)* You let us trample you. You made us. It was too simple. There was so much at stake and you didn't fight back.

RUBY: The line, Sigfrid…that was *your* speech…don't cross over the line.

SIGFRID: So much at stake…*you*…and you didn't fight back. Why, Clarence? Just tell us *why*.

LAKME: *(To herself, but seemingly in answer to Sigfrid.)* There is strength and there is weakness and there is only they.

RUBY: *(In direct answer.)* It *is* that simple, Sigfrid.

GRANDFA: *(Numbed now.)* No.

RUBY: We are the victors, Sigfrid. Remember that. Remember who we are. We are the victors.

GRANDFA: *(His voice always the most remote and distant sounding.)* "I'll never care what wickedness I do if this man come to good."

LAKME: *(An observation beginning a revery that will end in an outburst, but the beginning is low.)* Just like the dogs' are. I don't like dead.

SIGFRID: It was pointless, Clarence, what you did was pointless. We knew the fence was out there…that it could kill. We already knew that. You could have told us something else. You could have told us what was out there. What is finally out there. There might have been some point to it…some point to going out there…that we might have *known*…but *this*…

RUBY: *(Seizing on Sigfrid's "this.")* This…how it ends…the silence, Sigfrid…the silence.

SIGFRID: *YOU* WERE POINTLESS, CLARENCE!

RUBY: Gently, Sigfrid...*speak* gently...use gentle words. It is their *requiem*... the requiem for the weak.

SIGFRID: *(Obeying involuntarily.)* So pointless.

GRANDFA: *(Again and always as from afar.)* "If they live long and in the end meet the old course of death, mankind will all turn monsters." *(A pause; the thump.)*

LAKME: I don't *like* them to be dead.

RUBY: How pathetic to believe the world is anything but the way it is. What was your word for it, Clarence?

LAKME: I don't *want* them to be dead.

RUBY: *(Finding it.)* Unfortunate. Yes! Unfortunate. *(With a smile of remembrance.)* So judiciously.

LAKME: I don't want anyone to be dead...*ever!*

RUBY: To believe in anything but strength. To believe in weakness. How *unfortunate*. How unfortunate for *you*, Clarence.

LAKME: *(Beginning to climax.)* Dead is bad...I never saw dead...you didn't tell us, Ruby...you didn't tell us how bad dead was.

RUBY: *(Opening her arms to Lakme whose back is still to her.)* I couldn't...not until now...now, this night.

LAKME: I DON'T LIKE IT...DEATH! I DON'T LIKE IT AT ALL.

RUBY: *(As if Lakme were in her arms.)* Hush...hush now...yes! ...shhh...

LAKME: *(Wildly, turning on Ruby, the first time in the scene that anyone has confronted anyone else.)* WHY DIDN'T YOU TELL US HOW BAD DEAD WAS?

SIGFRID: *(Very low.)* Answer her, Ruby...answer *us*.

LAKME: *(With a sharp cry, rushing at last into Ruby's open arms)* JUST TELL US WHY!

RUBY: *(Comforting her.)* Some things can't be told, Lakme...best not...*(Then, for Sigfrid.)*...or answered. *(Again to Lakme.)* They just...happen.

LAKME: *(Her head buried in Ruby's arms.)* Death? You mean death?

RUBY: *(Her eyes on Sigfrid.)* The silence. *(A pause, the thump.)*

LAKME: *(Much, much calmer.)* But Clarence...that thing out there...

RUBY: *(At once.)* People like Clarence don't need something out there to come to a bad end.

LAKME: But we *made* him—

RUBY: *(She must make this point.)* People like Clarence don't even need *us*. They find it on their very own...even in broadest daylight...under the bluest skies. They sniff it out...hunt and scratch for it under every stump and log until they finally dig it up like some rotten truffle. It is their propensity. They are as attracted to a shabby, dismal, *futile* end as surely as...

SIGFRID: *(Alone and far away.)* We are.

RUBY: Are *not*. As surely as we are *not*. *(A pause; the thump.)* Consider the Clarences of this world...and they are out there...just as he was...millions upon millions of them...no different—not really—from this one...consider these Clarences...consider them *objectively*...with neither tears nor laughter...*objectively*...and you will know this: that no good will come to them.

SIGFRID: *(With a sad smile...perhaps.)* Objectively. The most important emotion...objectivity. The teaching emotion, Ruby? Isn't that what you told us?...*taught* us.

RUBY: They ...just as he ...do not understand what we have understood and we *have* ...*will* ...are *determined* to survive them. Understood that there *is* no ...

SIGFRID: Shakespeare...Florence...someone in the park.

RUBY: *(With finality.)* Anything. Just...us. *(A pause; the thump, a tiny bit louder.)* The litany, Sigfrid. I think we can begin now.

(He still does not, will not turn to her. Lakme, however, unburrows her head from Ruby's arms and, kneeling at her feet, looks up at her. Ruby has taken a deep breath and now begins a kind of chant.)

Fear is not strong.

LAKME: *(With the same cadences.)* Fear is not strong.

RUBY: Fear sickens.

LAKME: Fear...Come on, Sigfrid, do it!

RUBY: Fear corrupts.

LAKME: Fear corrupts.

RUBY: *We* were not strong...

LAKME: *We* were not strong...Sigfrid!

SIGFRID: *(Finally turning on and to Ruby directly; taking part, if he must, in the "litany.")* Are not. *Are* not strong.

RUBY: *(In deadly combat.)* ...once!

LAKME: ...once!

SIGFRID: Now!...still!...ALWAYS!

RUBY: *(Always a little louder, more forceful than Sigfrid.)* But we have dealt with fear...

LAKME: But we have dealt with fear...

SIGFRID: No! It has dealt with *us*. Warped...maimed...MUTILATED!

RUBY: *(Relentless.)* ...not succumbed to it.

LAKME: ...not succumbed to it.

SIGFRID: We *have* succumbed. We're suffocating with fear.

RUBY: But dealt with it.

LAKME: Dealt.

SIGFRID: *(Trying to reach Lakme.)* Don't listen to her.

RUBY: *(Stronger in his moment of weakening.)* Because we had to.

LAKME: *(Breaking out of the cadence of the litany, a simple concern for her brother now.)* We had to, Sigfrid.

SIGFRID: I've heard these words. All my life I've heard them.

RUBY: *(Never breaking the cadence of the litany, forcing it, in fact.)* Because demands were made on us...

LAKME: We agreed, Sigfrid. The three of us. We *agreed* to do it this way. The way we live...remember?

SIGFRID: *(Close to the breaking point.)* WE ARE NOT LIVING AND WE HAVE MURDERED FOR IT. WHY, RUBY, *WHY!!*

RUBY: Because we could no longer cope with...

SIGFRID: *(Now.)* OURSELVES!!!!!

LAKME: *(Shrinking.)* I'm frightened, Ruby, I'm frightened.

RUBY: *(Tremendous.)* ...IT!!! BECAUSE WE COULD NO LONGER COPE WITH IT!!!!

SIGFRID: *(A prayer, a desperate prayer.)* Please...someone...make it *stop*.

LAKME: Ruby!

SIGFRID: *Let* it stop.

RUBY: *(Ice.)* What stop, Sigfrid? Let "what" stop?

SIGFRID: Us...everything...the suffocation...

RUBY: What else is there, Sigfrid?

SIGFRID: I don't know...*some*thing...

RUBY: *(Caustic.)* Bridge?...anacrostics, maybe?...or tiddley-winks?

SIGFRID: I SAID I DON'T KNOW...SOMETHING...SOMETHING ELSE. THIS ISN'T ENOUGH, RUBY.

RUBY: *(Rapping it out.)* It will suffice!

SIGFRID: It's a mechanism, the way we live. That's all it is...a machine. It runs *us*. Sitting here...night after night...pretending—

RUBY: No, Sigfrid, no pretending.

SIGFRID: PRETENDING! Pretending not to feel ...to live. Rituals... requiems...litanies...guests...devices! Excuses for living. LOOK AT HIM! LOOK AT CLARENCE! That is the way we live ...the result of it. WE DON'T LIVE. WE ...

RUBY: Yes? Sigfrid. Go on.

SIGFRID: *(With a terrible anguish.)* WE *DO!* WE ARE NOT ALIVE ...WE *ARE!* *(A silence, the thump.)*

GRANDFA: *(Still from his remote position at the beginning of the act.)* Now, Sigfrid, yes...*now!*

RUBY: *(Not looking at him.)* You won't win him, Grandfa. I won't let you.

GRANDFA: Now...this night...*yes!*

SIGFRID: *(A quiet, careful beginning. The moment and what he will say are important. He knows this.)* The fact of us. There is the *fact* of us. That we *are!* What we are, who we are, where. *(Short pause.)* And *why*. Why we are. That, too. All these are the fact of us.

LAKME: *(Still cuddled in Ruby's arms.)* What's Sigfrid doing?

RUBY: Sshh, *cara,* sshh.

GRANDFA: Go on, Sigfrid, go *on.*

SIGFRID: I have no Message to the World...only a question. No, *questions!* I have questions to the world. Answer one...any *one* of them...and maybe, *maybe* we can start all over again.

LAKME: Is something bad happening? *(And again the thump.)*

GRANDFA: Yes! Oh thank God yes!

RUBY: He's only beginning, Grandfa. The questions are easy. But the answers, wait till the answers.

SIGFRID: This room...the fact of this stifling, wretched room. And yet there is a reason for it. Windows, none...the air, stale...the door, there, that door, locked. I would repudiate this place...I would *like* to...but I cannot. We each have bred the other and finally, yes, *deserve!* This room... we are safe in this room. This room...I AM SUFFOCATING IN THIS ROOM.

LAKME: It *is* something bad!

(Ruby comforts her, though never taking her eyes from Sigfrid.)

SIGFRID: Which is the way out of this room I cannot leave? Up there? Is it up there?

GRANDFA: Yes, Sigfrid, up!

SIGFRID: Or further down? Further down than we already are?

RUBY: Down. Our way is down, Sigfrid.

SIGFRID: I don't care anymore. The "fact" is that we are here. *(Sudden.)* WELL, WHO HAS THE KEYS TO IT? THE KEYS TO LET US OUT? THERE MUST BE KEYS! *(Vicious, to the picture.)* YOU, CLARENCE, YOU?

GRANDFA: You!

RUBY: No one. *(A silence; the thump.)* The fact of us, Grandfa. This is the fact of us.

SIGFRID: This house...there is the fact of this rotting, stinking house. Yes, there is an upstairs...with rooms...other rooms...darkened, empty daylight rooms. Rooms for when it's safe. Rooms we don't know how to live in. Rooms we've *forgotten* how to live in. There is a room up there with a bed in it. My room. A bed I can remember sleeping in. My bed. My bed before...*this.* Before we descended. Before we *had* to descend. It was a soft bed...a warm bed...a deep bed. I had a quilt on that bed...a quilt with calico patches. Every night... even the very coldest...I would sleep with the windows open. They were that warm...my bed and my quilt with the calico patches. And I would dream... real dreams. Not nightmares. Not like now. I would dream of Persia and flying carpets and every far-off place I'd ever read of. I *could* dream of them under my quilt with the calico patches, all snuggled deep in my soft, warm bed. *(Slight pause.)* But so what?

GRANDFA: *(Gently.)* Sigfrid.

SIGFRID: *(Ugly.)* SO WHAT? What does the memory of a warm bed have to do with anything? How does that *change* anything? How does a memory change *now?* I ASK YOU, CLARENCE, SO WHAT?

GRANDFA: So *everything.* Can't you see that, Sigfrid? Understand it. *Try.*

LAKME: Did I have a bed upstairs, Ruby, and a quilt with calico patches?

RUBY: No, child.

LAKME: Why?

RUBY: Sshh. *(A silence; the thump.)*

SIGFRID: This person…this residue of a possibility…this me. There is the fact of me. Yes, I am a monster and, yes, I have done damage…irreparable damage…to myself most of all, but others, too. *(An explanation.)* Because. *Because* this room, *because* this house, *because* this person. BECAUSE!

GRANDFA: But not always, Sigfrid. There was a time… "A sky, a blue sky."

SIGFRID: Monstrous! Now I am monstrous. I have *become* that. And who wants to make something out of it? *Why* doesn't someone want to make something out of it? Or am I to be allowed to happen?

RUBY: *(Mocking.)* Grandfa?

SIGFRID: ARE THERE NO MORE COCKED FISTS, CLARENCE?

GRANDFA: *Your* fist. Cock *your* fist, Sigfrid.

RUBY: Good *questions,* Sigfrid. Now try to *answer* them. *(A silence, the thump.)*

SIGFRID: That thing out there…the reason for this room, this house, this…maybe for this person. That thing out there.

   (Long pause; no one moves. And again the thump: a good deal louder than before but it might be possible not to hear it distinctly yet.)

WHAT *IS* THAT THING OUT THERE?…DID YOU SEE IT, CLARENCE? THEN TELL US…SOMEONE TELL US WHAT IT IS. IT HAS MADE US NECESSARY! AND WE MUST KNOW WHAT IT IS. *(A very, very long pause and again the thump.)*

LAKME: *(Low, scarcely breaking the quiet.)* Ruby, I want a bed like Sigfrid had and a quilt with calico patches.

SIGFRID: *(Husky.)* What?

RUBY: I've won him, Grandfa. With that one question I have won him.

SIGFRID: *(With that same mingling of sadness and contempt, turning directly to her for the first time since he began this long section.)* Have you, Ruby?

RUBY: *(Her eyes locked with Sigfrid's.)* What did I tell you, Grandfa?

SIGFRID: Not yet…not quite. *(Ruby laughs softly: that cruel, insinuating sound.)*

GRANDFA: Save yourself, Sigfrid…oh, sweet God, save yourself.

SIGFRID: *(A distinct, new beat; with a brighter vocal tone probably.)* The way we live…finally that. The way we do not live…and at long last the fact of that. Us. *(Then, making the suitable acknowledgments.)* My Ruby, my Lakme, my…*(He remembers.)*…and me. We are perfect people. We are especially perfect…people. Consider us.

RUBY: *(What's he up to?)* Is this necessary, Sigfrid?

SIGFRID: *We…we* are necessary. And perfect. I don't know about "this."

RUBY: *(Unwilling to explore this new territory; it is a resumption of the litany.)* "With hands…"

SIGFRID: *(Pow!)* LISTEN TO ME. *(He is obeyed.)* Consider first, consider my Ruby. *Che bella, eh?* The matriarch triumphant. The madonna entombed…excuse me, I meant enthroned. Medusa rampant on a field of…Medusa rampant. Call her any name but mother. It hurts her ears.

RUBY: *(Not amused.)* What is this all about, Sigfrid?

SIGFRID: We understand each other, my Ruby and I. That is *one* substitute for love. We also happen to be on to each other, which is *not*.

RUBY: I'm on to what you're doing and I'm asking you to stop.

SIGFRID: "Asking me?" Hoo hoo!

RUBY: *Telling* you!

SIGFRID: *(Charging ahead, delighted.)* What I most like about my Ruby are her teeth. She has always snapped them at anyone come to frighten me and hugged me close. At anyone come to take me away from here…our little nesty…which frightens *her*. My Ruby is a lion in that respect. A lady lion. A lioness. Tonight she snapped her teeth at Clarence…who didn't frighten anyone.

RUBY: *(Steel.)* If you are not like Clarence…

SIGFRID: *(Quick.)* I'm like Sigfrid?

RUBY: …if you are *not* like him…*if*…it is because of me. Because I wouldn't *let* you be like that. Because I insisted that you be stronger.

SIGFRID: You did do that. And I am! Clarence felt my muscles. He was impressed. I'm only sorry he didn't get a look at your biceps.

RUBY: He had a good look!

SIGFRID: Oh, you've taught us well to cope with a Clarence. Good Ruby, good mommy, good.

RUBY: Without me…

SIGFRID: *(At once.)* I might be free of all this.

RUBY: *(Continuing.)* …that would have been *you* in that dress.

SIGFRID: I'M IN A STRAIGHT JACKET.

RUBY: *(After a moment.)* There are the stairs, Sigfrid. Go on. Go out for a little stroll. And then when you come back you can tell us what your little friend didn't. You can report to us what's out there. Take a breath of air. I hate to see you stifling.

(A pause. The thump. Sigfrid looks up at the door. Ruby looks at him. Then, almost with a jerk, he turns to Lakme.)

SIGFRID: And Lakme. Little, little Lakme.

RUBY: *(A challenge.)* Admit your fear of what's through that door.

SIGFRID: Child of her time. Ruby's masterpiece. This century's.

RUBY: ADMIT!

SIGFRID: *(Moving in on Lakme.)* Too young to remember anything but this. And you have been forgiven much because of it. Because of your youth.

LAKME: *(Standing her ground.)* Don't start in on me, Sigfrid.

SIGFRID: No! Because of your non-youth. Thirteen years in this goddamn basement has made you five thousand years old.

LAKME: *(Not understanding, but sensing attack.)* I know plenty of bad things about you, too!

SIGFRID: You know everything and understand nothing. And you never will. You can't. Not down here. Nothing *happens* down here. Except us.

LAKME: I know how to get mad. I know that. *(Throwing it in his face.)* "Sky, a blue sky!"

SIGFRID: *(Immediately turning away from her.)* You don't have to, Lakme. Please…don't do that.

LAKME: *(In pursuit.)* "The eagle soars!"

SIGFRID: *(He hasn't said this in a long, long time. It hurts.)* I WANTED TO. I *WANTED* TO DEAL WITH WORDS. *DO* SOMETHING WITH THEM. AND I *TRIED*.

LAKME: *(Unappeased.)* "High soars, high soars the eagle."

SIGFRID: *(Bursting with it.)* IT WAS NOT GIVEN TO ME. I WAS DENIED THAT GIFT.

LAKME: *(Hard, in his ear.)* "Can I soar? Can I soar, too?"

SIGFRID: *(Burst.)* I COULD NOT DO IT. *(A pause.)*

LAKME: *(Low, almost toneless now.)* "For my longing is as great."

(Another pause; Ruby's laugh.)

Sigfrid?

RUBY: *(Serene.)* Shall we resume now, Sigfrid?

LAKME: I'm sorry, Sigfrid. Honest I am.

RUBY: *(Taking up the litany where she left off.)* "With hands…"

SIGFRID: *(Instantly getting hold of himself, yet more and more desperate with every word and gesture.)* You're not going to win tonight, Ruby. I am. I'm going to finish myself off this time! *(He has moved near Fa.)* I had a father who meant nothing to me. Nothing nothing nothing nothing nothing. Wake up, Fa, just once wake up and take a gander. See what's become of us. See what's become of your poor innocent bobbies. There is something out there and see how we've dealt with it. *YOU MEANT NOTHING!*

GRANDFA: Sigfrid!

SIGFRID: *(And with almost a skip he is over to him.)* Grandfa! Scribe and scrivener. How now, old wart!

GRANDFA: It's too *easy* this way, Sigfrid.

SIGFRID: How's your book coming along, Grandfa? How progresses that novel you're writing?

GRANDFA: It doesn't mean anything to give in to it like this.

SIGFRID: You're so old. You're so damnably old. Why do you continue? On what *grounds?* Why do you even bother to wake up in the morning?

GRANDFA: I will not despair! There was a time—

SIGFRID: I don't understand, Grandfa. I don't understand what keeps you from doing what we did years ago. You're so *old!* What keeps you from death?

GRANDFA: *(The most important point he can make.)* IT'S OUT THERE FOR *ALL OF US. (A pause; he has been heard.)* It's out there for all of us.

SIGFRID: Then what's the point of going on with it?

GRANDFA: *(Low, this is to Sigfrid.)* To stand *up* to it.

SIGFRID: From a wheelchair? *(A pause.)*

GRANDFA: *(Slow, with difficulty.)* Does there have to be a point to anything? Is that what men insist upon these days?

SIGFRID: *(In spite of himself.)* I suppose not, Grandfa. I suppose not…if you're nine thousand years old and you're standing up to it sitting down in a wheelchair. *Then* I suppose there doesn't have to be a point to it. *(A pause; the thump.)*

RUBY: *(Consoling, from across the room. She can afford to. Sigfrid is nearly done now.)* Soon, Grandfa. They'll be here for you soon. It won't be much longer now.

SIGFRID: *(Brightly again, moving all about the room during this speech.)* You're a Clarence, Grandfa. That's who you are. Clarence thought he could change things. Clarence even thought he could change us. Wasn't that sweet of him, Grandfa? And wasn't that sad. Sweet Clarence, sweet Grandfa. Sad Clarence, sad Grandfa. He couldn't do it, Grandfa. And neither can you. Things are the way they are. We are the way we are. Look what it took Clarence to find out he couldn't change anything…most of all himself. He stomped all over town…stomp, stomp, stomp…bells ringing…banners waving…his own little children's crusade…ta ta ta ta ta! Wanting to *change* things. And all he accomplished was this. Why he didn't even accomplish me. *(The viciousness, the hysteria are mounting now.)* I buggered him, Grandfa, I buggered him good. WE CAN'T HAVE BUGGERED SAINTS NOW CAN WE, GRANDFA? *(Turning to the picture and addressing it.)* We're sorry, Clarence, but your bid for martyrdom is rejected. It was a real good try, baby, but you just didn't have the stuff. This is the court of last resort down here and you and your ideals…your buggered ideals…have been found lacking. They lack the substance, they lack the granite, they lack the simple facts of life. The facts of *you!* (*And now, facing full front, his fists clenched against an imaginary antagonist.*) Yes, we're horrible. But *who*, who is there to make something of it? Stand up and be counted. This house is horrible. But do you know how to build a better one? The way we live is horrible. Then teach us *your* way. But don't send us this for an answer, world, don't send us a Clarence. It simply won't do. And tell us first…before you send us another Clarence…AND THERE WILL BE MORE OF THEM…tell us *why*. *Why* this horribleness. *Why* this room without windows. *Why* Clarence who does not move. *Why* Fa who meant nothing. *Why* that thing out there without a name. Why us. WHY! (*Then, turning to Ruby, but without breaking the tempo and emotion of the moment.*) All right, Ruby. We may resume now. (*He has begun the litany.*) With hands!

RUBY: (*Sinking back into her chair.*) Ah!

SIGFRID: …with mind!…

GRANDFA: (*Low, his head bowed.*) No, Sigfrid.

SIGFRID: …with *passion!*…we have managed an existence.

RUBY AND LAKME: (*Picking it up.*) An existence!

SIGFRID: …an arrangement…

RUBY AND LAKME: …an arrangement…

SIGFRID: …an arrangement that works…

RUBY AND LAKME: Yes!

SIGFRID: …something for *us!*

RUBY AND LAKME: Us!

SIGFRID, RUBY, AND LAKME: We have done that…

SIGFRID: …done that!…

SIGFRID, RUBY, AND LAKME: AND WE HAVE SURVIVED YOU!

> (*These last words are very loud: shouted almost. Now there is a sharp silence. No one moves. There should be the suggestion of a tableau. Sigfrid and Lakme are next to Ruby, their heads lower than hers. Grandfa is apart from them. We hear the thump. The moment looks and feels like the end of the play. Then Sigfrid, abruptly breaking his mood, crosses the stage and turns on the overhead lights. After so much darkness, the room should seem unbearably, unnecessarily bright.*)

RUBY: (*At once, and as she leisurely begins to remove her wig and costume ornaments.*) Your *viola de gamba* lesson, Lakme. Is it tomorrow or the day after? I can never remember which.

LAKME: (*Listless, removing her Green Hornet costume.*) Tomorrow. The day after. I don't know.

SIGFRID: I'm sorry, Grandfa. I tried. You know, I really tried this time. (*Grandfa turns away from him.*) All right, then, where's *your* Message to the World? Your little bundle of tidings and joy? (*He snatches the Chronicle from Grandfa's lap.*) I didn't *think* you had one! (*He throws down the Chronicle and moves away. The thump.*)

RUBY: Put something on the phonograph, Lakme. Something exhilarating. *La Grande Messe des Morts* should do very nicely.

(*Lakme goes over to the phonograph.*)

I understand the Libyans are agitating for land reforms. Or isn't that what they're saying? It's so difficult to keep up these days …nearly impossible. Turmoil under every bushel. (*No response. The thump: a little louder than before.*) I am an admirer of the works of Miss Jane Austen. In re-reading *Pride and Prejudice*…it was only last night…I was struck by the similarity of her writing to the music of Mozart. Each so precise, so balanced…so *controlled*, that's the word! Don't you think so? (*No response. The thump. Then, irritably:*) What are you doing, Lakme?

LAKME: It's broken.

RUBY: Don't be ridiculous.

LAKME: ALL RIGHT IT'S *NOT* BROKEN!

RUBY: Well! I can see that certain little girls get cranky when they're allowed to stay up after bedtime. You were wrong about your sister, Sigfrid. I'm afraid she's every inch a *twelve*. (*Sigfrid has removed his black shirt and is seen to be wearing a white one underneath.*) Soit une ange, caro, and snuff out the candles. It's so wasteful with the lights on.

(*Sigfrid obeys, almost mechanically. A silence. The thump. Then, clapping her hands together, joyfully:*)

Children! I just figured it out…finally! The reason your Ruby looks so young and glamorous. It's because she so seldom laughs. (*Then, this irritable aside:*) Lakme! Ne cueillez pas ton nez! (*She waits for Lakme's usual reply.*) "I'll pick it if I want to." You're not going to say that? So don't. (*And back to the joyful mood.*) Laugh! Go ahead, laugh. Or smile very broadly. (*She demonstrates.*) See the wrinkling it causes? Millions of horrible little crinkles.

(*Sigfrid and Lakme remain stony-faced.*)

Well, don't worry about it! Either of you. And turn off the projector. I'm sick of looking at him.

(*Again Sigfrid obeys. A silence. The thump.*)

Grandfa! Will you favor us with one of your dramatic recitations? And may I suggest the Richard II deposition scene. It should have particular significance for you this evening. No? An old trouper like you passing up an opportunity for a gala farewell performance? *Ein kleine schwanengesang?* Grandfa! (*A short silence. The thump. Then, turning to Sigfrid, with irritation, the projector is still on.*) I thought I asked you to—

SIGFRID: (*Curt.*) It's jammed.

RUBY: How long is *this* little sulk going to last?

SIGFRID: Try it yourself then!

RUBY: *(On her feet, going to the projector.)* Just tell me *when. (She fiddles with the projector.)* Oh…it is. And the phonograph. It really won't…? *(The thump. Then, with a nervous laugh:)* Retribution! Well what else could it be? Divine retribution! *(A taut silence. The thump.)* What shall we do now? No music, Grandfa won't recite, *les enfants sont* sulking…look at Clarence the rest of the night? *(The thump; it is becoming increasingly difficult not to acknowledge it.)*

LAKME: I'm going to bed. *(She is on her way.)*

RUBY: Lakme!

> *(Lakme returns and gives Ruby a perfunctory kiss. The thump.)*

LAKME: *(Perhaps she has heard it.)* I wish…

RUBY: For a deep, warm bed and a quilt with calico patches. I know.

LAKME: *(She means this.)* I wish we hadn't done this tonight.

RUBY: *(Ignoring this, yet comforting her.)* Now say good-bye to Grandfa. He won't be here in the morning.

> *(The thump. Lakme crosses to Grandfa.)*

LAKME: *(Simply.)* Grandfa. *(He only looks at her.)* We'll all miss you. And I hope you'll be very happy wherever it is you're going. I hope—

> *(He lunges at her with the chair.)*

I HOPE YOU DIE ON THAT FARM! I HOPE WE ALL DIE!

> *(She runs across on stage, on her way out, and as she passes in front of the picture of Clarence:)*

FINK! *(She is gone. Brief silence. The thump.)*

RUBY: Sigfrid?

> *(He looks at her.)*

Nothing.

SIGFRID: What, Ruby?

RUBY: Nothing.

> *(Sigfrid is moving toward the door now.)*

That is the most extraordinary photograph. Sigfrid! *(He turns.)* Please. Not just yet.

SIGFRID: It's late.

RUBY: *(With that forced gaiety.)* I'm not asking you to stay up all night with me! Just a little while longer. Besides, we don't have anything planned for tomorrow.

SIGFRID: Oh but we do.

RUBY: What on earth are you talking about?

SIGFRID: Another Clarence, Ruby. We have another Clarence planned for tomorrow.

RUBY: *(Always trying to keep him with her.)* Not if you don't want to, Sigfrid! *I'm* perfectly willing to…be here with you.

SIGFRID: *(Moving toward Grandfa.)* And all the poems, Grandfa, think of all the poems I must write tomorrow. Eagle poems. Little Sigfrid can't write his wondrous eagle poems with fuzz in his noggin, can he now, Grandfa?

GRANDFA: *(Vibrant.)* He never *tried.*

SIGFRID: Is that what the facts say, Grandfa? The facts of your fiction?

GRANDFA: *(His last chance with Sigfrid; he knows this.)* It's not fiction. You know it's not— *(A terrifically loud thump. Each of them, in his fashion, starts perceptibly. A loud silence.)*

SIGFRID: Ruby? *(She looks at him.)* Nothing.

RUBY: What, Sigfrid?

SIGFRID: Nothing. *(He is on his way out.)*

RUBY: Sigfrid! *(He stops but does not turn to her.)* Five minutes? *(He starts to go again.)* SIGFRID! *(Again he stops and again does not turn to her.)* What will become of us?

SIGFRID: *(After a moment.)* Nothing.

RUBY: No?

SIGFRID: We will continue. *(The thump.)*

RUBY: Yes?

SIGFRID: Ask Clarence. *(He is going.)* We will continue.

(He is gone. The thump. Ruby and Grandfa are alone.)

RUBY: We will continue. Did you hear that, Grandfa? Sigfrid said we will continue. *(A pause; the thump. Grandfa has begun and will continue to very slowly tear the pages, one by one, from the Chronicle.)*

And that nothing will happen to us. Ask Clarence, he said. *(A pause; the thump. Each time a little louder now.)* But Clarence doesn't have anything to say. Clarence is dead. *(A pause; the thump.)* Then what did Sigfrid mean by that? *(A pause; the thump. Then, like lightning:)* I AM NOT A STUPID PERSON. WHAT OTHER ALTERNATIVES WERE THERE? *(A pause; the thump.)* We are eagles, Grandfa, we are. We have, you see, some stature. We are not little people. We are not pathetic people. There is something heroic about us. *(A pause; the thump.)* WE ARE SAFE. DOWN HERE WE ARE SAFE. *(A pause; the thump.)* Ask Clarence? I have nothing to *ask* Clarence. I'll *tell* him. Tell him something he should have known. For all his talk about commitment, we were, after all, as it turned out, the committed ones. We were. *(A pause; the thump.)* IT WILL PASS. THIS THING WILL PASS US BY. *(A pause; the thump.)* You see, Clarence, we too, have taken a stand against these things, only we have *acted* on it. We have acted *accordingly.* We are no longer life-size. We are larger than you. We have transcended— *(An enormous THUMP. She falters. Then, forcing herself to continue:)* We have survived everything and we shall survive now this night. We shall do that. We are *prepared* for now this night. Our lives were meant for it. It is our meaning. We are vindicated…now this night…finally…totally…we are vindicated now this night! *(The thud: terrifying, overwhelming, crushing. Like a hard punch in the stomach. No reverberations. A dull, hard, crunching thud.)* SIGFRID SAID WE WILL CONTINUE!… WE…WILL…

(And again that devastating sound. And now silence, a very long one. Ruby and Grandfa like statues.)

RUBY: *(Without moving, numbed and toneless.)* Grandfa? *(THUMP.)* Sigfrid? *(THUMP.)* Lakme? *(THUMP.)* Fa? *(THUMP.)* No one?…No one!…NO ONE! *(THUMP. THUMP, THUMP.)*

GRANDFA: *(Tearing the last pages from the Chronicle.)* And then there is this…how it ends…the silence. *(And, indeed, there is one now. A very, very long silence. Sigfrid and Lakme come slowly into the room. They stop at the door and look at Ruby. No one moves. Silence.)* This is how the world is. This. And so be it. *(There is one last page left in the Chronicle. He writes on it with a large, decisive stroke.)* No. *(THUMP. Silence. Ruby has moved almost somnambulistically to the tape recorder. The wheels are spinning.)*

RUBY'S RECORDED VOICE: "…who thought they were to prevail. We shall *not* prevail …so be it. *(Thump.)* We shall *not* endure … *(Thump.)*…but who was ever meant to? *(Ruby is walking slowly back to her place in the center of the room.)* And we shall *not* inherit the earth…it has already disinherited *us*. *(THUMP. THUMP. Ruby sits. Staring straight ahead and not looking at them, she extends one hand each to Sigfrid and Lakme who come forward and sit one to each side of her. They do not move.)*

If we are without faith, we find our way in the darkness…it is light enough. *(Thump.)* If we are without hope, we turn to our despair…*(Thump.)*…it has its own consolations.

(Grandfa has gotten out of his chair.)

And if we are without charity, we suckle the bitter root of its absence… wherefrom we shall draw the sustenance to destroy you.

(THUMP. Grandfa has begun to climb the stairs: slowly, slowly.)

Go…seek not to know us…to understand…the compassion of it will exhaust you and there is so little strength left us now…so little.

(Grandfa is nearly there. Ruby, Sigfrid, and Lakme never move. Even their eyes do not move. They stare straight ahead and nothing more. The lights are beginning to fade.)

Spoken by me this December morning. Unwitnessed, unheard, alone."

(The Thump. Silence. Grandfa is out. No one moves. The Thump. Silence. The Thump. Silence. The thump. And silence. The stage is completely dark. THE THUMP.)

END OF PLAY

Where Has
Tommy Flowers Gone?

for my friends

WHERE HAS TOMMY FLOWERS GONE? by Terrence McNally was first presented on January 7, 1971, by the Yale Repertory Theatre, New Haven, Connecticut. It was directed by Larry Arrick. Set and costumes designed by Steven Rubin. Lighting and graphics coordinated by William B. Warfel. Lighting designed by Dennis G. Daluiso. Slides by Michael Shane. Music arranged by Barbara Damashek. Sound created by Eugene Kimball. The production stage managers were Frank S. Torok and Carol M. Waaser.

Tommy Flowers	Robert Drivas
Greta Rapp	Barbara Damashek
Showgirl	Lydia Fisher
Needa Lemon	Sarah Albertson
Bunny Barnum	Katherine De Hetre
Tommy's Mother	
First Lady	Elizabeth Parrish
Woman Customer	
Tommy's Brother	James Naughton
Tommy's Nephew	Henry Winkler
Ben Delight	Jeremy Geidt
Arnold	Steve Van Benschoten
Taxi Driver	David Ackroyd
Moderator	

Also in the cast were: Louis Plante, Charles Turner, Peter Covette, James Brick, Maxime Lieberman, and Lisa Carling.

Subsequently, WHERE HAS TOMMY FLOWERS GONE? was presented on August 11, 1971, at the Berkshire Theatre Festival, Stockbridge, Massachusetts.

This same production opened in New York City on October 7, 1971, at the Eastside Playhouse. It was produced by Richard Scanga and Adela Holzer. It was directed by Jacques Levy. Sets by David Capman. Lighting by Marc B. Weiss. Costumes by James Berton Harris. Visuals by Ed Bowes and Bernadette Mayer. The production stage managers were Nicholas Russiyan and Kate M. Pollock.

Tommy Flowers	Robert Drivas
Ben Delight	Wallace Rooney
Nedda Lemon	Kathleen Dabney
Arnold	Toppy
The Girls	Barbara Worthington
The Men	F. Murray Abraham
The Women	Marion Paone

THE CHARACTERS

TOMMY FLOWERS
BEN DELIGHT
ARNOLD
THE MEN
THE WOMEN
THE GIRLS

THE SETTING

The time of the play is now. The places of the play are here, there, and everywhere in New York City.

OVERTURE

Special spotlight on the Conductor. He bows to the audience, acknowledging their applause—on tape, raps his baton on the podium for attention and waits. Special spotlight comes up center stage on a gleaming stainless steel and glass phonograph. More applause. There is a shiny black record on the changer ready to play.

The Conductor raises both arms. The record drops into the playing position and begins to spin. The tone arm hovers over the record a moment and then falls heavily onto it—but missing the lead-in groove so that what we hear is the horrible (and mightily amplified) clunking sound of the phonograph needle banging along the edge of the record. Clunk. Clunk. Clunk.

The Conductor just stands there with both arms raised. After what will seem like an interminable length of time, the Black Stagehand comes shuffling out of the wings. You have never seen anyone shuffle more and get to where he is going less. He does the kind of vaudeville/minstrel show shuffle that takes three steps forward then two steps back. He has a portable cassette tape recorder slung over one shoulder and the music he shuffles to is Otis Redding's "(Sittin' On) The Dock of the Bay." When he finally makes it over to the clunk-clunk-clunking phonograph (he can take five minutes for all I care if he's an expert shuffler; the longer the better, in any case), he stands looking down at the spinning record. He starts moving his head and neck in a circle until they are going at 33-$\frac{1}{3}$ r.p.m. and he can read the label.

BLACK STAGEHAND: Where has Tommy Flowers gone? Side one. *(He laughs hugely and looks out at the audience.)* Shee-it! *(He gives the phonograph a good hard swat and the needle drops into the proper groove.*

The Conductor gives the downbeat and we hear the three opening chords of the overture to The Magic Flute. *What follows next is pretty much up to the imagination of a composer or a sound man but some of the songs and sounds that make up the* Where Has Tommy Flowers Gone? *Overture are:*

A baby crying.
"The Star Spangled Banner."
The Andrews Sisters' "Rum and Coca Cola."
"I'm Looking Over a Four Leaf Clover."
War sounds.
The theme music from "Let's Pretend" and the "Lone Ranger."
A voice calling "Henry! Henry Aldrich!"
"Abba Dabba Honeymoon."
Yma Sumac.
A big explosion.
Bill Haley and the Comets' "Rock Around the Clock."
A woman's screams.
Elvis Presley's "Heartbreak Hotel."
More gunfire.
Early Dylan.
Sirens.
Many gunshots.
More sirens.
Early Beatles.
"We Shall Overcome."
The Zarathustra music from 2001.
The conclusion of the Magic Flute Overture *itself.)*

    During the Overture we will see many images flashed on a series of screens above the stage. Some of these images of Tommy Flowers, his life and times, will surely include:
Tommy as a baby boy.
FDR.
The baby boy getting bigger.
Truman.
As a little boy dressed in a sailor suit.
A birthday cake.
Now he's riding a pony.
Another birthday cake.
It's his first Holy Communion.
V-Day celebrations.
He's quite the little man now.
A Studebaker.
As a teenager with a crewcut.

Eisenhower.

At a high school prom with a flat top.

Then as a college graduate with somewhat longer hair.

Then as a tourist in Paris with even longer hair.

Kennedy.

Then as a soldier in front of the Berlin Wall with a crewcut again.

Johnson.

Then a series of pictures in which our hero's hair gets longer and longer and longer
and his clothes become funky and hip.

Nixon.

In the final picture, Tommy is smiling broadly and looking right at us. With one
hand he forms the "V," with the other he is giving us The Finger.

At this point the Overture reaches its climax, the phonograph blows up and the
picture of Tommy Flowers is extinguished.)

ACT ONE

DEDICATION

TOMMY: I would like to thank the following people for making me what I am
today: Mom and Dad; my big brother Harry; my wonderful Nana; my
beloved Grandpa; Walt Disney; The Little Engine That Could; Golden
Books; American nuns; Batman and Robin and all the gang over at Dell
Comics; Little Lulu; Wonder Woman; Betty and Jughead; Rossini, the Lone
Ranger and Tonto, too; Cream of Wheat for Let's Pretend; all MGM musi-
cals but especially the one with Abba Dabba Honeymoon; Ringling Brothers,
Barnum and Bailey; Francis the Talking Mule; Ma and Pa Kettle and their
farm; B.O. Plenty and Sparkle; Henry Aldrich in the Haunted House;
Abbott and Costello; the Wolf Man; Kukla, Fran and Ollie; Uncle Miltie and
my real Uncle Fred; Harry S. Truman; Margaret S. Truman; Gene Autrey and
his girdle (if he ever really wore one); Roy Rogers and Dale Evans; Johnny
Weismuller; Johnny Sheffield; Sabu; Esther Williams; Joe Di Maggio; Pee
Wee Reese; Jackie Robinson; Ralph Buche; Trygve Lie; Miss America; Mr.
America; the Weavers; Patty Page; Babe Diedrickson Zaharias; Mme. Chiang
Kai-shek; Chuck Berry; the Coasters; Candy Barr; Lili St. Cyr; all strippers
who worked with animals but especially snakes; Ava Gardner; Hal Wallis;
Corinne Calvet; Jerry Lee and plain Jerry Lewis; Johnny Mathis; Terry
Moore; ol' Marilyn up there, of course; James Dean; Elvis Presley; John F.
Kennedy; Rose F. Kennedy; Fidel Castro; Bernadette Castro (hell, why not?);
Che Guevara; Bob Dylan; Ho Chi Minh; the Beatles; Miss Teenage America;

Mme. Nhu; Lady Bird Johnson; Lyndon Bird Johnson; Lynda Bird Johnson Robb; Luci Bird Johnson Nugent; the Rolling Stones; Janis Joplin; The Man From Glad; Richard M. Nixon; the last girl I balled and all the sisters of mercy to come *and…*whew!…we really do get by with a little help from our friends…Mr. Thomas Jefferson, who said something about God forbid we should ever be twenty years without a rebellion! To all of them I dedicate this act. Oh, yeah, I'm Tommy Flowers. Hi.

(A really statuesque Showgirl has appeared. Her costume is revealing, her manner intensely sincere.)

SHOWGIRL: Dynamite! Of all the good stuff that is the stuff! Place this in the immediate vicinity of a lot of rich loafers who live by the sweat of other people's brows, and light the fuse. A most cheerful and gratifying result will follow. A pound of this good stuff beats a bushel of ballots all hollow—and don't you forget it. Our lawmakers might as well try to sit down on the crater of a volcano or on a point of a bayonet as to endeavor to stop the manufacture and use of dynamite. Albert Parsons, 1885. Thank you. *(Showgirl exits. The stage is empty.)*

ANNOUNCER'S VOICE: May I have your attention please. A mink stole with the monogrammed initials DKR has been found on the floor of the ladies room on the mezzanine level. Thank you.

THE LAST OF THE LINCOLN CENTER FOR
THE PERFORMING ARTS

(On the screens above the stage we see a photographic montage/mural of Lincoln Center. In the left panel is the New York State Theatre. In the center panel we see the Metropolitan Opera House. At the right are the Vivian Beaumont Theatre and Philharmonic Hall. On the stage level and in the middle of all this is the Lincoln Center fountain. It isn't working. A girl guide, Greta Rapp, enters and greets us.)

GRETA: Hello, welcome to Lincoln Center. I'm Greta Rapp, your guide for today's tour. *(Consulting a piece of paper.) Bonjour, bienvenu á Lincoln Center. Je suis Greta Rapp, votre guide pour le tour d'aujourd'hui. Buon giorno, Benvenuto a Lincoln Center, Io sono—*

VOICES: *(Unseen, grumbling.)* Speak English…yeah, lady, whadda ya think?…what did she say? what did she say?

GRETA: Then we're all Americans? Well that's something! Most days it's like the United Nations around here. *(She laughs.)* The Lincoln Center for the Performing Arts is the nation's cultural capital. Naturally, it's in New York. *(She waits.)* That usually gets a laugh. *(She laughs.)* It was built *by* the people of New York City *for* the people of New York City to the tune of two hundred and thirty-five million, six hundred and seventy-eight thousand, four hundred and eighty-two dollars and eleven cents. There have been an awful lot of jokes made about where all those eleven cents went, too, let me tell you! *(She laughs.)* And just try to get a ticket for something! *(She makes one final effort to amuse her apparently stony-faced charges.)* Of course there are some people who consider themselves fortunate that they can't! *(Again nothing. She braces herself.)* Shall we begin? Once we're inside, no smoking, positively no picture taking and quiet, *s'il vous plaît.* This way please and mind the construction. *(She crosses to underneath the picture of the New York State Theatre.)* The New York State Theatre is home for the brilliant New York City Ballet. The theatre boasts three hundred and forty-six miles, that's right, *miles*, of carpeting; thirty-one separate but equal rest rooms with a combined total of one hundred and eighty-six individual conveniences, and uses in excess of fifty tons of paper towels and bathroom tissues in one season. Fifty tons, ladies. Imagine. Sshh! We're in luck. They're holding auditions. Let's tiptoe in. *(Lights come up center stage on Tommy. He is disguised as a Ballerina. He wears a pink tutu and toe shoes. He carries a bright red shopping bag which he promptly sets down.)*

VOICE: *(Russian accent.) (Unseen, from the rear of the theatre.)* Miss Heather Begg.

TOMMY/BALLERINA: *(Thick cockney accent.)* That's Begg with two g's, ducky, but that's ain't what I'm doing. Swan Lake, guvnor. The whole bleeding thing. *(Music begins. Tommy dances an outlandish ballet. His concentration is fierce but he moves with all the grace of an elephant.)*

VOICE: *(After only a few moments of this madness.)* Thank you, Miss Begg! That will do, Miss Begg!

TOMMY/BALLERINA: *(In the middle of a pirouette.)* I can't stop now, luv! Wheeeeeeee! *(He whirls and dances to his conclusion. Stunned silence in the theatre. He looks out hopefully.)*

TOMMY/BALLERINA: Well, luv?

VOICE: No, luv.

TOMMY/BALLERINA. *(Eliza Doolittle.)* Caaaaaaaa!

VOICE: Thank you, Miss Begg.

TOMMY/BALLERINA: *(Smiling sweetly; it sounds like thank you.)* Fuck you, ducky, fuck you very much. Nice place you got here, guvnor. Pity. *(He exits, leaving the red shopping bag where he first placed it. Pin spot on the shopping bag. Other stage lights fade.)*

GRETA: As you can see, they don't call Lincoln Center the Boulevard of Broken Dreams for nothing. Many are called here by the Muses but few are chosen. We can't all be a Leontyne Price. Mind the scaffoldings. *(She crosses to underneath the picture of Philharmonic Hall.)* Philharmonic Hall, as you may have heard, heard, heard…! *(She laughs.)*…has had more than its fair share of acoustical problems.

AN ECHO: …fair share of acoustical problems.

GRETA: But I think you'll find they're pretty well under control by now.

AN ECHO:…under control by now.

GRETA: For those of you with a more scientific bent of mind, recent tests now rank PH as the 19th most acoustically perfect concert hall to be erected since the Second World War. That's three places up since the last time and we're still climbing! And actually, the slight echo that remains has proved an interesting challenge to conductors, composers, and soloists alike. We'll go this way now. Careful on the stairs here, they're meant to be lit. Now this is strictly off the record. For those of you who were fortunate enough to catch the telecast of the historic opening concert, where you're standing right now is the famous spot where Lenny kissed Jackie much to Jack's chagrin. Remember, I didn't say that. Hmmm? Leonard Bernstein. Jacqueline Kennedy. President Kennedy. Never mind. Sshh! Someone's on stage.

(Lights come up center stage on Tommy disguised as a Musician. He has long, wild, unruly hair; a big mustache and glasses. He carries a pair of cymbals and another red shopping bag which he promptly sets down.)

VOICE: *(Italian accent.)* Giuseppe Bonatella.

TOMMY/MUSICIAN: *(Heavy Italian accent.)* That's a me! Giuseppe Bonatella! The most a musical fella! The big a noise on Bleecker Street! What I'm a gonna play for you now, mister, is a the Beethoven Ninth a Symphony in a C sharp a major, as arranged for a solo a cymbal. It's a my own arrangement. And a one, and a two, and a three…! *(He crashes the cymbals violently for several minutes.)*

VOICE: Mr. Bonatella! *Signor* Bonatella! Ehi, Bonatella!

TOMMY/MUSICIAN: I can't a hear you! Too much a noise! *(He continues crashing the cymbals a while. Finally he stops.)*

VOICE: *Grazie.*

TOMMY/MUSICIAN: Ehi, paisano, you speak a Italian! Bravo! You want a more music? I play a more music! *(He crashes away again for several moments. Stops at last.)*

VOICE: That's enough., Signor Bonatella, *basta*, please!

TOMMY/MUSICIAN: Giuseppe Bonatella! That's a me! *(He crashes the cymbals.)* I getta the job, mister?

VOICE: We a letta you know.

TOMMY/MUSICIAN: I don't getta the job, mister, you gonna getta the boom-boom! *(He crashes the cymbals together one more time and exits, leaving the shopping bag behind again. Lights down center stage except for pin spot on the shopping bag.)*

GRETA: We can't all be a Van Cliburn either. The standards at Lincoln Center couldn't possibly be any lower than they are now. Let in one like that and pretty soon you're letting in them all. One thing about the level of performance here, it's consistent. That's two broken hearts today and it's not even noon. Lincoln Center is a bitch. Let's all stay together now in a tight little group. Watch out for the broken glass. That's the famous Henry Moore fountain those men are repairing. It was leaking right into the underground garages directly beneath, capacity 3126, and people coming out of the theatres kept walking into it and getting wet and then their cars wouldn't start and so they drained the fountain! It's people who don't look where they're going they should fix. Careful, it's a little tricky here. Are we all here? *(She has crossed to underneath the picture of the Vivian Beaumont Theatre.)* The Vivian Beaumont Theatre is the home of theatre at its best. Its actors and actresses, its directors, its plays, its scenery and costumes, its lighting effects, its fully annotated programs, its backstage facilities, everything! are without question the finest in the land. Just think of all the wonderful plays that have been done here and all the great stars of today who got their start on this very stage so that lucky audiences could later boast "We saw her when." Those who say the theatre is dying certainly ought to drop in at the Vivian Beaumont Theatre. Let's see what exciting young talent they're auditioning today for their Salute to the Polish Expressionists season.

(The lights come up center stage on Tommy disguised as an Actor. He wears tights, sunglasses and a T-shirt. He lies on the floor making strange noises and jerking convulsively. There is another red shopping bag beside him. The noises and jerking continue for a very long time.)

VOICE: *(American accent.)* Mr. Takinas?

(Tommy makes intense, violent, waving gestures as if to say "I'm concentrating. Don't rush me." He groans. He jerks. the whole Grotowski-trained actor bit.)

GRETA: *(Stage whisper.)* I think we're seeing one of those Method actors at work.

TOMMY/ACTOR: *(An insane, inarticulate howl in the direction of Greta.)* Aaaaaaarrrrrgggggghhhhh!!!!!

GRETA: *(Covering her mouth.)* Sorry!

VOICE: We don't have all day, Mr. Takinas.

(Tommy nods violently as if to say "I know, I know! I'm almost ready." When he finally begins to speak it is with a rather pronounced speech impediment.)

TOMMY/ACTOR: Speak the speech, I pray you, as I pronounced it to you, trippingly on the tongue. But if you mouth it, as many of our players do, I had as lief the town crier spoke my lines. Nor do not saw the air too much with your hand, thus, but use all gently, for in the very torrent, tempest, and (as I may say) whirlwind of your passion, you must acquire and beget a temperance that may give it smoothness. O, it offends me—

VOICE: Thank you, Mr. Takinas.

TOMMY/ACTOR: Tikanis. Orestes Tikanis. Greek.

VOICE: Yes, Mr. Tikanis. Don't call us, we'll call you.

TOMMY/ACTOR: I also do French farce, some musical comedy and I'll work in the nude. Wanna see?

VOICE: That's all right, Mr. Tikanis, and thank you.

TOMMY/ACTOR: How come you don't do more American plays?

VOICE: We'd like to, only there aren't enough of them.

TOMMY/ACTOR: I've got a whole shitload of 'em. Wanna hear one?

VOICE: Maybe next time. Who's next?

TOMMY/ACTOR: You know something funny? There ain't gonna be a next time.

(He laughs and exits, leaving the shopping bag behind. Lights come down center stage except for pin spot on the shopping bag.)

GRETA: The way he bit my head off you'd think it was my fault. Actors! They're so temperamental. And for what? We'll take the tunnel here. Careful of the railings. They're loose. A woman fell and broke her hip last week and now she's suing us. Suing Lincoln Center! *(She has crossed to underneath the picture of the Metropolitan Opera House.)* The Metropolitan Opera House is the crown jewel in the Lincoln Center tiara. From the Chagall murals in the lobby to the Austrian cut-crystal chandeliers and African rosewood walls in the auditorium proper, truly it deserves its appellation as the Fountainbleau of the New World. And surely it is the dream of every great singer to lift his voice in song here. Indeed, one cannot truly say one has sung until one has sung at the Met, as it is so affectionately called. We seem to be in luck all around today. The legendary Metropolitan Auditions of the Air are in progress. Let's listen in.

VOICE: *(Viennese accent.)* Madame Anita Dorfmeister-Gluck.

(Lights come up center stage on Tommy disguised as a great Diva. He wears a large picture hat and a floor-length mink coat. He carries another red shopping bag which he will set down.)

TOMMY/DIVA: *(Thick German accent.)* I am from the Stuttgart Opera. You know Stuttgart? Stuttgart is fabulous. Stuttgart looks just like Los Angeles. Los Angeles looks just like Stuttgart. New York looks like Dusseldorf.

VOICE: Madame Dorfmeister, if you please.

TOMMY/DIVA: Dorfmeister-Gluck, if *you* please. I shall sing, what I shall sing is *Tosca* by Puccini. The great aria, "Vissi d'arte, Vissi d'amore."

VOICE: Very good. Maestro.

TOMMY/DIVA: Which means—it's in Italian, *ja?*—she lived for art, she lived for love. I love this woman!

VOICE: May we begin then?

TOMMY/DIVA: *(Setting the scene.)* Act two. Napoleonic Rome. The Rome of Napoleon. Floria Tosca, the fabulous, the beautiful, the tempestuous grand diva, I *am* this woman to my tips! begs the evil Baron Scarpia on her hands and knees—

VOICE: Please, Madame Dorfmeister, there are others behind you!

TOMMY/DIVA: Dorfmeister-Gluck, *liebchen.* Where are they? *(Raucous German laugh.)* I begin. They go out of their heads when I do this in Stuttgart. *(Nods to accompanist after much throat clearing.)* Otto. Play, gypsy, play.
(He begins the aria in the most horrendous falsetto soprano imaginable. He is only a few bars into the aria when the Voice calls out.)

VOICE: Thank you, Madame Dorfmeister-Gluck, thank you!

TOMMY/DIVA: *(Without missing a beat.)* You're welcome, you're welcome! *(He goes right on singing.)*

VOICE: Throw that woman out of here!

TOMMY/DIVA: *(Injured majesty.)* Don't touch me. Don't nobody lay a finger. I go. But you see those pretty Austrian cut-crystal chandeliers, *ja?*

GRETA: *(Stage whisper.)* I was telling you about them.

TOMMY/DIVA: Pretty soon you don't see those pretty Austrian cut-crystal chandeliers. I take this to the ambassador. Otto, my limousine!
(He sweeps out majestically, leaving the red shopping bag behind. Lights fade center stage except for pin spot on shopping bag. All four shopping bags glowing in their special pin spots now.)

GRETA: We'll go outside now. Careful not to slip. These marble floors are murder. *(She moves downstage.)* Our tour of Lincoln Center for the Performing Arts wouldn't be complete without a stop at the famous Lincoln Center fountain with its beautiful dancing waters whose intricate patterns are programmed by an IBM computer. It's been estimated that you'd have to stand here ninety-three hours and forty-six minutes to see the fountain repeat itself. Of course when the fountain's actually working—Tuesdays, Wednesdays and alternate Saturdays—it's never been left on that long so nobody's had a chance to prove it, but I can't see any reason to doubt IBM. I thought I'd throw in a little plug there. My father's with IBM. *Are* you? Maybe you know him. Ira Rapp? Small world, isn't it? *(She laughs.)* Anyway, the fountain with its geometrically-patterned-after-a-design-by-Michelangelo-plaza is a popular gathering place at intermission *and* for some of New York City's weirdest weirdoes. And believe me, this town is full of them. There's one now.
(Tommy enters disguised as a crazy, tattered Old Lady. He carries another red shopping bag and a violin. He mutters to himself as he makes ready to play.)

TOMMY/OLD LADY: They want some of Ma Picker's mince pie, they're gonna get some of Ma Picker's mince pie. With arsenic and ground glass in it. No respect, no respect at all for an old lady anymore! Ma Picker's mince pie, that's the ticket! Those sons of bitches. *(He continues in this vein.)*

GRETA: I must say I haven't seen that one before. If any of you would care to make a donation and a request, I'm sure she'd be very happy to oblige.

TOMMY/OLD LADY: I don't do no requests, mister. I take donations but I don't do no requests. *(He accompanies himself on the violin and sings.)*

Lincoln Center falling down.

Lincoln Center falling down.

Lincoln Center falling down.

There's mice in the lobby.

(Lunging out with his bowstick.) Go on, get out of here! Everybody beat it! Scram! Shoo!

GRETA: *(Ignoring this.)* What did I tell you?

TOMMY/OLD LADY: And don't come back!

GRETA: That concludes our tour of Lincoln Center. I hope you've enjoyed yourself. And please, please don't litter. New York is a nice place to visit but we have to live here. Good-bye.

TOMMY/OLD LADY: Anybody make litter, I kill them! Go on, get away from here! Buzz off! Hit the road! Take a powder! Vamoose!

GRETA: Who do you think you are?

TOMMY/OLD LADY: You, too, mister, you, too!

GRETA: You can't do that to people!

TOMMY/OLD LADY: Who says, who says?

GRETA: The law for one.

TOMMY/OLD LADY: What law? Whose law? I don't see no law.

GRETA: Stop poking at me with that!

TOMMY/OLD LADY: I said you better beat it, mister!

GRETA: I don't want to beat it. It's a free country. I can't beat it. I work here. And you're crazy. Now leave me alone or I'll call the police.

TOMMY/OLD LADY: *(Hog-calling.)* Sooowwwiiieee! Sooowwwiiieee!

GRETA: I mean it! *(But we can see she is amused.)*

TOMMY/OLD LADY: Okay, mister.

GRETA: Stop calling me that. I'm a girl.

TOMMY/OLD LADY: Okay, girl. *(He starts to play the violin.)*

GRETA: Must you?

TOMMY/OLD LADY: It's a free country, honey.

GRETA: Unfortunately. *(She turns her back to him, apparently for good.)*

TOMMY/OLD LADY: *(Sings.)*

Lincoln Center falling down.

Lincoln Center falling down.

Lincoln Center falling down.

(Speaks.) You know something?

GRETA: What?

TOMMY/OLD LADY: For a girl guide you got a very nice pair of stems on you. *(Sings.)* There's a bomb in the lobby!

GRETA: *(Turning.)* Hunh?

TOMMY/OLD LADY: It wouldn't be a show without some tippy tap toe! *(He starts tap dancing. He drops coins at his own feet but pretends they were thrown.)* Thank you! Thank you! Much obliged, much obliged!

GRETA: What are you talking about? What bombs?

TOMMY/OLD LADY: Show time! Show Time! God bless you, sir! Thank you, madame!

GRETA: You said something about bombs! You're not an old lady! You really are crazy! *(She quickly breaks off.)* Hello, welcome to Lincoln Center. I'm Greta Rapp, your guide for today's tour. The New York State Theatre—
(As she pronounces the words, the New York State Theatre is blown up in a terrific roar of explosives and a beautiful cloud of smoke. Its photograph on the screen above the stage is extinguished and the pin spot on that particular shopping bag goes out.)

TOMMY/OLD LADY: *(Cockney accent.)* The New York State Theatre…? Go on, ducky, finish what you was saying.

GRETA: Oh oh oh!

TOMMY/OLD LADY: How do you like them apples, guvnor?

GRETA: It's all blowing up!

TOMMY/OLD LADY: There's plenty more where that came from, luvy!

GRETA: There *was* a bomb!

TOMMY/OLD LADY: You bet your blooming arse there was!

GRETA: I thought you were kidding.

TOMMY/OLD LADY: I'm just beginning.

GRETA: Who are you?

TOMMY/OLD LADY: *(Italian accent.)* Giuseppe Bonatella; That's a me! And a one, and a two, and a three!
(And with that Philharmonic Hall goes down in a roar of explosives and a cloud of smoke. Its photograph and the pin spot on the red shopping bag beneath it both go out.)

TOMMY/OLD LADY: That's right, pigs, you heard me. Burn, baby, burn! The fire this time!

GRETA: Look at Lincoln Center!

TOMMY/OLD LADY: Fuck Lincoln Center.

GRETA: Who are you?

TOMMY/OLD LADY: *(Thick speech impediment.)* You wanna see something, lady?
(The words are no sooner out of his mouth than the Vivian Beaumont Theatre goes up in a cloud of smoke. Its picture and the light on the shopping bag beneath go out.)

GRETA: Ooooooooooooo!

TOMMY/OLD LADY: You ain't seen nothing yet. The best for last, baby, the best for last.

GRETA: That was beautiful!

TOMMY/OLD LADY: You dig what I'm doing?

GRETA: Oh, absolutely! Do it again, do more! I just realized it: I hate Lincoln Center! This is fun!

TOMMY/OLD LADY: You know something?

GRETA: Don't talk, don't talk!

TOMMY/OLD LADY: *You're* crazy!

GRETA: I know, I know!

TOMMY/OLD LADY: And I love crazy chicks!

GRETA: Especially ones with nice pairs of stems on them!

TOMMY/OLD LADY: Right on, sister!

GRETA: Do more, do it again, do more!

TOMMY/OLD LADY: *(Thick German accent.) Das ist ein kleine* opera house? *Ja, ist das ein kleine* opera house!
(The Metropolitan Opera House explodes with an enormous roar of dynamite and lots of smoke. Its photograph fades and the pin spot on the red shopping bag goes out. All the screens are dark now.)

GRETA: Thank you, Madame Dorfmeister! Thank you!

TOMMY/OLD LADY: Dorfmeister-Gluck, *liebchen.*

GRETA: There go the Chagalls!

TOMMY/OLD LADY: I'm sorry.

GRETA: I hated them, too!

TOMMY/OLD LADY: Nice stems all the way up?

GRETA: Unh-hunh! I never knew how much I hated Lincoln Center until I saw it like this. Do more, do more!

TOMMY/OLD LADY: I can't. There is no more. *(Remembers.)* No, wait a minute.
(This time there is an offstage explosion.)

GRETA: The Walter Damrosch Band Shell, too! Fantastic! I'm Greta Rapp. I live around here.

TOMMY/OLD LADY: Then what do you say we split?

GRETA: *(A hesitation.)* You really did all this? I mean the bombs and everything, they were you?

TOMMY/OLD LADY: There's a connection?

GRETA: Yes or no?

TOMMY/OLD LADY: Yes! Because I—

GRETA: Don't tell me why. I don't care why. It'll just spoil it. I'll find out you're a Communist or something. I hate political men. Come on.

TOMMY/OLD LADY: Men? Men? I'm not men, man! Don't you know who I am?

GRETA: No.

TOMMY/OLD LADY: Oh wow!

GRETA: Should I?

TOMMY/OLD LADY: You really mean you still don't know who I am yet?

GRETA: I'm sorry, but no.

TOMMY/OLD LADY: O wow, baby, oh wow!

(There is another offstage explosion.)

GRETA: The underground garages! Well who are you?

TOMMY: *(Taking off his wig.)* Tommy Flowers!

GRETA: *(Overcome.)* Tommy Flowers!

TOMMY: Tommy Flowers, Revolutionary!

(Greta has swooned by now. Tommy catches her in his arms.)

TOMMY: Oh shit, I forgot Juilliard!

(He carries her off Tarzan-style, letting out a jungle yell as he goes. There is one final explosion and a puff of smoke as the fountain explodes. The Showgirl appears dressed in the French tricolors.)

SHOWGIRL: Louis XVI: Is it a revolt? Duc de la Rochefoucauld-Liancourt *(She has trouble with the name.)*: No, sire, it is a revolution. When the news arrived at Versailles of the Fall of the Bastille, 1789. Thank you. *(She exits rapidly.)*

ANNOUNCER'S VOICE: May I have your attention, please. I have a correction. A mink stole with the monogrammed initials DKR has been found on the floor of the *men's* room on the mezzanine level. Thank you.

SUMMER OF '52

(Tommy appears in a red baseball cap worn backwards and a scarf. He starts skimming stones.)

TOMMY: In the first place, it was a dumb question. "Who are the ten most admired men in America today and why?" That's almost as dumb as when they ask you what you want to be when you grow up. And so I wrote your name ten times. Holden Caulfield. Holden Caulfield. Holden Caulfield. Holden Caulfield. Holden Caulfield. Holden Caulfield. Holden Caulfield. Holden Caulfield. Holden Caulfield. Holden Caulfield. "Because he's not a phony" and I got an F. *(To audience, as he stops skimming stones.)* I always knew it would happen like this. I'd just be walking along the beach one night, skimming stones, and I'd see this kid just my age, looking just like me, and wearing the same red baseball cap and he'd just be walking and skimming, too, and when we finally got close together we'd both stop walking and start skimming together and without really saying anything—anything phony like "What school do you go to?"—we'd just kind of drift into this really natural conversation. *(Tommy starts skimming stones again.)* And then my parents had to go talk to Mr. Bartlett, our principal, and they all decided they didn't know what to do with me and then I had to go see Mr. Bartlett with them and they told me there was no way anyone anywhere could answer Holden Caulfield is even *one* of the ten most admired men in America today on his civics test and get away with it and how Miss Pearce had practically had a hemorrhage when she read my paper because she had such high hopes for me this semester and I would have to apologize to her and who the hell was Holden Caulfield anyway? and no wonder I was smoking in the boys' lavatory between classes and if I kept it up my growth would be stunted and I was short enough for my age as it was and hadn't my parents promised me a convertible if I didn't smoke until I graduated from high school? which is such a phony offer I almost puked because who wants a convertible *after* they graduate from high school, I'll probably be married by then or in the army or college maybe, and all the time we're in Bartlett's office he's scratching his balls, right in front of everyone, I was getting sick to my stomach, and my father is trying to sound stern and my mother is shaking her head, and all I'm thinking is how much I'd like to get out of there and have a Lucky Strike and maybe go over to Jan Moody's and hack around if her parents were still out of town—she is probably the most developed girl for her age in this state, 38D, I heard. You know, cup size. Sound good to you?—when Bartlett, still scratching his balls, and my mother's right in front of him, I should've called his bluff, "Stop scratching your balls, Bartlett!" when Bartlett asks if I want to take the test again and answer it properly this time and I looked at the three of them very calmly and said "okay" and went into another room and wrote "The ten most admired men in America today are Eisenhower, Truman, Acheson, etc., etc., etc., *because* etc., etc., etc." and I came back and handed it to them and Bartlett read it and smiled at my parents and then he smiled at me and said "You see, that wasn't so hard, was it now?" and I said "No, sir. It was very easy and now *I'm* a phony" and Bartlett was so shook up he even forgot to scratch his balls and said something about expelling me and they all agreed they'd talk about it later and we drove home with nobody saying a word and when we got there the phone was ringing and it was my big brother calling from California before he got shipped off to Korea and I couldn't think of much to say to him and so I said "Just don't get killed over there," which is just about the best and least phony thing I can think of to say to someone who's going off to Korea, especially your brother, and that started a new outburst from my mother and so I walked out of the house and went over to Jan Moody's, only her parents were back, but I tried to peek in her window anyway, she likes to sit around *nude* practically, and all I did was get my shoes muddy and ruin some of her mother's goddamn prize-winning roses and so I came down here and I'm very glad to have this opportunity to offer you a Lucky Strike, tell you I really do consider you the most admired man in America today because you're not a phony and ask you about Times Square. When I finally get to New York City I'm going to stand there for the entire first week just looking at people. You know what they call it? The Crossroads of the World. That's right where I want to be. There's nothing to look at in this town except Jan Moody's knockers. Maybe we could go together. I mean you know about subways and things. *(Pause.)* Seventh Avenue and 42nd St. I was there. Holden wasn't.

TOMMY'S MOTHER OR I AM THE WALRUS

TOMMY'S MOTHER: Your father and I certainly enjoyed your last collect call. Tell me, don't they sell pens and writing paper up in that neck of the woods anymore? I'm joshing, of course. It's better than not hearing from you at all. I just worry about you. What with all the violence and murders and bombings, etc., New York certainly doesn't sound like a very safe place to be right now. I'm very glad I'm right here in St. Pete in my own house. I don't miss it up there one second. Thank God, we don't have those problems down here. Your father is the same as ever. Smokes his head off, coughs all night, and smokes his head off again all next day. I'm so worried he has emphysema. I'm fine, of course. My back went out again last week and I was laid up for three days but I can't complain. I think I need a psychologist instead of an orthopedist but you even mention the word to your father and he sees red. All my friends who have therapists look and feel 100% better and we're all the same age, have the same problems, etc. I'm convinced nearly everything is psychosomatic nowadays. The good TV is on the blink so we're back to watching all the shows in black and white. It's like the Middle Ages. Well, I don't want to depress you with all our little problems and travails, so I'll sign off. I just missed you tonight. Say hello to Manhattan for me and have one on me while you're at it. Love you, Mom.

CHEZ GRETA

GRETA: *(In and out as she undresses.)* Tommy!

TOMMY: I'll be right in! *(To audience.)* You'll have to excuse me. I'm a little bushed. At my age, it catches up with you. I'm thirty years old which is neither as young as I was nor as old as I'm going to be but still kind of late in the ball game. You know what I mean. I'm just a child of the fifties, a little seedy and the worse for wear, but who isn't lately?

GRETA: It's true what they say about girl guides!

TOMMY: I'm finding out!

GRETA: Then hurry up!

TOMMY: What else should you know about me? I've got a *summa cum* something from somewhere in my head, no prospects in mind and lots of bridges burned behind me, an honorable discharge from Uncle Sam and a three-dollar bill in my wallet, call it lead in my pencil or love in my heart, Greta Prince in the next room lusting for my perfect body, no place to live, and a terrific dog named Arnold who's staying with a terrific girl who just kicked me out, which wasn't so terrific of her.

GRETA: Tommy!

TOMMY: I'm coming! I'm coming!

GRETA: Well hurry up!

TOMMY: I don't always think about girls. I don't want you to get the wrong impression. I also think about blowing this country up so we can start all over again. I sort of dig this country, see? That's why I think about blowing it up so we can start all over again. Now we can blow it up nice or we can blow it up tough. What I'm doing now is nice. What some of my friends are doing is tough. I'd prefer nice. Wouldn't you?

GRETA: Tommy!

TOMMY: She really does have nice legs all the way up.

GRETA: Tommy!!

TOMMY: A little weak in the chest department but her heart's in the right place. Okay, Greta, here I come!

TOMMY'S NEPHEW SPEAKS HIS PIECE

TOMMY'S NEPHEW: Power to the people! Off the pigs! Right on! Peace. What are you up to these days, Uncle Tommy? Nobody ever hears from you anymore. St. Petersburg is the same as ever. I don't blame you for not coming back. They still think anybody with hair over an inch long is some kind of freak. Right now they're pissed off at me because they caught me with a little grass again. Big deal! They should see what I got stashed in the garage. My mother is a real ball-breaker when it comes to dope and I know he's your brother, but my father is a creep. You, Uncle Tommy, on the other hand, are probably the finest person I know. Where you painted your name on the big water tower when you were in high school still shows through and they just painted it again. I see it every day. I'm planning to run away. I'd like to join you in NYC. I hear it's good for kids up there. We could really tear that town apart. I'd have to get a job and help pay my own way, of course, but I bet you know a lot of people who could help me out. I know I can trust you. You're the only one in this whole family I can. I'm really serious about running away. I'm also thinking about Mexico or some places in Peru. I don't care if you think this is corny, but I have plans for a wonderful life. You'd still be my favorite uncle even if you weren't my only one. Your loving, spaced out, increasingly radicalized, funky, freaky nephew, Charles Flowers the First.

TRAVEL LIGHT

GRETA: *(Off.)* I love you, Tommy Flowers!!

TOMMY: I love you, too, Greta Rapp! I had two wonderful weeks. She had two wonderful weeks. Fair enough. I'm back to zero but something will turn up. I'd like you to meet someone. Come on Arnold—come here, meet some people. This is Arnold. He's my dog. I say that because some people confuse their dogs with people. I'm not one of those people, and I'd hate to meet that person Arnold could be confused with. I have him all entered in the Westminster Dog Show as a chihuahua. Well, what can they do? I've paid the entry fee. I'll just say he's a little large for his breed. I'm going to tie-dye him, too, one day. I've even bought the colors. In my book, he's right up there with Lassie and Rin Tin Tin among your all-time dog stars. Hello.

MAN: No.

TOMMY: No what, man?

MAN: Just no.

TOMMY: I didn't ask for anything.

MAN: I don't have any.

TOMMY: I said hello.

MAN: The answer is no.

TOMMY: Thank you. Thank you very much. *(To audience.)* Travel light. That's my first piece of advice. Yes sir, travel light. Everything I own is right in here. A toothbrush, a change of shorts, my autographed picture of James Dean, my nun's habit. This is a true play and already you don't believe me. That's about it from the permanent collection. Everything else is temporary, disposable and eminently replaceable. Everything breaks, nothing works anymore. Hot enough for you?

MAN: Get a job.

TOMMY: I have one, thank you. Creep. *(To audience.)* And don't encumber yourself with a lot of junk. The only junk I take with me is right up here. Facts about famous people, world capitals and useless dates. Franz Liszt contracted cholera while vacationing in Baden-Baden on July 7, 1873. It wasn't even fatal. Otherwise, I'm as fluid as fluid can be…Excuse me, sir, would you happen to have any spare change?

MAN: It's exactly eleven after two.

TOMMY: I'm a little fast.

MAN: It happens.

TOMMY: Don't mention it.

MAN: Don't mention it.

TOMMY: You're welcome. And don't be ashamed of being a mooch. You can't very well live out of a shopping bag if you're ashamed of being a mooch. Like the man says, we all get by with a little help from our friends.

BEN: Brother, can you spare a dime?

TOMMY: Listen, chief, this is sort of my corner and things are kind of slow today. So keep it down, hunh? Just sort of fade into the sidewalk. I wouldn't want to see you crowding my style, know what I mean?

BEN: Got you.

TOMMY: Thanks.

BEN: Money's tight.

TOMMY: I know, man, I know.

BEN: Tighter than a drum.

TOMMY: Boom, boom, boom! He's not a friend. Don't worry. I'll score. I'm very optimistic. What else could I be? I'm an American.

MAN: Hare Krishna.

TOMMY: Hare Krishna.

MAN: Krishna Hare.

TOGETHER: Ommmm.

TOMMY: Where are you from?

MAN: Queens.

TOMMY: You got any coins on you?

MAN: Fuck off, man.

Together: Ommm.

TOMMY: God bless you, too, asshole. *(To Ben.)* This used to be a good street for us until those goddamn fake monks started hitting it up. Some Joe Blow Betty Boop from Peoria, Illinois, shaves his head, mops a salad bowl from Prexy's and tells everybody he's a fucking Buddhist monk!

BEN: Is that your dog?

TOMMY: Yep.

BEN: I hate dogs.

TOMMY: Who asked you?

BEN: I had a dog once. He committed suicide. We were watching television, Ed Sullivan, and he got up and jumped right out the window.

TOMMY: It's been nice talking to you.

BEN: His name was Arnold.

TOMMY: Arnold's my dog.

BEN: He was a Siamese. A real thoroughbred. I'll move over there. I'm crowding your style.

TOMMY: Thanks, old timer, we'll be talking to you.

GIRL: Taxi!

TOMMY: Now that's more like it!

GIRL: Taxi!

TOMMY: Miss! Yoo hoo, miss! Aren't you Miss Subways?

GIRL: Yes!

TOMMY: You are?

GIRL: Yes, I am!

TOMMY: You're a great looking chick.

GIRL: I know!

TOMMY: My dog and I haven't eaten in twenty-four hours.

GIRL: Here.

TOMMY: Thank you, thank you very much. I hope you win many such elections. *(Sees it's a subway token she's given him.)* Hey! I don't ride the subways.

GIRL: Me either. They're too dangerous. Taxi! Yoo hoo, cab! *(She is gone.)*

TOMMY: I didn't even vote for you! Miss Subways, Miss Subways! Miss *Shitways*, Miss Subways! I thought I had her pegged. Come on, seven, come on, baby. *(To Ben.)* Here, take a subway somewhere. *(Flips Ben the token.)*

BEN: *(Flipping it back.)* I don't ride the subways, young man.

TOMMY: Then take a bus.

BEN: Them either.

TOMMY: Then take a walk.

BEN: *(He's found a movie magazine in Tommy's shopping bag.)* Is this yours?

TOMMY: Hey!

BEN: You mind if I look at it?

TOMMY: You can have it. Take it to the park with you.

BEN: I hate the park.

TOMMY: What's wrong with the park?

BEN: Too many damn dogs.

TOMMY: Buzz off, why don't you?

BEN: It's a free country, young man.

TOMMY: Unfortunately. *(He "reads" the subway token.)* The Metropolitan Transit Authority. Even the names of things in this country are literature. The Great Atlantic and Pacific Tea Company. Northwest Passage. Lorna Doone cookies. Lorna Doone, mind you! Thom with a "h," Thom McCann Shoes. The A. B. Dick Repeating Company. That's not penis fixation, lady, hell, no, it's poetry! God, how we loved that one in grammar school. To see the word *dick* on a ditto machine! *Dick.*

MAN: Hi there.

TOMMY: You got any spare change, brother? I'm strapped, really and truly strapped.

MAN: That depends.

TOMMY: Can I guess what it depends on?

MAN: You're a big boy, you should be able to.

TOMMY: You're the best offer I've had all day. Thanks, but no thanks.

MAN: Hostile bitch.

TOMMY: I love talking to people. I majored in conversation in college.

BEN: "Lucille Ball's Night of Terror."

TOMMY: It's a terrific story.

BEN: "Bob Hope's Biggest Fear."

TOMMY: The whole issue's great.

BEN: "Mia Farrow's Cry for Help."

TOMMY: It's heart-breaking.

BEN: "Marlon Brando's Night of Terror."

TOMMY: Yeah, they're all scared shitless on the West Coast, too. *(To audience.)* Franchot Tone once bought my mother a Singapore Sling at the bar in the Stork Club. No more Stork Club, no more Singapore Sling.

BEN: No more Franchot Tone.

TOMMY: And my father claims he spent a pretty memorable weekend with Lana Turner in Westport, Connecticut. They're nice people, my folks are. You'd like them. Just your average neighborhood star-fuckers, geriatric groupies. I don't mean that. Though actually I did meet Franchot Tone once and it just seemed kind of stupid to say, "Hello, Mr. Tone, you may not remember this but you bought my mother a Singapore Sling in the Stork Club before she married my father and I'm their son." He would have thought I was crazy. Or he might have thought it was nice.

BEN: Or he might have thought it was nice, young man.

TOMMY: You think?

BEN: I knew Mr. Tone.

TOMMY: No kidding?

BEN: I didn't like him.

TOMMY: Of course you didn't.

BEN: He didn't like me much either.

TOMMY: I'm not surprised. *(To audience.)* But stories like that only seem to happen in this country. Did you ever meet a kid from La Paz, Bolivia, with a tale to tell like mine? No sir, you did not! Where is everybody? What happens to them anymore? Whose mind hasn't been blown lately? Who hasn't freaked out? Alger Hiss sells stationery. J. D. Salinger has an unlisted number. Sabu's been busted. My high school English teacher, write-what-you-know-about McIlvey, where is she? Hit by a bolt of lightning while making a deposit at a drive-in bank. Her, the car, the money. Rumble! Zing! Pfft! Zap! Really. Only in America could your high school English teacher die like that. I mean it just wouldn't happen to a Laplander, an awful thing like that.

(A pedestrian has entered and crossed.)

TOMMY: Hey! Hey, come back here! No fair! I wasn't looking. Shit! See how you got me started? You gotta concentrate every second if you're gonna hustle. You get distracted and they could be handing out free money and you wouldn't score. So knock it off. I told you, this is my corner. Can I have my *Screen World* back now?

BEN: I was an actor, too, you know.

TOMMY: The magazine, chief.

BEN: Take it, it's yours. Never heard of anybody in it anyhow. I like my movies all right but give me good ol' live theatre any day of the week. That Lana Turner of yours couldn't cut the mustard up here. None of them movie personalities could. I was in the original production of *Kismet* with Otis Skinner.

TOMMY: Sorry I missed it.

BEN: Lots of feathers in that one.

TOMMY: It sounds terrific.

BEN: Me and Paul Muni were bitter rivals.

TOMMY: *The* Paul Muni?

BEN: He had my career.

TOMMY: I've seen *Fugitive from a Chain Gang* a dozen times.

BEN: I was up for that part, nearly had it, too.

TOMMY: What's your name?

BEN: My stage name was Ben Delight.

TOMMY: Ben Delight? I never heard of you.

BEN: It's the kind of name you can't forget.

TOMMY: What was your name before you changed it?

BEN: Jack Wonder.

TOMMY: You changed your name from Jack Wonder to Ben Delight?

BEN: It's a long story.

TOMMY: I bet.

(A woman passes by.)

TOMMY: Excuse me, madam, I'm not going to hassle you. I'm just taking a little poll for charity.

WOMAN: We already gave.

TOMMY: I'm sure you haven't. We're just getting started. And this one's fun. Now who's your favorite movie star?

WOMAN: Oh that's hard. That's very, very hard.

TOMMY: Well, think. It's for charity. *(Helping her out.)* Slim Pickens?

WOMAN: *(Shaking her head.)* No.

TOMMY: Mario Lanza? Franchot Tone? Me?

WOMAN: What's your name?

TOMMY: Tommy Flowers.

WOMAN: What have you been in?

TOMMY: Tommy Flowers.

WOMAN: I missed that one, I'm sorry.

TOMMY: It hasn't been released yet. Now come on, who?

WOMAN: *(Blushing.)* Well…

TOMMY: Cary Grant, I knew it!

WOMAN: Charlton Heston.

TOMMY: Charlton Heston!

WOMAN: Is that all right?

TOMMY: It's terrific! I was just reading this article about him. He's a woman.

WOMAN: What a terrible thing to say about the man who played Moses!

TOMMY: Well, you know, these fan magazines.

WOMAN: Oh, I'm just sick.

TOMMY: Well *I* didn't say it. See? "Hollywood's best kept secret." "Charlton Heston Is A Woman" in great big letters.

WOMAN: They spoil everything nowadays.

TOMMY: Hey! *(She is gone. To audience.)* Fuck Charlton Heston. Well maybe he is. Fuck him anyway. She'd like to. *(To Ben.)* I was an actor once myself. It shits. I've been a lot of things once. They all shit, too. What I am now, you see, is free.

(Sees Ben fiddling in the shopping bag.)

TOMMY: Do you mind?

BEN: Who is it?

TOMMY: Careful of that, will you?

BEN: Looks like some kind of an actor.

TOMMY: It's James Dean, for Christ's sake!

BEN: I've seen that face somewhere.

TOMMY: I should hope so.

BEN: Name some plays he was in.

TOMMY: *The Immoralist* and *See the Jaguar.*

BEN: That's all he was in, two plays?

TOMMY: I'm afraid so.

BEN: What's the matter? Wasn't he any good?

TOMMY: He was terrific. The best.

BEN: I don't see how terrific he could've been if all he was in was two plays.

TOMMY: You'll just have to take my word for it.

BEN: Never heard of him.

TOMMY: He was a movie star.

BEN: Not in my book.

TOMMY: *East of Eden. Rebel Without a Cause. Giant.*

BEN: Go on.

TOMMY: That's it.

BEN: Two plays and three movies?

TOMMY: He died young.

BEN: No wonder you don't hear his name mentioned much.

TOMMY: May I have my picture back?

BEN: I thought I knew all the greats. But James Dean. That's a new one on me. A real star, hunh?

TOMMY: One of the biggest.

BEN: You could've fooled me.

TOMMY: *(To audience.)* How can anybody not have heard of James Dean? And how do you tell somebody who hasn't what he was like? He was just like you, only he was your big brother, too. I know this for a fact: James Dean, the movie star, like me, Thomas P. for Prospers Flowers, a high school kid with pimples.

JIMMY

(Warner Brothers logo appears. East of Eden theme music is heard.)

BAR: Two Schlitz. That kid shouldn't be in here, Jimmy.

TOMMY: It's okay, Lois, he's with me.

(She goes.)

TOMMY: Listen, Tom Flowers, I'm gonna have to split.

YOUNG TOMMY: Where you going, Jimmy?

TOMMY: Nowhere.

YOUNG TOMMY: Why don't you stay then?

TOMMY: You see the Porsche Spider out there? They told me it'll do 160. I'm gonna find out.

YOUNG TOMMY: That's too fast, Jimmy.

TOMMY: I've got to.

YOUNG TOMMY: Okay, Jimmy.

TOMMY: Hey, and listen, Tom. Your father likes you. He just don't know how to say it. Just try talking to him, man to man. He's…unh…shy, Tom. It's hard for him to tell you he loves you. Try making it easy for him, what do you say?

YOUNG TOMMY: Thanks, Jimmy.

TOMMY: And, hey, you know something else? Gretchen Selby likes you, too.

YOUNG TOMMY: I don't think so, Jimmy. Not after what I done.

TOMMY: That's not what she told me.

YOUNG TOMMY: You talked to her?

TOMMY: I said, hey, Gretchen, what's so wrong if my friend Tom Flowers drinks a few beers and raises a little hell and maybe he ain't an A+ student like you and maybe your mother thinks he's a hellion and won't let you go out with him and your father thinks he's a bad kid and wants you to go out with Buba Walsh. Buba Walsh is a square, baby. And then she started crying and saying "Tell Tommy"…is that what she calls you, Tom?…"Tell Tommy I love him and I know he's not bad."

YOUNG TOMMY: Gretchen really said that?

TOMMY: Yeah, she did.

YOUNG TOMMY: Gretchen Selby, 108 Surf Street, St. Petersburg, Florida?

TOMMY: Hey, Tom, it's me, Jimmy talking. Ain't I always been straight with you?

YOUNG TOMMY: Sure thing, Jimmy.

TOMMY: Then what are you waiting for? I gotta split now. You see that Porsche Spider out there? They told me it'll do 160. I'm gonna find out.

YOUNG TOMMY: I'll go with you.

TOMMY: I've got to find out all by myself. See you later, Tom. Hey, it's gonna be all right.

YOUNG TOMMY: Yeah?

TOMMY: It's got to.

YOUNG TOMMY: Thanks, Jimmy. Stay happy.

TOMMY: Happy! Who says I ain't.

(*Car sounds, screeching of tires, a crash.*)

YOUNG TOMMY: Jimmy? Jimmy? Jimmy!!

TOMMY: If I'd've been there that never would have happened. The best friend I ever had and I wasn't with him!

(*The Warner Brothers logo and music have faded.*)

BEN: *Kumquats!*

TOMMY: Kumquats?

BEN: *Kumquats!* I saw you in *Kumquats.*

TOMMY: You're putting me on now.

BEN: The Belasco Theatre. The season of...let's see...

TOMMY: Five or six years ago.

BEN: I never forget a face.

TOMMY: You don't know who Jimmy Dean is but you remember me in *Kumquats?*

BEN: I forget names but I can't shake faces.

TOMMY: I had ten lines!

BEN: There are no small parts, young man, only—

TOMMY: I know, but I had green stripes on my face and was wearing feathers!

BEN: I remember those stripes.

TOMMY: It only ran one night.

BEN: That's why I try to make most openings.

TOMMY: You really saw it?

BEN: Oh indeed I did, sir.

TOMMY: You've got to be kidding.

BEN: I was there all right.

TOMMY: That was some play, hunh?

BEN: One of your all-time super-flops, that one.

TOMMY: I told them it was ahead of its time.

BEN: That it was, sir, that it was.

TOMMY: What…unh…well what did you think of it?

BEN: That *Kumquats* show?

TOMMY: It's *Kumquat*, actually. Singular. Just one kumquat. We could never figure out why people insisted on pluralizing it.

BEN: I guess when you think of kumquats you just naturally think of more than one.

TOMMY: Yeah, I guess so.

BEN: *Kumquat*, singular, was a badly written, ill-structured, poorly motivated, humorless, pedantic, philosophically sophomoric, cliché-ridden *and* plagiarized (and that takes some doing!), three-and-a-half hour, $5.50, from where I sat, piece of shit.

TOMMY: Oh really?

BEN: *Kumquats*, plural, would have been a double piece of shit.

TOMMY: No kidding?

BEN: You were pretty four thumbs yourself.

TOMMY: Oh?

BEN: All nerves, no style.

TOMMY: Unh-hunh!

BEN: And you tripped. I remember you tripped.

TOMMY: Oh you remember that?

BEN: You came in, said one line and fell right over your feathers!

TOMMY: Thanks for reminding me.

BEN: Tell me… *(He's laughing so hard he can barely speak.)* Tell me, is that your own voice you use when you act?

TOMMY: Are you through?

BEN: *(Drying his eyes.)* I guess.

TOMMY: You know what the trouble with old people like you is? Exactly what they are: they're old. Their bodies are old, their minds are old, their skin is old, their hair is old, their eyes are old their glands are old, their cocks and cunts are old. They look old, they act old, and they smell old. Everything about them is old, it's old, man, it's old. And because they're old they hate anything young and most of all they hate young people. They hate young people's clothes, they hate long hair, they hate grass and acid, they hate words like fuck but most of all they hate to fuck because they can't do it anymore. Well I'm young, mister, and I can fuck and when I'm not fucking or getting stoned or just grooving, I'm out finding out every good way I can to fuck up this whole fucking system that produces fucked up old people like you. You're dead, mister, you're already dead. You've already lost and we've already won.

BEN: *(Simply.)* All right, son.

TOMMY: Erase that. Erase everything I just said.

BEN: That's all right, too.

TOMMY: I didn't mean it and I'm truly and deeply ashamed of myself and you'll just have to take my word for it.

BEN: Okay.

TOMMY: No, really!

BEN: It's okay, son, it's okay.

TOMMY: It's not and you don't have to say it is.

BEN: Me and my friend here, we understand, don't we, boy, hunh?

(Tommy suddenly hugs Ben and kisses him.)

TOMMY: You know what my wonderful grandfather taught me? God, why couldn't the whole world have known him? I wanted money for the movies and he wouldn't give me any. Maybe he didn't even have it. He only worked for the post office. He said "Walk in backwards and they'll think you're coming out." Isn't that beautiful? Hunh? "Walk in backwards and they'll think you're coming out." But I was a little boy then and I never liked him after that. It took me twenty-five years to realize the almost ancient wisdom of that remark. "Walk in backwards and they'll think you're coming out." You know something? They do.

BEN: Why of course they do, son.

TOMMY: You knew about that?

BEN: How do you think I saw you in the *Kumquats* show?

TOMMY: Look at that coat. It's worse than mine. Come on, we'll go to Bloomingdale's. I'll get you a new one.

BEN: That's all right.

TOMMY: I want to.

BEN: I'm perfectly fine in this.

TOMMY: Bullshit. We'll hop a cab and have you fixed up in no time.

BEN: But you don't have that kind of money.

TOMMY: I don't have any money. Dig?

BEN: I don't know, kid.

TOMMY: You know how long it's been since anyone's called me kid? You just got yourself an entire fall wardrobe. Now what do you say?

BEN: Well…

TOMMY: This street's dead anyway. Bloomingdale's is loaded with easy-to-score-with chicks. I'll find myself something while I'm at it. *(Calls.)* Taxi! *(Jumping back.)* Cocksucker! *(Pretending to jot down license number.)* 4Z 5505. *(To Ben.)* I'm used to this.

BEN: So am I.

TOMMY: When I finally get one, I love to tell 'em 136th Street and Lenox Avenue. They have cardiac arrests. Taxi! He's stopped for a light. Come on, let's grab him, if the doors aren't locked. *(They approach a cab.)*

HACK: *(New York accent.)* Bonjour, bonjour.

TOMMY: You go uptown?

HACK: I go uptown, downtown, crosstown, Chinatown, Brooklyn, Queens, the Bronx, Jersey, all three airports and Westchester County, what can I tell you? You want to go to Grand Rapids, Michigan? I'll take you to Grand Rapids, Michigan. *Bonjour, bonjour!*

TOMMY: We're only going to Bloomingdale's today, thank you.

HACK: Bloomingdale's it is. Just thought I'd mention it. Climb in.

(Tommy, Ben and Arnold get into the cab.) Allons enfants de la patrie!

TOMMY: Don't throw the meter.

HACK: Meter? What meter? I don't see no meter. As far as I'm concerned, this cab is empty. I ain't picked up a fare all day, you know what I mean? I'm gonna take 11th Avenue, just in case. I bet you two was surprised when I even stopped for you, weren't you? Hunh? Hunh?

TOMMY: We certainly were, sir.

HACK: Most drivers would rather pick up your mutt than you two and no offense.

TOMMY: We're very grateful.

HACK: I'll tell you why. See, the point is you gotta accept life. That's right, you heard me, accept it. Too many drivers don't accept life, so they're always locking their doors and refusing to pick up fares like maybe that was gonna keep 'em from getting mugged or stiffed or murdered even. But not me, mac, no sir. If some nigger wants to mug me, he's gonna mug me, know what I mean? God's will be done and all that, I ain't religious. Figure that one out.

TOMMY: We're working on it.

HACK: I been mugged 16 times...17 if you count that Spic bitch...but I've been pushing a hack for 20 years and if you do some long dividing you'll find that I been mugged on the average of less than once a year, which ain't so bad. 'Course all these muggings have happened in the past three years but my boss says you gotta figure it over the whole twenty. *C'est la vie, c'est la vie!* Look at the tits on that one! *(Out the window.)* That's right, honey, if you got 'em, flaunt 'em! *(Back into the cab.)* Would you mind not smoking? I'm allergic. *(Tommy has lit a joint.)*

TOMMY: This is a French cigarette.

HACK: Oh, *Parlez-vous français*, either of you two?

TOMMY: I'm afraid not.

HACK: I had one of them Indian women in here a couple of minutes ago. Right where you're sitting. Indian from the country India. She was even wearing one o' them things they wear, that's how Indian she was.

TOMMY: Sari.

HACK: That's okay.

TOMMY: No, they're called a sari, what she was wearing.

HACK: Oh! Sari, hunh? That's a terrific word. *Aimez-vous saris? Non je n'aime pas* saris. Christ, it's a terrific language that French stuff. I'm teaching myself so I can talk to foreign people, too. If there's one thing I like it's exchanging views and if there's one thing this town is full of, it's foreign people. It was either French or Spanish, if you know what I mean. She spoke French. Say, either of you two gambling men?

BEN: That depends, sir.

HACK: I bet you a dollar you can't guess how old I am and I already told you I been pushing this thing 20 years. Go ahead, take a guess. I'll give you five years either side of it, too. I'm listening.

BEN: Forty-five.

TOMMY: No, much younger. Forty-one at most.

HACK: Hah! Don't I wish I'd see either of them two again. Fifty-five and me are old friends, too. I'm 63 years old this May, my friends. *Soixante-trois.*

TOMMY: That's amazing.

BEN: It's depressing.

HACK: You don't believe me.

TOMMY: We believe you.

HACK: Look at that and call me a liar.

TOMMY: You're 63 years old this May all right.

HACK: Okay, so cough it up. If there's one thing that gets me going it's people who welsh on their debts. Know what I mean?

TOMMY: Absolutely. I'm sorry, Ben, but he's got a point.

(Tommy and Ben pool their resources.)

HACK: This one guy, this little kike bastard, he guessed I was 47 and then he wouldn't pay up and said he thought it was just a game. Ask me, what's a game anymore? I'll tell you, nothing's a game anymore. Brother, he pissed me off.

TOMMY: You've got a colorful vocabulary.

HACK: Thank you. I pride myself on it. One thing I ain't ever been accused of is boring my passengers half to death. Most drivers just yak-yak-yak and who asked 'em? Who asked 'em? Honor the passenger. Respect his intelligence. And keep your GD mouth shut. That's my philosophy. *(Out the window.)* What's the matter with you? You paraplegic or something? *(Back into cab.)* C'est la vie! C'est la vie! You know what my son Benedict says?

TOMMY: No, what?

HACK: He's a veterinarian up in Maine, he got out of this rat race, nice wife, nice family, nice house, nice car, nice neighborhood, so far, but like Benny says: the quality of life, pa, it's the quality of life that ain't so hot anymore.

TOMMY: That's true.

HACK: My dear dead wife, Rosa, Rosa Capri her maiden name was, how's that for a monicker? Rosa Capri, God bless her, you'd a thought she was a Guinea with a handle like that, when we'd be stuck in traffic like this she'd say "What's the race, Mayo, what's the big race?" Wonderful woman. I don't know. I don't know anymore. Your friend don't say much.

BEN: I'm asleep.

HACK: God bless you, mac.

BEN: I'm old. I'm tired.

HACK: Who ain't, who ain't? *Voici* Bloomingdale's. There she is.

TOMMY: Thanks for the lift. That's all you've got, Ben?

BEN: You're the one who wanted to take a cab.

HACK: *(Last of the big spenders.)* Let's just say three dollars and call it even. Two for the ride and the buck you just lost to me.

TOMMY: Let's just say *none* for the ride and ninety-nine cents for what we lost to you.

HACK: Hey, what's this?

TOMMY: A subway token and sixty-four cents. We owe you a penny. Unless you want to wait for us.

HACK: Wait for you??

TOMMY: I didn't think so. Officer! Officer!

HACK: What are you doing?

TOMMY: This driver didn't throw his meter and I'm making a citizen's arrest!

HACK: You said you was gonna take care of me!

TOMMY: I am. Hey, officer!

HACK: Stop for you? I shoulda run over you! *(He flees.)*

TOMMY: There'll be a four-state dragnet out for you, 5Z-6022! *(To Ben.)* You're not coming in?

BEN: I hate Bloomingdale's. I'll wait out here.

TOMMY: Then keep an eye on Arnold.

BEN: One of those trench coats with a zip-in lining would be nice. An Aquascrotum.

TOMMY: You start big. Only it's Aquascutum, okay? *(He goes.)*

BEN: I thought Aquascrotum sounded funny.

(Lights down on Ben and Arnold.)

LOVE IS WHERE YOU FIND IT

(The lights come up on a row of pay toilets. From behind one of the closed doors we hear Tommy singing "Shenandoah." After a while, he stands up and looks down into the adjoining booth.)

TOMMY: Beautiful song, isn't it?

(A woman screams.)

TOMMY: Got a match?

NEDDA: I'm trying not to get hysterical and start yelling for the cops or anything but this is the ladies' room!

TOMMY: I know.

NEDDA: Don't you think you ought to be in the men's room, sir?

TOMMY: I was in the men's room. I didn't like it. It's not so hot in here either, now that you mention it, but compared to the men's room it's Chock Full O'Nuts.

NEDDA: You're not meant to be in here!

TOMMY: I know.

NEDDA: It's against the law.

TOMMY: No, it's not.

(Nedda comes charging out of her booth carrying a cello case.)

TOMMY: Where are you going?

NEDDA: I'm going to call a policeman is where I'm going, you...you rapist!

TOMMY: You forgot your purse.

(Nedda puts down the cello case and goes back into her booth while Tommy darts out, grabs the cello case and takes it into his booth. When Nedda comes back out, she can't find her cello case.)

NEDDA: Where's my...? Give me that!

TOMMY: *(From behind the door of his booth.)* What is it?

NEDDA: *(Trying to reach over.)* Never mind! Now give it to me!

TOMMY: Tell me what it is first.

NEDDA: A cello case!

TOMMY: What's in it?

NEDDA: A cello.

TOMMY: I've always wanted to play the cello.

NEDDA: Don't open that!

TOMMY: It's so light for a cello!

NEDDA: It's a Stradivarius!

TOMMY: A real Stradivarius?

NEDDA: It's very fragile. Please don't open it!

TOMMY: I've always wanted to see a Stradivarius.

NEDDA: I said don't open that!

TOMMY: I'll be very careful! Oh! What have we here? No wonder you didn't want me to open it. *(Handing the objects mentioned up to her.)* A red-and-white umbrella. The price tag's still on it. It must be a Stradivarius. And what's this? A Westinghouse Stradivarius alarm clock out of its box. Two Stradivarius dresses. Feels like a Stradivarius cashmere sweater. No, Stradivarius vicuna. Stradivarius shoes. And a tube of Charles of the Ritz Stradivarius Rose Blush Lipstick! They're very unusual cellos, these Stradivariuses: no strings.

NEDDA: *(Her arms full now.)* I'm going to pay for it.

TOMMY: Boy, you really cleaned them out, didn't you?

NEDDA: You can't do anything to me, I haven't left the store yet!

TOMMY: *(Standing up.)* Mr. Pinkerton guard! Mr. Pinkerton guard! We've got a shoplifter in stall eleven. Help! Help!

NEDDA: It's not what you're thinking.

TOMMY: *(Nailing her.)* What is it then?

NEDDA: *(Squirming.)* I don't know but it's not what you're thinking.

TOMMY: Then about that policeman: what do you say we call a truce?

NEDDA: Okay, okay!

TOMMY: I bet you feel pretty rotten now, don't you?

NEDDA: I've never done anything like this in my life.

TOMMY: Rip off Bloomingdale's?

NEDDA: I didn't know I'd feel so guilty.

TOMMY: You didn't know you were gonna get caught.

NEDDA: I'm going to take it all back. Yes, yes! That's exactly what I'm going to do: put everything back right where I found it.

TOMMY: Relax. You should see the haul I've got down here. It's not as big as yours, of course, whose is? but...

NEDDA: You stole something, too?

TOMMY: Bloomingdale's runs a terrific free store. Listen to this.

(A radio is heard.)

NEDDA: You took a radio?

TOMMY: Nice tone quality for a Jap import, don't you think? I'd have preferred a Zenith but they were all out.

NEDDA: I took the last Zenith.

TOMMY: Where?

NEDDA: It's inside the boots.

TOMMY: Hot shit, she did! Are you sure this is the first time you've ripped off Bloomingdale's?

NEDDA: First and last.

TOMMY: But you're off to such a terrific start.

NEDDA: I don't have the nerves for it. I'm shaking like a leaf. Look at me.

TOMMY: Okay. *(He gets up and looks at her.)* Hi.

NEDDA: Hi. *(Short pause.)*

TOMMY: Somebody's coming.

NEDDA: You better hide!

(Tommy and Nedda duck down in their respective booths. A woman enters and goes in to the third booth. Pause. We hear her sigh in relief.)

TOMMY: Hey, Mac! Did you see where the Mets are in first place again? I tell you! What a ball club! What a ball club! They should've dropped that Minny Minoza three seasons ago.

(Tommy is standing up in his booth waiting for her as the woman's head slowly appears over the top of the door.)

WOMAN: Oh dear. I'm sorry. I'm most terribly sorry. I thought this was the…I had no idea…!

TOMMY: That's okay, lady, that's okay. Think nothing of it.

WOMAN: I could have sworn it was the ladies' room!

TOMMY: It is. Now sit down!

(Woman's head disappears as she sits.)

TOMMY: Now the Orioles are a whole other ball team! You see them against the Senators last week? The ninth inning, two men out, the bases loaded and they put Herlihy in against Braverman!

(The woman stands up again, runs out of her booth and is gone.)

TOMMY: Don't you want to know who won? *(Knocks on Nedda's door.)* Do you?

NEDDA: What am I going to do now?

TOMMY: You can come out of there for openers.

(Nedda reappears.)

TOMMY: Hello again.

NEDDA: What do I do with all this?

TOMMY: Pack up your Stradivarius and wait till the coast clears. You're better off in here with me. You like rock or classical?

NEDDA: Hunh?

TOMMY: A little music will calm you down. Rock or classical?

NEDDA: Classical.

TOMMY: Classical? Fancy! Classical it is. *(He turns on the radio again.)* Listen to that resonance. Must be all the tile. Hey, this is nice.

NEDDA: *(Repacking her cello case.)* Are you sure it's not against the law for you to be in here?

TOMMY: Unh-hunh.

NEDDA: I can't believe it.

TOMMY: You'd be surprised how many laws against things they haven't gotten around to thinking of yet. Did you know you can have a complete Chicken Delight dinner delivered to your seat in a movie theatre? They don't like it, they discourage it, in fact, but it's not against the law. And you know those tags on mattresses that say Do Not Remove Under Penalty of Law? There's no such law? Rip 'em off, rip 'em off. It's your fucking mattress and you can do anything you want with it. And you can, too, return a bathing suit. They just say the Board of Health says you can't so they don't have to be bothered. I pee in them first and then I return them, that's how un-against the law returning a bathing suit is.

NEDDA: Well it was nice talking to you…

TOMMY: It's Flowers, ma'am, Tommy Flowers.

NEDDA: It was nice talking to you, Mr. Flowers.

TOMMY: Aren't you going to wash your hands?

NEDDA: Is there some law about that, too?

TOMMY: No, but it's a nice habit.

NEDDA: I think the coast is clear now.

TOMMY: Don't go.

NEDDA: Hunh?

TOMMY: Stay.

NEDDA: I can't.

TOMMY: Okay.

NEDDA: And thanks for not turning me in.

TOMMY: It's not my store. I mean if this place were called Tommy Flowers then maybe I'd get a little uptight about people like you.

NEDDA: I told you! I never did anything like this in my life. I don't know what came over me today.

TOMMY: Yes, you do.

NEDDA: Yes, I do. Greed. Wish me luck.

TOMMY: Good luck.

(She still hesitates.)

TOMMY: You're scared?

NEDDA: Well aren't you when you…?

(Tommy is drawing on a joint.)

NEDDA: Is that what I think it is?

TOMMY: It ain't oregano. You want some?

NEDDA: You could get in a lot of trouble doing that.

TOMMY: No worse than we're both in now. You better take some. It's a cold and heartless city out there, full of store detectives and vicious little meter maids.

NEDDA: I hate this city. I hate it, I hate it!

TOMMY: What's the matter?

NEDDA: I don't know. Everything!

TOMMY: What's your big rush anyway?

NEDDA: I wish I knew.

TOMMY: You know something? You really are better off in here with me.

NEDDA: I know! *(She takes the joint.)* My father was right. Three months in New York City and I'm a fallen woman. *(She smokes.)*

TOMMY: Nice, hunh?

NEDDA: Wonderful! I'm ruining my entire life.

TOMMY: So what's your name, fallen woman?

NEDDA: *(Smoking in earnest.)* Nedda Lemon.

TOMMY: Any relation to Jack?

NEDDA: No.

TOMMY: I bet you're sick of people asking you that question?

NEDDA: Not particularly. May I ask you something? Are you trying to pick me up?

TOMMY: What do you think?

NEDDA: I just wanted to make sure.

TOMMY: So what do you do besides shoplift Bloomingdale's?

NEDDA: I told you I've never...!

TOMMY: I said what else.

NEDDA: *(Pointing to cello.)* This.

TOMMY: That?

NEDDA: I'm a cellist.

TOMMY: A real cellist?

NEDDA: A real cellist.

TOMMY: No shit?

NEDDA: No kidding.

TOMMY: A serious cellist?

NEDDA: Too serious.

TOMMY: I better watch my step then.

NEDDA: If you'd said you were Pablo Casals or Rostropovitch, I'd've done cart-wheels.

TOMMY: I'm Pablo Casals or Rostropovitch.

NEDDA: I can't do cartwheels.

TOMMY: Are you famous?

NEDDA: A real biggy.

TOMMY: I can do cartwheels.

NEDDA: With a lot of practice and a little luck, I may one day be asked to play the Lord's Prayer at somebody's bar mitzvah in Brooklyn.

TOMMY: That would be quite a stunt if you could pull it off.

NEDDA: I'm just a nobody.

TOMMY: Don't say that, man.

NEDDA: Living in this city I feel about this big most of the time.

TOMMY: How big is that?

NEDDA: Infinitesimal.

TOMMY: That's pretty small.

NEDDA: I know.

TOMMY: Well you're not. Not to me you're not. To me, you're one of the all-time super biggy cellists.

NEDDA: Thank you.

TOMMY: I guess you're bowlegged?

NEDDA: No!

TOMMY: Where do you live?

NEDDA: The Village, where else?

TOMMY: Alone?

NEDDA: You really are trying to pick me up.

TOMMY: But wait'll you tell your father you smoked with Pablo Casals or Rostropovitch in the ladies' room at Bloomingdale's.

(They are both pretty high and giggly by now.)

NEDDA: He'll never believe me.

TOMMY: I know.

NEDDA: I don't believe it either. My father wants me to go back home and marry this creep lawyer and be a creep music teacher until we start having creep babies and then I can become a creep housewife and maybe he's right, only I don't want to, and I just broke up with this creep oboist who all he did was suck on his reeds and now I'm a criminal and the only reason I'm telling you all this is I'm stoned and you're a stranger and no one ever tried to pick me up in the ladies room before and I guess I'm flattered but I'm too much of a creep to let you and it was very nice talking to you, Mr. Flowers. *(There is a pause.)*

TOMMY: I need a place to stay, Miss Lemon.

NEDDA: You do?

TOMMY: Me and Arnold.

NEDDA: Who's Arnold?

TOMMY: My dog. He's very nice. You'll like him. He's beautifully housebroken and he's very unusual in that he never gets that doggy odor which can be so offensive to some people or sheds any hair. Believe me, he won't be any trouble.

NEDDA: It's not Arnold I was worrying about.

TOMMY: You mean it's me?

NEDDA: Don't get me wrong. I think I like you and everything. Only, well, you know…

TOMMY: You're a virgin.

NEDDA: No, it's not that.

TOMMY: Yes or no?

NEDDA: No.

TOMMY: You got a social disease?

NEDDA: That's not very funny, Mr. Flowers.

TOMMY: Tommy, please, Miss Lemon, it's Tommy! I just thought I'd ask. There's practically an epidemic.

NEDDA: I like men, I like being with someone. I'm just not terribly promiscuous that way.

TOMMY: Okay, I'll tell you what: if you don't want to make love, we won't make love.

NEDDA: What about you?

TOMMY: I always want to make love.

NEDDA: You do?

TOMMY: It's my curse. I'll tell you what: we'll pick up Arnold and this friend of mine who's out having coffee...

NEDDA: There's someone else?

TOMMY: Ben Delight.

NEDDA: Ben Delight?

TOMMY: But that's just his stage name. He changed it from Jack Wonder.

NEDDA: Jack Wonder?

TOMMY: Don't worry, you'll like him. He knew Paul Muni.

NEDDA: Paul Muni?

TOMMY: Paul Muni! How old are you? Ten? And then we'll all head for your place and you can cook us a spaghetti dinner. I'm crazy for Italian food. So's Arnold.

NEDDA: I don't know what to say.

TOMMY: I do. I like your name, I like your style, I like the sound of your voice. I also like what I see, I like it a lot, and I'm really desperate for a pad tonight. So come on, Nedda Lemon, no-relation-to-Jack, what do you say?

POLICEMAN: *(Off.)* All right, buddy, come out with your hands up!

TOMMY: Kill the joint!

(Tommy hides in the booth, Nedda pops the joint in her mouth.)

POLICEMAN: *(Off.)* I know you're in there! Now are you coming out or am I coming in there after you? One, two, three. I'm coming in. *(Policeman enters with woman.)*

NEDDA: *(Indignant.)* I beg your pardon?

POLICEMAN: Step aside, miss, there's a man in there.

NEDDA: There's no one in here. You're the only man in here.

POLICEMAN: Now sshh!

NEDDA: This is the ladies' room!

POLICEMAN: And I'm going to keep it that way! All right, buddy, I know you're in there. Now come out of there. Come out I say. Now open up or I'll shoot. *(To woman.)* There better be a man in there.

NEDDA: If there is a man in there, I don't think you have to shoot him.

POLICEMAN: One.

NEDDA: You must be crazy.

POLICEMAN: Two.

NEDDA: He's got a gun!

POLICEMAN: Three!

NEDDA: No.

(The door swings open to reveal Tommy disguised in a nun's habit.)

TOMMY: Yes, officer?

POLICEMAN: I'm terribly sorry, sister. Some nut told me there was a man in here.

TOMMY: That's perfectly all right.

POLICEMAN: I don't know what to say, sister.

TOMMY: God bless you.

POLICEMAN: Thank you, sister.

TOMMY: *(Taking Nedda's arm.)* Excuse us. She's a nun and look at her. It's the third time this month she's tried to escape. Sister Rose, control yourself! You're not even supposed to be in Bloomingdale's.

(On their way out.)

TOMMY: You know something? I am going to want to make love to you.

NEDDA: You know something? Me, too, Sister Rose.

TOMMY: You're Rose; I'm Mary.

(They are gone.)

POLICEMAN: What's happening to holy mother church? I'm taking me kids out of parochial school so fast those nuns won't know what hit'em.

(He goes. Woman sighs, goes into a booth, closes the door and sits.)

STORE ANNOUNCER: Your attention, may I have your attention, please. For your shopping convenience, Bloomingdale's will be open until 9 P.M. this evening. I repeat, for your shopping convenience…what is this?

TOMMY'S VOICE: This is Tommy Flowers. For your shopping convenience Bloomingdale's is going to be bombed. Grab what you can before it's too late and split. You've got three minutes to split.

(The woman screams and comes charging out of her booth. Lights up on Tommy taking off his improvised nun's habit: he's used his white jockey shorts for the head-piece.)

TOMMY: I haven't really put a bomb in Bloomingdale's but don't think it hasn't crossed my mind. A lot of things have crossed my mind…but so far I'm still playing it nice. Well why not? Somebody might get hurt. Besides, so far nice is fun. Try it some time. Try the ladies' room, try the men's room. You might be pleasantly surprised. You've got fifteen minutes. That's a lot.

ENTR'ACTE

(Special spotlight on Conductor. He turns, bows to audience, accepts the rose that has been thrown to him, turns again and waits. The lights come up center stage on another gleaming stainless steel and glass phonograph. Again there is a shiny black record on the changer all ready to play. The Conductor raps for attention, then raises both arms ready to conduct.

The Black Stagehand shuffles out of the wings still playing his portable cassette, watches and waits. The record drops into the playing position and begins to spin. The tone arm hovers over the record a moment and then drops noiselessly into the spinning grooves. At once: Music! Loud! Stereophonic sound! What we hear is a luscious choral rendition of "America, The Beautiful" sung by an invisible chorus in the ripest Mormon Tabernacle Choir style. The Black Stagehand shrugs and shuffles off. What we see on the screens above the stage are images of America, The Beautiful in vibrant Kodachrome. Think of the large photographic murals in Grand Central Station. Pictures of her spacious skies, her amber waves of grain, her purple mountains majesty above her fruited plains from sea to shining sea.

After one full verse of "America, The Beautiful" there is a musical/visual transition. The lush stereophonic sound changes to the scratchy, tinnier tone of an old 78 r.p.m. record and we will hear a medley of old popular American songs. The Conductor will turn to face the audience and lead them in a sing-along. He's suddenly sprouted a goatee and looks remarkably like Mitch Miller now. What we will see on the screens is what has become of those spacious skies, amber waves of grain, fruited plains and shining seas of America, The Beautiful. The Showgirl will help out by holding up cue cards with the song lyrics. Some of the old popular American songs we hear are: "Moonlight Bay," "Harvest Moon," "In the Good Old Summertime," "April Showers," "June Is Busting Out All Over," "This Was a Real Nice Clambake," "White Christmas," "Blue Skies," "By the Beautiful Sea," and so forth. Some of the images of America we see are: factories belching smoke, over-crowded beaches, littered campsites, trash-strewn streets, clogged sewers, billboard-gutted highways, the astronauts' litter on the moon, traffic jams, polluted rivers, oil slicks, mutant sea life, crops being spray-dusted, and so on.

During this sing-along of an old popular American music medley, the Black Stagehand appears and dances a very elegant soft-shoe routine. He moves with an indefinable grace. He is elegant the way Mozart is elegant. His slow, easy, fluid dance movements evoke nostalgia for an America that was. It is almost an elegy, in fact. After his soft-shoe ends, the Black Stagehand glides off into the wings, the Conductor turns his back To audience and again begins to conduct his invisible forces and the beautiful stereo returns with a reprise of "America, The Beautiful."

On the screens we now see pictures of the Stock Exchange, the Statue of Liberty, and Rockefeller Center. The music fills the theatre. The Kodachrome pictures are gorgeous.

"America, The Beautiful" hits its final chord. Then again. Then again. Then again. Clearly the record is stuck. With each repeat of the final chord, there is the sound of an explosion and one of the pictures is extinguished only to be replaced by another. Some of the places and landmarks exterminated in this fashion are: Con Edison, The Induction Center, Chase Manhattan Bank, Columbia University, Grant's Tomb, The George Washington Bridge, The Metropolitan Museum of Art, The Empire State Building, Madison Square Garden, Howard Johnson's, and so on. The Conductor is powerless to do anything. Instead, he can only conduct the final chord over and over again.

The Black Stagehand comes shuffling out of the wings, taking all the time in the world, a big "I told you so" grin on his face and clearly enjoying the sound and *sight of all this carnage. He stands by the phonograph, recognizing his power to stop the bombings and taking his own sweet time to do so. Several times he is about to reach down to "unstick" the record, only to stop at the last moment and let the building in question explode. Clearly, he's playing a game of Cat and Mouse and having a good time at it, too. It is only when a picture of this theatre itself, the one we are all in now, appears that he moves quickly to avert another disaster. He hits the phonograph hard and the final chord is played and this time stays played. The Black Stagehand grins triumphantly.)*

BLACK STAGEHAND: Where Has Tommy Flowers Gone? Side two. Shee-it! *(He is still grinning and gloating when the phonograph explodes.)*

ACT TWO

COMRADE MARILYN

(The Twentieth Century Fox fanfare. The blonde hair and pretty face of Marilyn appear in a special light. That is all we see of her. Tommy Flowers is Marilyn.)

MARILYN: *(Fielding questions like an old pro.)*…which will lead to the violent over-throw of the corrupt and decadent institutions that control our capitalistic, materialistic, racist society. That's what I think, comrade.

VOICE: That doesn't sound like you.

MARILYN: It wasn't. *(Piano introduction.)* Mr. President. Ladies and gentlemen. Lennie. *(She sings.)*
Happy birthday to you.
Happy birthday to you.
Happy birthday, dear America.
Happy…*(She does some quick adding.)*
195th birthday to you!
(The song ends, taped applause.)

VOICE: Hold it, Marilyn! Atta girl! *(Flashbulbs pop. Marilyn poses.)*

MARILYN: Thanks, honey.

VOICE: How is it up there, Marilyn?

MARILYN: Oh it's just peachy! How is it down there?

VOICE: Do you have a new love interest?

MARILYN: I always have a love interest, honey.

VOICE: Who's the lucky man?

MARILYN: I think all men are lucky.

VOICE: Come on, what's his name?

MARILYN: Kay. Isn't that too much?

VOICE: Kay? His name is Kay?

MARILYN: That's what I told him. Kay Guevara. What kind of a name for a man is that?

VOICE: You mean Che Guevara? That Che?

MARILYN: That's what I said. Shay.

VOICE: The Cuban revolutionary?

MARILYN: Cuban? He told me he was from Havana.

VOICE: Tell us, does Señor Guevara think the CIA plotted his murder?

MARILYN: Whose murder, honey?

VOICE: His. In Bolivia.

MARILYN: Oh, no, sweetie, then it's not the same Kay Guevara. This one's not dead. We're having what the French call an *affaire du coeur*. You know what I call it, honey? That Old Black Magic! Is that okay to say anymore? Everybody's so touchy these days! Can I do my number now?

VOICE: Of all the men in the world, why him?

MARILYN: That's easy. He's very nice and extremely well read and he's told me all sorts of things I didn't know before.

VOICE: Like what?

MARILYN: Also, he's kind of cute with that little beard and beret! *(More flashbulbs. Marilyn is happily posing for them.)* Oooooooo!

VOICE: Like what?

MARILYN: Aaaaaaaaa!

VOICE: Marilyn, like what?

MARILYN: Hunh?

VOICE: Skip it.

MARILYN: All these questions. All I want to do is sing, honey.

VOICE: Just one more question. If you had it all to do all over again, would you do it any differently?

MARILYN: Had what, honey?

VOICE: Life.

MARILYN: What life, sweetie?

VOICE: Yours.

MARILYN: You mean I'm not alive?

VOICE: You didn't know?

MARILYN: I told you: nobody ever tells me anything.

VOICE: I just assumed.

MARILYN: But I'll tell you something! You're morbid, mister. You think everyone's dead. And I'll tell you something else! I'm not the one who's dead. You are. I'm glad I didn't do my number for you. Why don't you try fucking yourself!

VOICE: We're sorry.

MARILYN: Sure you are.

VOICE: We all remember you.

MARILYN: I remember you, too.

VOICE: We all love you.

MARILYN: I know.

VOICE: We all need you.

MARILYN: Don't, honey, you'll make me cry.

VOICE: We all miss you.

MARILYN: I miss you, too.

VOICE: And you're still very much alive.

MARILYN: I am?

CUBAN ACCENT: *(Off.)* Marileen, *vamonos, muchacha!*

MARILYN: I've got to split, honey. He hits me when I'm late.

VOICE: Just tell us what you think of what's going on down here?

MARILYN: You mean all the bombs?

VOICE: Right.

MARILYN: From where I am they look very pretty. And that Tommy Flowers is kind of cute, *n'est-ce pas?* if you know what I mean. I'm no politician. I just think people should be nicer to one another.

CUBAN ACCENT: Marileen!

MARILYN: That's what he says, too, only it takes longer and it's more complicated.

CUBAN ACCENT: *Ay, muchacha, vamonos!*

MARILYN: Next time I'll do "Running Wild" from *Some Like It Hot* in which I had first star billing over Jack Lemmon and Tony Curtis, only it was for United Artists. Even Kay likes that one. Bye, honey! *(She starts to wiggle off, then turns and speaks over her shoulder.)* You know something? I knew I wasn't dead! *(And with a shimmy and a wiggle and a squeal, Marilyn is gone.)*

ANNOUNCER'S VOICE: This just came in. A man who the police say blamed Eastern Airlines for the death of his champion Irish wolfhound walked up to an Eastern jet today and chopped eighteen holes in its underbelly with an ax, airport officers said. Thank you.

(The Showgirl appears.)

SHOWGIRL: Revolution is the only thing, the only power that ever worked out freedom for any people. The powers that have ruled long, and learned to love ruling, will never give up that prerogative till they find they must, till they see the certainty of overthrow and destruction if they do not! To plant—to revolutionize—those are the twin stars that have ruled our pathway. What have we then to dread in the word *revolution?* We, the children of rebels! We were born to be rebels—it runs in our blood! Wendell Phillips, 1848. Thank you. *(She goes.)*

THE GREAT ATLANTIC & PACIFIC TEA PARTY

(The lights come up on Tommy with a shopping cart. He is eating yogurt.)

TOMMY: I can't help smiling. Life is just too much fun lately. I've got a fairly permanent roof over my head, Bach's Sonatas for Unaccompanied Cello running out of both ears and two wonderful friends. Three, if you include Arnold. The health department has a thing about dogs in supermarkets. Afraid they'll crap in the aisles or something. I suppose they have a point.

(Nedda enters with a shopping cart. She looks very pregnant.)

TOMMY: It's not what you're thinking. Good God, no. We're doing our shopping.

NEDDA: *(Through clenched teeth.)* As soon as we get out of here, *you* take the turkey. It's leaking. Now what do I do with these?

TOMMY: Find some 39¢ tops to fit the 96¢ jars and play it cool at the checkout. *(Wrinkling his nose at what he sees.)* Mama Lucia's Frozen Pizza?

NEDDA: Beethoven's Six Symphonies. The last three didn't fit. Anything else, maestro?

TOMMY: How are we fixed for fruit?

NEDDA: *(Nodding to her bosom.)* Apples, oranges…take your pick.

TOMMY: You're catching on.

NEDDA: I've got a good teacher.

(She goes. Ben enters walking rather stiffly.)

BEN: I've got six eggs in my drawers.

TOMMY: I think maybe five now.

BEN: I was afraid I felt something.

TOMMY: Put the lamb chops *under* the potatoes, not on top. They'll overcharge us. You're a novice in crime, Ben.

BEN: I can't seem to get the swing of it, Tom.

TOMMY: Hang in there, you will. And walk tall!

(An egg rolls out of Ben's pants as he walks off. Tommy takes out a can opener and helps himself to some food. Also a straw for a twist-open pop bottle.)

TOMMY: *Bourgeois, vous n'avez rien compris.* Bourgeoisie, you have understood nothing. French rebellion poster. But I look at it this way: America's a rich country. It can afford me. Of course if I really had balls I'd light a can of Sterno and rustle me up a Spanish Omelet right here in Aisle D. This is delicious!

ANNOUNCER'S VOICE: Is there a doctor in the house? We need you, man, we really need you. There's a young chick in the manager's office who's really freaked out on some bad acid. She's having a really bad trip. So help her out, hunh, man? Peace.

(The Showgirl appears. She is half out of her last costume and half into her new one.)

SHOWGIRL: Who do they think I am with these quick changes? Plastic Woman?

(Composing herself, but still surly.) We can't have education without revolution. We have tried peace education for nineteen hundred years and it has failed. Let us try revolution and see what it will do now. Helen Keller, 1916. *(Showgirl exits.)*

TOMMY'S OLD FLAME

TOMMY'S OLD GIRLFRIEND: Hi, Tommy. Remember me? If you said you didn't, I'd come up there and scratch whoever-she-is' eyes out for her! It's me, all right. Only it's Beverly Swantner now. You remember Norman. Just listen to him. *(We hear snoring.)*

You know what I've been thinking about tonight? A pink and white Ford Fairlane with a chrome dip in the door. The back seat in particular. Sound familiar? We were just terrible together, Tommy! I bet everyone at Paine High School knew about us. You probably told them. Well don't look at me. Shelly Pape is the only girl I ever told and *she* was hardly in any position to talk.

Do you ever think about what it might've been like if we'd gotten married? I'm serious. I could've gotten you to, you know. I didn't have to make you use those things. And don't think I didn't think about it. Right at the end I practically made a scene about them. Remember? It wasn't anybody's fault. You wanted something else. I ended up wanting this. I've got it. What about you? Only, well, it was different with you. Happier, better, more different I guess. Listen to me! We were just so young then, that's all. We thought we were very, very old but all we really were was young. If you're ever back in St. Petersburg, and I wouldn't wish that on my worst enemy, please look us up. Norman would get a kick out of seeing you again, too. Oh, Tommy!

A QUIET EVENING AT HOME

(Lights up on Nedda playing her cello. Ben is reading Variety. *Arnold is at his side. Tommy is lying on the floor.)*

TOMMY: *(Regarding Nedda fondly.)* Hey!

(Nedda shakes her head, too busy concentrating on the music to look up even.)

TOMMY: You're biting your tongue again.

NEDDA: I am not! *(A moment later and she is doing it again.)*

TOMMY: That's nice.

NEDDA: It's hard.

TOMMY: Just keep your tongue in.

NEDDA: Sshh!

BEN: It says here there's twin strippers in Tulsa with identical forty-nine-inch busts. They call themselves Stress N' Strain. I played Tulsa. *Shanghai Gesture.*

TOMMY: Must have been a lot of feathers in that one, too.

BEN: No feathers but a hell of a lot of fans.

(*Tommy has settled back to smoke.*)

TOMMY: I like this. I like this whole evening. I even liked your lasagna tonight.

NEDDA: It was ravioli.

TOMMY: It was so good it tasted like lasagna. What do I know? Now shut up and fiddle.

(*Pause. Only the cello music.*)

BEN: I like the kid. He's been good to me. I sleep over there. It's a little lumpy but I've done worse. What I can't always figure is why the kid likes *me*. I knew Eugene O'Neill. Tommy can't get over it. Hell, I toured the *Count of Monte Cristo* five straight seasons with his father! Hick towns then like Waco, Texas, or Topeka, Kansas, real flea bags, and he's impressed. I've been everywhere and seen everything and there's nothing new under the sun. But try telling Tommy that. I checked up on that Mr. James Dean of his. Seems he was pretty good. But as Tommy says, he died young. Poor sonofabitch. Me, I want to live forever and I nearly have. You can add ten years to what you're thinking and you'll still be off by twenty. I like the girl, too. She's a lady. Not too many of them around anymore either, let me tell you. 'Course I can't stand all that damn fiddling but it's nice here with them. While it lasts. I'm even kind of fond of Arnold tonight. Not crazy about him, mind you, just fond. I'm getting mellow. I've got to watch that. That damn spaghetti of hers is coming up on me!

(*Nedda stops playing.*)

NEDDA: Tommy?

TOMMY: I'm, right here, Nedda. I'm so right here I can't believe it.

NEDDA: Me, too. Good, I'm glad.

BEN: They're making another musical out of *Peter Pan.* They're auditioning fairies.

(*Nedda resumes playing. Pause. Only the cello music.*)

NEDDA: I'd like to ask Tommy if he loves me. I wonder what he'd say. I'm sorry, but I'm a very conventional budding girl cellist from Tampa, Florida, that way. Tommy's from St. Petersburg. Small world, isn't it? I grew up thinking life could be very nice if you just let it. I still do. It's certainly full of surprises and most of them are good. Like my music. That happened when I was ten years old and went to my first concert. ·I came home in a dream. Or like Tommy Flowers! That happened...well, you *saw* where that happened and we came home in a cab Tommy didn't pay for. I love my music. Whenever I get the teeniest bit depressed I think about it and I'm all right again. The notes are hard for me, I can't always play them at first, but if practice makes perfect then I'm going to be a very good cellist one day. That's what I want. And now there's Tommy. Someone I hadn't counted on at all. A small world but so many different people in it! I don't know what Tommy wants, so I have to play it by ear with him. That's hard for me and I'm pretty smart about men. It's not like practicing my music; Tommy has to help, too. And which is real or which is realer? All these little, wonderful, difficult notes some man wrote once upon a time somewhere or me, right now, in a whole other place, trying to play them and wanting to ask Tommy Flowers if he loves me and wanting him to answer, "I love you, Nedda Lemon"? They're both real. I don't want to change the world. I just want to be in it with someone. For someone with such a sour name, I could be a very happy person. *(Nedda stops playing.)* Tommy?

TOMMY: You stopped.

NEDDA: Do you love me?

TOMMY: I love you, Nedda Lemon. I'm here. You're there. We're together and it's nice.

NEDDA: I know. How about another cup of coffee?

TOMMY: Only no Pream in it this time, hunh? It has cyclamates or something. *(Nedda has gone by now.)*
Somebody ought to blow that place up. Maybe I will. *(The phone rings. Tommy answers it in an exaggerated Southern black accent.)* Nedda's place. Rosco speaking. I work at the Mobil station on the corner. Miss Nedda said I might come over here to use her shower when I wanted to…well, suh, who is *this?*…Oh.
(Nedda has returned.)

NEDDA: Pream was all we had. You'll have to drink it black. Who is it?

TOMMY: It's for you.

NEDDA: Who is it?

TOMMY: It's your father.

NEDDA: *(She takes the phone from Tommy.)* Hi, daddy, how are you?…Hunh?

TOMMY: I should've guessed it might be him.

NEDDA: Just a friend…no, of course not!…what do you mean?

TOMMY: Nedda hasn't called home to ask for money in weeks. I'm trying to get her to be more independent.

NEDDA: *(Looking at Tommy now.)* It was just a joke, daddy.

TOMMY: You said he was a big liberal.

NEDDA: Of course I don't…Well what if I did? *(Still talking she takes the phone into the other room.)*

TOMMY: Bet you can't count to ten without smiling!
(Ben is standing up.)

TOMMY: So what's up, Ben?

BEN: I'm going to bed. Come on, Arnold. And no snoring this time.

TOMMY: Good night, Ben.

BEN: Good night, Tommy.

(Ben and Arnold go. Tommy waits until the coast is clear.)

TOMMY: I've been doing some interesting reading lately. I've got something I want to show you. *(He brings the makings of a homemade bomb and an instruction manual from out of a hiding place.)* A cigar box. A dry cell battery. Some wire. An alarm clock. And dynamite. I know it doesn't look like much but according to this pamphlet it packs some little wallop. *The Civilian Guide to Explosives.* It's free from the United States Army Corps of Engineers. All this talk about bombs…even the government wants to get in on the act. I'm up to lesson four. *(He turns on the television and settles back to work.)* Maybe there's a good revolution on.

ANNOUNCER'S VOICE: …told reporters today that there was no "real danger" of a black or Puerto Rican shooting the President because "they can't shoot very straight."

TOMMY: You want to bet?

ANNOUNCER'S VOICE: Mr. Hoover, who is 74, went on to deny rumors that he intends to retire this year.

TOMMY: Hang in there, you old fairy!

ANNOUNCER'S VOICE: The First Lady was in town today to officially open the Carmen Hernandez Center for Blind Child Study. The multi-million dollar center is named for the nine-year-old girl who got her wish to meet the President a few short weeks before she succumbed to leukemia. Blind at birth, Carmen was also mentally retarded. "She was the bravest little girl who ever lived," said her father, Hector Hernandez. Carmen had her big day in Washington and now there's a center named for her but her parents are still on relief. I'll be right back with Frank Cross and the weather.

INSTANT REPLAY

(The First Lady and the interviewer have appeared.)

FIRST LADY: I declare this center open. *(She snips the ribbon. Applause.)* Thank you.

INTERVIEWER: It's a wonderful facility, isn't it?

FIRST LADY: My, my, my, my, my!

INTERVIEWER: And you'll notice that even the water fountains are so designed that the children confined to wheelchairs can reach them without assistance.

FIRST LADY: My, my, my, my, my!

INTERVIEWER: Perhaps you'd care to comment?

FIRST LADY: It's a wonderful facility, Bob. I'm speechless. My, my, my, my, my!

INTERVIEWER: The children here at Carmen Hernandez have asked me to give you this small token of their affection that was made for you in their new crafts center with their very own little hands.

FIRST LADY: You know, Gene, it's touching when this sort of thing happens. No matter how many times it happens, I'm just completely touched. What is it?

INTERVIEWER: I believe it's a pot holder.

FIRST LADY: A pot holder, Frank! My, my, my, my, my!

INTERVIEWER: Unh, it's Flo, Ma'am. The name is Flo.

FIRST LADY: Flo! Of course it's Flo! I know it's Flo! Why do I keep calling you Ted? But you see, Flo, I genuinely like poor people and minority groups and the physically handicapped. Yes, I do. I've been lucky enough to be able to sit down and have a real heart-to-heart with people less fortunate than myself. I'm convinced we all should. I'm sorry more people haven't. It's such an en-riching experience, Gabe, let me tell you. It's because of something like this little...*potholder*...I can say this to you today, Chet: there are no poor peo-ple...no, not really!...only poor hearts. *(Ovation.)* May I say something? Young people. That's right. You heard me. It's you young people, that's who. You kids. I think you young people in this country are pretty darn wonder-ful. W-o-n-d-e-r-f-u-l. I know that's a pretty unfashionable statement to make these days, Hugh, but the youth of America are number one in my book. I'm sorry, Dan, but I say exactly what's on my mind.

INTERVIEWER: It's Flo, ma'am, it's Flo.

FIRST LADY: No, I'm sorry, Flo. But I'm just crazy about today's kids. My recent tour of North Dakota college campus really rammed that point home to me in no uncertain terms, Gabe, let me tell you!

INTERVIEWER: Perhaps you'd care to tell us about it?

FIRST LADY: I just did.

(There is an awkward moment happily broken by the appearance of Rachel Gonzalez who gropes her way uncertainly onto the stage and stands now with her back to the audience. Rachel Gonzalez is a very tall Puerto Rican girl, ten years old, dressed in a pink satin party dress, gold cross around her neck and a religious medallion pinned to her dress, high socks and black patent leather slippers with taps. There is a big rose in her hair, too. Rachel Gonzalez is Tommy Flowers.)

MODERATOR: Thank you. And now we'd like you to meet Rachel Gonzalez, our own little mentally retarded, leukemia-stricken, Fight For Sight poster girl of the year. Let's hear it for Rachel!

(Applause on tape.)

RACHEL: *(Blowing kisses, her back to the audience.)* Hello. Hello, everybody. I wish I could see you, the way you can see me. Hello. Hello, everybody.

MODERATOR: We're over here, Rachel, that's the girl!

RACHEL: *(Facing front now, blowing more kisses.)* Hello. Hello, everybody. You gonna donate? You better donate!

MODERATOR: Rachel's a Puerto Rican, aren't we, sweetheart?

RACHEL: *Si.*

MODERATOR: My, but aren't we big for our age!

RACHEL: *Si.*

MODERATOR: *Muy, muy grande.*

RACHEL: *Si. (Rachel is touching the First Lady's face.)*

MODERATOR: Unh, Rachel…!

FIRST LADY: It's all right, Walter. It's just her way of seeing me.

RACHEL: You smell funny.

FIRST LADY: That's my perfume.

RACHEL: It smells like my neighborhood.

MODERATOR: Unh, how old are we, Rachel?

RACHEL: *Si.*

MODERATOR: We're nine years old going on ten, aren't we, sweetheart?

RACHEL: No.

MODERATOR: What are those you're carrying, Rachel?

RACHEL: Flowers.

MODERATOR: And who are those flowers for?

RACHEL: Her.

FIRST LADY: More flowers! My! What's my name, Rachel?

RACHEL: *Si.*

FIRST LADY: What is my name?

RACHEL: No.

MODERATOR: Why that's the…

FIRST LADY: Wait, Walter, let me do it. Rachel?

RACHEL: Don't hit me, mister, don't hit me, don't hit me!

FIRST LADY: No one's going to hurt you, Rachel. Now: *como*…unh, *como,* it's coming back!…*como, como, como…Como me!…Como me llamo?*

MODERATOR: *Muy bien,* yourself.

FIRST LADY: It's very simple. We honeymooned in San Juan and I've always had this knack for picking up foreign languages. You see, Dell, my feeling is that—

RACHEL: *(Yanking at First Lady's skirt.)* Hey! What about me?

FIRST LADY: I'm sorry, darling! Hmmm? *Como mi llamo?* (The poor thing!) *Como mi llamo?*

RACHEL: What's my name?

FIRST LADY: You understood! She understood! *(First Lady clutches Rachel to her. Studio audience applauds.)*

MODERATOR: *(Stage whisper.)* What Rachel doesn't know is that she has only six weeks to live.

(The First Lady is being pawed all over.)

MODERATOR: Unh, Rachel!

FIRST LADY: I don't mind, David, really I don't.

RACHEL: You have big *carrangas.* This man in our slum tenement try to play with my little *carrangas* all the time and make *puñetas* with me but I stab him in the eye with an ice pick, like that! and he go to Bellevue and maybe he never get out or else he have to get a dog and sell pencils. I don't care. I been to Bellevue too. It's a big dirty place. I been there after the *raton* bit me. The *raton* was that big. It bit my *clamato*. I cried like a little devil. I cried so much my big sister the *puta* tied me to the bed and stuffed rags down my throat for five days until my father got back from San Juan and he beat the shit out of her and then he took us *both* to the hospital. I'm hungry. I want a cheeseburger and a chocolate malt and french fries and a piece of apple pie à la mode. Can I have those things, First Lady? Oh please, oh please, oh please!

FIRST LADY: Of course you can, Rachel. You can have anything you want. Just as soon as we're off the air I'm going to buy you the biggest hamburger you ever saw.

RACHEL: I can't see! And I said a cheeseburger!

FIRST LADY: Of course, Rachel, of course! How I love that fiery Latin temperament, Ray.

RACHEL: You better believe it. I have gypsy blood in my veins. I was born with castanets in my fingers and a rose in my teeth. I will now sing and dance *Clavelitos*.

FIRST LADY: One of my favorites!

RACHEL: No shit.

FIRST LADY: Absolutely!

RACHEL: You're a nice lady. That's too bad. *(She comes downstage.)* Hit it, chicos! *(Rachel goes into her number like a hard-driving little professional. All traces of the shy little girl vanish when she entertains. The full stage lights come up fast, as Rachel socks into her grand finale. Ovation.)* Good-bye, good-bye, everyone! I love you! *(Blowing kisses, she is on her way out, stumbling, tripping, groping, when she suddenly whirls around to face us and makes the clenched fist salute.)* Venceremos! *(And Rachel/Tommy is gone.)*

FIRST LADY: *(Smiles, sighs.)* So afflicted and yet so full of life!

MODERATOR: If that isn't the cutest little Puerto Rican child I've ever seen I'll eat my hat.

FIRST LADY: She forgot all about her cheeseburger! No, a sight like Rachel Gonzalez really tears the heart out of you. If only she were more retarded, then maybe it wouldn't occur to her that she was blind. As our President is so fond of saying, "What they don't know, won't hurt them."

MODERATOR: This is in reference to Rachel?

FIRST LADY: No. I think it's in reference to just about everyone.

(Explosion. The bouquet of flowers Rachel has given her blows up in her face. The First Lady and the Moderator are gone.)

THE LAST OF THE BIG SPENDERS

(Howard Johnson's. Nedda and Tommy are finishing dinner.)

TOMMY: No, I think my prepubescent fascination with Wonder Woman influenced my entire attitude toward women. In fact, I know it has. I probably would have grown up a raging lesbian if I'd been born a girl because of her. I didn't just read Wonder Woman comic books like some of the other kids (she was never very popular; not like Superman or Captain Marvel anyway); I was obsessed with them. I even considered asking my mother to run up a copy of that red, white and blue, stars and stripes, halter and panties outfit she ran around in (Wonder Woman, wise guy, not my mother) on the old family Singer— *(Points to Nedda's plate.)* Aren't you going to finish those? *(Nedda shakes her head.)*

TOMMY: Waitress! *(Resuming at once.)* —but I knew my father would kick *both* our asses around the block if he ever came home and caught me in that getup. Don't laugh. At least I turned out straight. All my friends who read Batman ended up queer.

(Waitress has appeared.)

WAITRESS: Not more clams?

TOMMY: We can't finish these. Would you put them in a guppy bag?

WAITRESS: A what?

TOMMY: Guppy bag. For our fish.

WAITRESS: We only got doggy bags.

TOMMY: I don't think they'll notice. They're piranhas. Now hop to it.

(Waitress regards him warily, quickly clears the table.)

TOMMY: God, she was a tough cooz, old Wonder Woman was! Remember her invisible airplane?

NEDDA: Tommy!

TOMMY: All the other characters kept talking about how invisible it was. To them it looked like she was sitting on air. But *I* could see it. To me it just looked like she was sitting in a plastic airplane. Whoever drew that comic really botched that one up. Relax will you?

NEDDA: This is all I have!

(She has a bill. Tommy takes it from her.)

TOMMY: Remember her truth lasso? Her magic bracelets?

NEDDA: What are we going to do?

TOMMY: Jesus Christ, you don't remember anything about Wonder Woman! Didn't you read? You really are ten!

NEDDA: What are you doing?!

(Tommy has set fire to the bill with a match. Next he will light another cigarette with it.)

TOMMY: If she got you in her truth lasso you'd confess to anything. I love you, I hate you, you've got bad breath—that sort of thing. The magic bracelets were for warding off bullets. She could move them so fast the bullets were deflected right off them. Now the same artist did a terrific job there. All these squiggly lines around her wrists to indicate how fast she was moving them. *(He demonstrates.)* You know?

NEDDA: People are looking!

TOMMY: *(Waving, the flaming bill in one hand.)* Hi! Hello there! Enjoying your meal?

NEDDA: Tommy!

TOMMY: And she had this fantastic headband she could plug into this sort of television receiver kind of thing to talk to her mother and the other chicks back home on the isle of Lesbos. They were always practicing archery or doing gymnastics or something when she'd ring up. Very dykey, the whole setup. Hey, calm down, it's just money.

NEDDA: I know!

TOMMY: Get hung up on that stuff and you're right back in the system right up to here.

NEDDA: That was all I had. There's no more.

TOMMY: Good!

NEDDA: You may like to wash dishes, I don't

TOMMY: Nobody likes to wash dishes. How are we doing on silverware?

NEDDA: We've got a service for eight.

TOMMY: *(Gathering more.)* There's never enough.
   (Waitress has appeared.)

TOMMY: That's just what I was telling the little lady here. What month were you born, honey?

WAITRESS: November, why?

TOMMY: A Scorpio, I knew it. I can always tell. Very passionate women, those Scorpios.

WAITRESS: November 29th. I'm a Sagittarius and I'm about as passionate as that plate. Is that it? *(She starts to total the check.)*

TOMMY: May I ask you another personal question, Jeanette?

WAITRESS: Who Jeanette? What Jeanette?

TOMMY: Your badge says Jeanette.

WAITRESS: It came with the uniform. I'm Dolores.

TOMMY: For Dolores Del Rio! What did I tell you, Nedda?

WAITRESS: For Dolores Del Flushing.

TOMMY: Just between you and me, Dolores, and this won't get any further: are you getting much around here?

WAITRESS: What does it look like?

TOMMY: I meant salary.

WAITRESS: So did I. $1.30 an hour plus tips. Why?

TOMMY: That's bad, man, that's really bad.

WAITRESS: You want to make a better offer?

TOMMY: Howard Johnson should be ashamed of himself.

WAITRESS: I'll tell him you said so.

TOMMY: $1.30 an hour plus tips! Did you hear that, Nedda? If I were you, Dolores, I'd take off my apron, rip up that check and go on strike.

WAITRESS: They *are* on strike. That's why they hired me. What are you, a Communist? Pay up front. *(She leaves Tommy with the check and goes.)*

TOMMY: Fucking scab.

NEDDA: Tommy!

TOMMY: $8.68.

NEDDA: Look at me.

TOMMY: Fucking tax.

NEDDA: You said you were taking me to dinner.

TOMMY: I'm trying to.

NEDDA: By beating the check?

TOMMY: Hey, calm down, it's just Howard Johnson's. The clams weren't that good.

NEDDA: If we were married, we'd be divorced, you know that, don't you?

TOMMY: Two minutes ago you loved me.

NEDDA: Two minutes ago I thought this was going to be a nice evening.

TOMMY: It still is. Happy birthday, Nedda.

NEDDA: It's not my birthday.

TOMMY: It is now!

(Restaurant lights dim fast as manager appears with a cupcake and a candle.)

MANAGER: *(Greek accent.)*

Happy birthday to you.

Happy birthday to you.

Happy birthday...

(Tommy joins in.)

...Nedda Lemon

Happy birthday to you.

TOGETHER: Speech! Speech! Speech!

NEDDA: *(Standing.)* I want everyone in this restaurant to know I've never been un- happier in my life! *(She can't continue. She sits down.)*

MANAGER: *(Clapping happily.)* Ella! Ella!

TOMMY: Thank you. Thank you. Wasn't that nice of him, Nedda? She's 47 years old, would you believe it? We're expecting our first child. That was very kind of you...

(Manager is adding price of cupcake to bill.)

MANAGER: Cupcake.

TOMMY: It's not on the house?

MANAGER: In Howard Johnson's nothing is on the house.

TOMMY: What happened to Greek hospitality?

MANAGER: Gone with the junta. Kaput! *(He laughs at his own joke.)*

TOMMY: I didn't want to mention this, but what about this *roach* I found in my food? Think quick, Tino, people are watching.

(Manager takes the roach from Tommy's plate, looks at it.)

MANAGER: Tony's Novelty Shop, 46th and 8th, three for a dollar, right?

TOMMY: Two for a dollar. You handled yourself magnificently. You see, Miss Lemon here is the restaurant and food editor for an exciting new gourmet magazine, it's all very hush-hush and I shouldn't be revealing her identity but you're a nice guy and I thought I'd give you a break. How many stars did you say you were giving this place, darling? Four? Four stars! *(Handing the check to the manager.)* Take care of this, will you? Thanks, Tino.

MANAGER: What's the name of this magazine?

TOMMY: *Free Eats.*

MANAGER: They were already in here.

TOMMY: No kidding?

MANAGER: About five times so far today.

TOMMY: It's got a big circulation.

MANAGER: Too big. *(Handing the check to Nedda.)* Happy birthday, lady.

TOMMY: Could I have my cockroach back?

MANAGER: I'm keeping it hostage up at the register. *(He goes.)*

TOMMY: You're not Greek! You're some kind of Turk! $8.98! Thirty cents for this shit! Fucking inflation. You want some? You hate me.

NEDDA: I guess I'm in love with you in theory because in reality you give me the hives.

TOMMY: 1, 2, 3, 4…

NEDDA: 5, 6, 7, 8, 9, 10.

TOMMY: You're not laughing.

NEDDA: Just once I wanted to enjoy my meal, pay the check and walk out like a normal person.

TOMMY: Go ahead, I'll wait for you. Come back tomorrow with the bread and bail me out.

NEDDA: I'm thinking of it.

TOMMY: You want to call your father?

NEDDA: I'm thinking of that, too. I'm tired, Tommy. People can't live like this.

TOMMY: Like what?

NEDDA: Like we are!

TOMMY: We could always blow this place up.

NEDDA: I'm being serious!

TOMMY: So am I. Now hang on. *(He suddenly stands up and begins shouting.)* I've had it with you, Fred! I'm fed up to here with you!

NEDDA: People are looking!

TOMMY: Of course people are looking, Fred! I don't blame them, Fred! They can look all they want! The analyst told us he was over all this. Maybe you can fool these people, Fred, but you can't fool me. I wanted to be proud of you, Fred, but you're a disgrace. Pay for your own dinner. I don't take that shit from any man. Hell, you can earn it right here. *(He violently overturns the table.)* Do a little floor show for them, you…tatty transvestite! Out of my way, please, out of my way. I can't bear it.

(He storms out, leaving Nedda, overwhelmed to say the least, sitting alone at the table.)

TOMMY: The ability to improvise in my line of work can't be overemphasized. That's called the Tommy Flowers Foolproof Free Eats Plan, emergency phase three. I just thought of it. You loved that one, right, Grandpa? Let's see if Nedda did.

(The manager has escorted Nedda out of the restaurant and onto the street. Tommy watches her standing there, so thoroughly and totally wretched, and then to audience.)

TOMMY: I didn't want this. Honest. *(Calling for her.)* Psst!

NEDDA: What?

TOMMY: Get over here.

NEDDA: I don't ever want to see you again.

TOMMY: You can take that wig off now, Fred. I beat the check, didn't I?

NEDDA: I don't care.

TOMMY: Hey, look at me.

NEDDA: No.

TOMMY: A little smile already, Fred.

NEDDA: That's what you think!

TOMMY: It's getting bigger.

NEDDA: Smiles aren't enough, Tommy. Just because you make someone happy…

TOMMY: I make you happy, Fred?

NEDDA: I mean smile. Just because you make someone smile doesn't mean you're making them happy. So leave me alone. Please, just go away. If you knew how unhappy I was, you wouldn't stand there trying to make me laugh. I can't stand being happy with you, it's making me miserable. I just want to be unhappy all by myself. *(This is too much, even for her.)*

TOMMY: I'm sorry I make you so happy, Fred.

NEDDA: My name's not Fred. It's Nedda Lemon and I hate you!

(She's in his arms by now.)

TOMMY: I know.

NEDDA: I loathe you.

TOMMY: Don't stop.

NEDDA: I can't stand you.

TOMMY: Of course you can't.

NEDDA: You're not even that good in bed.

TOMMY: You go too far, Miss Lemon.

NEDDA: What am I doing with you?

TOMMY: That's the breaks.

NEDDA: I want a nice doctor with a good practice who smokes a pipe.

TOMMY: So do I.

NEDDA: I want to live in the suburbs and drive a station wagon.

TOMMY: So did Eva Braun.

NEDDA: I want a big family.

TOMMY: So lay off the pills.

NEDDA: What if I did?

TOMMY: Look, I'm not a doctor and I hate pipes. I like who I am and where I am. I like you.

NEDDA: Why does everything have to be guerrilla warfare with you?

TOMMY: You're not the enemy.

NEDDA: I don't see the point.

TOMMY: The point is, get it while you can.

NEDDA: I don't see any future in it.

TOMMY: Future? The whole thing's gonna collapse.

NEDDA: What do you want?

TOMMY: I don't know.

NEDDA: That's childish.

TOMMY: It's honest.

NEDDA: What do you want from me?

TOMMY: I want to go home and make love to you.

NEDDA: Tommy!

TOMMY: Fuck the movie. Unless you want to do it right here on the street. I feel much better about it now that your name's not Fred.

NEDDA: Answer me!

TOMMY: I think maybe I want everything.

NEDDA: That's impossible.

TOMMY: I know I want you.

NEDDA: You've already got me.

TOMMY: Now do you want to make puñetas with me or go to the Waverly?

NEDDA: I don't know what I want anymore.

TOMMY: I'm giving you a choice.

NEDDA: Puñetas *and* the Waverly.

TOMMY: In which order?

NEDDA: *(Opening her purse.)* Get a paper.

TOMMY: I don't need that. I'm surprised you didn't leave it on the table for Ataturk.

NEDDA: Aren't we ever going to pay for anything?

TOMMY: Not if I can help it.

NEDDA: What about the movie?

TOMMY: We'll walk in backwards.

NEDDA: Tommy!

(He goes. Nedda stands a moment, looks at the money in her hand, makes a face, makes a decision and goes back into Howard Johnson's.)

TOMMY: That's how Nedda Lemon ended up in the Women's House of Detention. When I came back with the *Post*, she wasn't there. I looked up and down Sixth Avenue for her, everywhere, even that crummy paperback bookstore. There wasn't a trace of her. And then there was a police car in front of Howard Johnson's and there was Nedda getting into it with two policemen. No wonder I couldn't find her. The last place I would've looked for Nedda was back in Howard Johnson's. *(Calling off.)* Come on, Arnold, let's go visit Nedda.

NEDDA INCARCERATED

TOMMY: Nedda!

NEDDA: *(Off.)* Tommy!

TOMMY: Nedda.

NEDDA: Are you there?

TOMMY: Yes!

NEDDA: *(Appearing at another stage level.)* I can't see you!

TOMMY: I'm down here! On the street!

NEDDA: I can't see you!

TOMMY: It doesn't matter! I'm here! What happened?

NEDDA: I went back!

TOMMY: Why?

NEDDA: To pay him!

TOMMY: Pay him?

NEDDA: It didn't seem right!

TOMMY: It didn't seem what?

NEDDA: Right!

TOMMY: That was dumb!

NEDDA: He wouldn't even listen to me!

TOMMY: I said that was dumb!

NEDDA: He just called the police!

TOMMY: How are you?

NEDDA: I hate it here!

TOMMY: I know!

NEDDA: I hate it a lot!

TOMMY: I'm sorry!

NEDDA: I just hate it!

TOMMY: Did you hear me say I was sorry? How are you?

NEDDA: How are you?

TOMMY: I'm fine!

NEDDA: And Arnold?

TOMMY: He's right here! He says hello!

NEDDA: And Ben?

TOMMY: Unh, fine.

NEDDA: Hunh?

TOMMY: He's fine! Everybody's just fine! *(To audience.)* We were just sitting in the Automat, Ben and me, having a cup of coffee when this awful rattle sound started coming out of him. It was awful trying to get him out of there or anyone to help us. Don't ever be old and sick and poor in this town. Just don't you ever.

> *(The lights have come up on Ben.)*

BEN: They don't like that.

TOMMY: He was just sick, ol' Ben was, you know? And they were asking for deposits like.

BEN: Admittance fees, they're called admittance fees.

TOMMY: Jesus Christ, Jesus Christ, Jesus Christ.

BEN: Finally Tommy got me into Bellevue.

TOMMY: After I told the nurse on admissions I'd personally take that stethoscope and ram it down her fat dumb throat if she didn't let Ben in.

BEN: He meant it, too, and she knew he did.

TOMMY: He's been there ever since on the critical list. They put him in a ward with ten other old men on the critical list. Nice. I'll come again tomorrow.

BEN: That's okay.

TOMMY: You can count on it. I still want to hear about you and Paul Muni.

BEN: Tom.

TOMMY: What?

BEN: I never knew Paul Muni. Any of those people.

TOMMY: Sure you did.

BEN: No. I was a vagabond, gypsy, third-rate barnstormer. I had a lot of fun, but that's all I was.

TOMMY: I don't believe you.

BEN: It's off my chest. You can believe any damn thing you want.

TOMMY: You and Paul Muni, right down the line.

BEN: If you say so.

TOMMY: Don't die on me, Ben.

BEN: Who said anything about dying?

TOMMY: What are you laughing at?

BEN: You in that *Kumquats* show! Green stripes, feathers, one line and you tripped!

TOMMY: Hey, take it easy, Ben! You're not supposed to laugh.

BEN: Who says? Now beat it! I'll see you tomorrow. You and *Kumquats!* Hey, kid, walk in backwards and they'll think you're coming out! *(The lights fade down on Ben.)*

TOMMY: He died at 7:51 A.M. this morning. I wasn't there. Peacefully, they said, when I telephoned. He died peacefully. But I think they have orders to tell everyone that. I mean, did you ever call a hospital and they said the patient died violently?

NEDDA: Give him my love!

TOMMY: He's just fine! He sends you his love! And I'll get you out of there, too! I'll blow the place up if I have to, but I'll get you out!

NEDDA: I called my father.

TOMMY: Hunh?

NEDDA: He's flying in.

TOMMY: What did you do that for?

NEDDA: I want to get out of this place. I'm sorry!

TOMMY: Don't you trust me?

NEDDA: It's not like that!

TOMMY: What is it then? I thought we were in this together! *(Pause.)* Well say something! Nedda! Nedda!

NEDDA: Maybe you better take your things out for a while!

TOMMY: Yeah, sure.

NEDDA: I mean…!

TOMMY: Don't worry about it!

NEDDA: You know…!

TOMMY: Sure I know! *(More to himself.)* Fuck! *(Pause.)* Am I going to see you? Nedda! Nedda!

(The lights are fading on Nedda. Tommy gives up, goes to Arnold.)

TOMMY: What did she have to call her father for? You wouldn't do that on me, would you? Chin up, Arnold, I'll think of something. Shit! *(Lights down on Tommy.)*

TOMMY'S BIG BROTHER

TOMMY'S BROTHER: You've got the right idea, Tommy. Don't get married. Don't ever get married. Take it from your big brother: he's been there and back. I wish to hell I had a telephone number for you. All I've got is a page of crazy "care of's." I really need to talk to you. I'm putting Charlie into a military academy. I feel like hell about it but I just don't have the time or patience for him anymore and Rita is no help at all in that department. You remember Rita. She's my wife. We're married. It might interfere with her golf lessons at the club. Or her sleeping around. She does, Tommy. I know it. Jesus Christ, I've practically caught her in bed with some of the sons of bitches. The dumbest move I ever made was not taking your advice about heading north for awhile before settling down. Now I'm so settled I couldn't move if I wanted to. I guess I never really took the time to find myself. I envy you up there, footloose, single, no responsibilities, laying everything in sight if I know you. You've got my number. Call collect, if that's the problem. I just want to talk to you. I'm very down. I did something terrible to Rita last night. She didn't want to make love. She lets me get on top of her but she never wants to make love. Well last night I didn't feel much like making love myself, so I just grabbed her by the hair and got going at her like she was just some flesh. I wanted to hurt her that way. You know. Then I made her take me in her mouth. She would never do that for me. She said that was what whores did and I said I know. Afterwards we just looked at each other a long time. She didn't say anything. She knew. I love you like hell, Tommy, but you're never around. No one is.

(The lights come up on Tommy in a telephone booth.)

OPERATOR'S VOICE: I have a collect call for anyone at this number.

TOMMY'S BROTHER'S VOICE: Where's the call from, operator?

OPERATOR'S VOICE: New York City.

TOMMY'S BROTHER'S VOICE: I don't know, Rita! Who's calling, operator?

OPERATOR'S VOICE: Your party wishes to know who's calling, sir.

TOMMY: No one.

OPERATOR'S VOICE: I can't hear you, sir.

TOMMY: Tell him no one.

TOMMY'S BROTHER'S VOICE: Hey, Tommy! Tommy, is that you, Tommy?

OPERATOR'S VOICE: Do you wish to accept charges, sir?

TOMMY'S BROTHER'S VOICE: You're damn right I do!

OPERATOR'S VOICE: Go ahead, New York.

TOMMY'S BROTHER'S VOICE: Hey, Tommy, old man! What's this "no one" business? I—!

(Tommy hangs up.)

CALIFORNIA DREAMIN'

(A young girl, 16, 17 years old tops, has entered and been watching Tommy. Her name is Bunny Barnum and she carries a map and a camera. Obviously Bunny Barnum is from out of town. Also, she is a knockout. Fantastic legs and tan.)

BUNNY BARNUM: Hello. My name is Bunny Barnum from Tarzana, California, outside of Los Angeles? It's where Edgar Rice Burroughs is from, he wrote *Tarzan*, that's why it's called Tarzana and I'm here for five days with my high school civics class on our annual "Know America" trip, the Tarzana Kiwanis Club and American Legion post are sponsoring us, and everyone else is taking that Circle Line boat trip around the island right now except me; I snuck off, and I believe that people should really try to talk to one another and I'd like to talk to you. *(She's already taken Tommy's picture with her Instamatic camera.)* You're a hippie, aren't you?

TOMMY: *(Dazzled.)* Oh wow!

BUNNY: That's okay. We have hippies in Tarzana, too. Mildred Miller's taken LSD three whole times.

TOMMY: She has?

BUNNY: It made all her hair fall out. I bet you smoke marijuana, too.

TOMMY: I do, miss, I most surely do.

BUNNY: I don't. I think people who smoke marijuana should be electrocuted.

TOMMY: You do?

BUNNY: Oh yes. My parents started turning on—my daddy's a nuclear physicist, he was born in Mannheim, that's in Germany, but I was born in Tarzana and he's a naturalized American now; my mother's a real Okie, ugh!—anyway, they were stoned half the time, real heads, the two of them, and they were growing their own stuff right in the backyard and so I turned them in. Citizen's arrest. Here. You look poor. How old are you?

TOMMY: Your parents were electrocuted for growing pot?

BUNNY: No! They were just busted! What's the matter? Wax in your ears? How old are you?

TOMMY: Thirty.

BUNNY: Thirty? You're thirty? Yikes!

TOMMY: *(Pleased.)* I know.

BUNNY: Drugs, hunh? You should see what Cubby Dodge looks like. A real wreck. I hate her. Do you mind if I say something? You're too pale. It's against the law practically to be that pale in California. Why don't you go to California? Too poor, hunh? I'd hate to be poor. I couldn't stand it. I'd probably have another nervous breakdown.

TOMMY: How many have you had?

BUNNY: *(Dismissing this.)* Just one! How many does it look like?

TOMMY: Oh, no more than that certainly.

BUNNY: I was Student Council recording secretary, head cheerleader and going steady with Rusty Winkler all in one semester! No wonder I flipped. Boy, I'd hate to live in New York City. Do you know how to surf?

TOMMY: Oh sure.

BUNNY: Randy Nelson is from Tarzana.

TOMMY: He is?

BUNNY: You don't know who Randy Nelson is? From what rock are you under? He's the world champion seventeen-year-old surfer. I'm supposed to be going with him. He's on the boat, looking for me probably. But I just had to ditch him today, you know? He's got fantastic knobs on both knees. He may even need surgery.

TOMMY: Knobs?

BUNNY: From surfing, dolt! We're reading Shakespeare on the bus and dolt's a very big word with everybody right now. Dolt, varlet, and bared bodkin. Have you ever taken a bus from California to New York? It's a drag. I told Mrs. Burmeinster, our chaperone, do you believe it? that if she didn't make them do something about the restroom I was going to call my father collect.

TOMMY: What would you like Mrs. Burmeister to do?

BUNNY: Bur*mein*ster. It's filthy in there. Please, can we change the subject? Thirty years old! I can't believe it. Yikes, that girl looks like Connie Nugent when she had both legs! Talk about resemblances! *(Calling off.)* Connie! Connie Nugent! *(Shrugs.)* You never know. Boy, I'd love some tacos and a chocolate milk shake right now. Mmmmmm! With French fries. I used to have pimples. Acne practically. I couldn't go anywhere. Ecch! What's the matter?

TOMMY: Connie Nugent when she had both legs.

BUNNY: Oh that! She was my brother Fritz's fiancée and they were driving home from somewhere, Disneyland, I think, and they had this terrible accident and they cut off Connie's leg. That girl looked just like her. Listen, stranger things have happened, right? Donna Barr lost the tip of her nose in a refrigerator door and they sewed it back on and all she has is a teen-tiny bump right there. Granted, it was a freak accident but *still*. Big Sur! They were coming back from group encounter in Big Sur.

TOMMY: Connie and Fritz?

BUNNY: Right. I almost lost my faith in God when that happened. But then I realized Fritz would have had to marry her and who wants a one-legged sister-in-law? I don't mean that cruelly, believe me, that is not a vicious remark. I'm just being realistic.

TOMMY: Then he didn't marry her?

BUNNY: Of course not! He was killed! That's why I almost lost my faith in God! It's true, people *don't* listen to one another.

TOMMY: I'm listening to you, all right, only I'm having trouble following you.

BUNNY: Drugs again, hunh? Boy, I'd love to see your chromosomes under a microscope! I bet they're really bent.

TOMMY: That's the most erotic thing anybody's ever said to me.

BUNNY: Erotic! Don't get me started on that!

TOMMY: On what?

BUNNY: Smut. I'll talk your ear off. There was a man in Tarzana we found out was making pornographic movies.

TOMMY: Let me guess: citizen's arrest.

BUNNY: We burned his house down.

TOMMY: We...?

BUNNY: The Hi-Y's. This stupid girls' club my mother made me join. Coke parties, slumber parties, swimming parties, the whole schmear.

TOMMY: I don't suppose there's any chance we could continue this conversation somewhere else?

BUNNY: There's a very big one. I hope that's not your dog. I hate dogs. I'm allergic to them, as a matter of fact. If I'm fucking someone, pardon the expression, who's been even near a dog in the past six months I break out in hives. Isn't that a crazy thing to be allergic to?

TOMMY: Dogs?

BUNNY: Yes, dogs. Of course, dogs. How could anyone be allergic to fucking? They'd have to be a freak or something. *(Breaks off, points.)* There's one! Will you look at that? One thing we *don't* have in Tarzana is queers. Unless you count Trevor Sloane, but he must be close to 90. He uses a cigarette holder and wears Capezio ballet slippers to work. I hate him. *Now* what's the matter?

TOMMY: I think you said the magic word.

BUNNY: You mean f-u-c-k? There's a reason. Notice I haven't used a single other bad word. I hate bad words, they sicken me, I actually vomit. But I also think the word *love* is the most overworked word in the English language. You hippies have just ruined it. I love chocolate ice cream, you love bull fights, he loves abalone sandwiches, we love pedal pushers, they love Hawaii. Everything is love nowadays. I can't stand that. I'm sorry but that word is just too sacred to me to throw it around like that. F-u-c-k is something else. At least I can look a boy in the eye when I say it. I mean, just ask yourself, how could you and I make love? I don't even know you. But I can f-u-c-k you.

TOMMY: You have a point.

BUNNY: What time is it? We're giving a concert tonight in Collegiate Marble Church, wherever that is. If I miss that one, too, I'll really be in Dutch.

TOMMY: Who's giving the concert?

BUNNY: We are, my civics class. What did you think, it's all fun and games? Hah! We're also a chorus. The Tarzana Youth Tones present "Up, America, Up!" It's this sort of musical pageant we do in different churches. It's supposed to help pay for the trip or something. Not that any of us ever sees a penny from it. Oh well, it's for a good cause and I like the theme. I think people who don't like America should be electrocuted, too, don't you?

(Tommy dumbly nods, hypnotized by her bosom.)

BUNNY: Of course in California we only have gas chambers. When I was co-chairman of our Decent Teens club I got to go to Las Vegas. They shoot people in Nevada. I mean they have a real firing squad. Isn't that gruesome? What are you staring at? Oh that! Who wears a bra anymore? I'd have to be Doris Day or something. I hope you live around here.

(Tommy only nods.)

BUNNY: Now what?

TOMMY: You're a very desirable person, Bunny.

BUNNY: *(Shrugs.)* I guess.

TOMMY: Very desirable and very terrifying.

BUNNY: Terrifying? Me? Go on!

TOMMY: Terrifying.

(He takes her by the arm and they start moving off.)

BUNNY: I'm glad that wasn't your dog.

TOMMY: Me, too; me, too.

BUNNY: *(Pointing.)* There's another one. This town is crawling with them. I'd hate that a whole lot. Hey, I don't even know your name!

TOMMY: It's Cohen, ma'am, Leonard Cohen.

(They are gone. Stage lights fade except for pin spot on Arnold, left there on his leash.)

ARNOLD'S SPEECH

ARNOLD: I didn't always have Tommy Flowers and I'm not at all sure I always will. I got him when I was given back to him by a friend of his who didn't want me after Tommy had given me to him in the first place. It's complicated, I know. This friend was a very lonely sort of person and Tommy decided that he should have a dog. Only he didn't want a dog. But when he saw me something inside of him must have snapped because his eyes kind of filled up like he was going to cry and he held me very close. I was this big then! And he didn't say anything and he walked a few feet away from everyone and stood with his back to them and just held me like a little baby. No one had to ask if he wanted me. You could just tell. I was so happy. But the next morning he didn't want me at all. There I was, just kind of slumped in my box, all droopy-eyed and warm-nosed and not looking at all too hot. Puppy chill is all it was. Tommy said they'd just take me to the vet but the friend didn't want a sick dog. He didn't want any dog. And you know what his reason was? They die on you. That's what he said. They die on you. We do, you know. Everything does. But is that a reason? How could anyone not want me? Oh, don't get any ideas. I'm not a talking dog. I'm a thinking one. There's a difference! *(Lights out on Arnold.)*

ANOTHER QUIET EVENING AT HOME

TOMMY: *(Appears with a towel—the American flag—around his waist.)* This is going to take a little longer than I thought. It must have been those banana splits she insisted on in Howard Johnson's because this is a highly irregular condition for me to be in. I've done it with real dogs, mercy fucks, and had less trouble.

BUNNY: *(Off.)* Mark!

TOMMY: And she is so gorgeous with all her clothes off, this Bunny Barnum creature is! Maybe that's it. Maybe I ought to put her in high stiletto heels and chase her around the bed a while.

BUNNY: *(Off.)* Mark!

TOMMY: Maybe I ought to put myself in high stiletto heels!

BUNNY: *(Off.)* Hey, Mark!

TOMMY: Mark? Oh shit, that's me! I switched it to Mark Rudd. She hasn't heard of him either. *(Calling off.)* What, Bunny?

BUNNY: *(Off.)* You want me to come in there?

(Tommy is rolling a joint.)

TOMMY: No! Stay right where you are!

BUNNY: *(Off.)* Well hurry up!

TOMMY: I'm sorry but I couldn't do it out here with you people watching. Bunny could probably; hell, she'd love it, but not me. That's the way I am. But here, I want to show you something. It's—

(Sounds of someone trying to play a cello and badly, too.)

TOMMY: Bunny, please, don't touch that.

BUNNY: *(Off.)* It's so big!

TOMMY: It's a cello.

BUNNY: *(Off.)* It's still so big!

TOMMY: It's a Stradivarius! *(To audience.)* Nedda's cello. She'd shit.

(Music has stopped.)

TOMMY: Thank you! Go back to bed! I'll be right in!

BUNNY: *(Off.)* You want to bet? What are you doing in there anyway?

TOMMY: Resting!

BUNNY: *(Off.)* From what?

TOMMY: *(Letting it pass, to audience.)* Start that argument with a chick and you'll never get it up. But here, I was going to show you something. *(He is coming down into the audience.)* This business about people not being able to communicate, I just don't buy any. Everyone's got at least one true story in him if you're just willing to listen. You, sir, would you mind coming with me? I'm kind of busy right now and I could use a little help. Out here, wise guy, I could use a little help *out here!* Christ! Give one a spotlight and he turns into Lenny Bruce! I'm only kidding. Will you? Thanks.

(Tommy leads a man from the audience back up onto the stage.)

TOMMY: Buy someone a drink, it doesn't have to be real booze, a beer even, a total stranger, and see what you get for your sixty cents. People love to talk. What's your name?

(Man answers.)

TOMMY: The last time I was home, *(Name of man.)*, I was hitching back East through our Great Southwest when I stopped off in this little roadhouse and saw this woman sitting alone at the bar. I dug her, not sexually, but dug her. She looked like she was waiting for someone to buy her a beer. She didn't look like a hooker. Oh no. She just looked like she wanted a beer. I bet she's still there.

(Lights coming up on Woman in Sunglasses sitting on a bar stool.)

TOMMY: I told her I'd buy her that beer if she'd tell me a true story. She didn't even hesitate.

WOMAN IN SUNGLASSES: Lou! Hey, Lou, make that another Falstaff!

TOMMY: What did she have to lose? We were total strangers. I'd never see her again. You'll never see her again either.

(Tommy has sat the man from the audience on a stool next to the Woman in Sunglasses.)

TOMMY: Hi. Remember me?

(Woman shakes her head.)

TOMMY: About six years ago?

(Woman shakes her head.)

TOMMY: Do you know my friend?

(Woman shakes her head.)

TOMMY: Tell him your true story and he'll buy you a beer.

WOMAN IN SUNGLASSES: Hey, Lou, make that *two* bottles.

(Bunny appears.)

TOMMY: Hey!

BUNNY: Are you sure that wasn't your dog? I'm breaking out.

TOMMY: Those are goosebumps, Bunny, good old-fashioned goosebumps. I'm covered with 'em myself!

BUNNY: What's that?

TOMMY: A therapeutic cigarette, doctor's orders.

BUNNY: I hope it works.

TOMMY: In there, Bunny, in there! *(To audience, indicating the flag around his waist.)* Many a bum show has been saved by the flag. George M. Cohan, showman, 1919.

(Bunny squeals delightedly as Tommy takes her offstage. The lights come down except for necessary playing area for scene that follows.)

(We hear a jukebox playing. The Woman in Sunglasses has been served by now. She pours herself a glass of beer. The man from the audience will be sitting next to her. She begins to speak now.)

A TRUE STORY

WOMAN IN SUNGLASSES: This is a true story. When I was a sophomore at Moodus King Senior High School in Crystal City, Oklahoma—it's about twenty-eight miles north of Norman, Oklahoma—there was a beer joint on the outskirts of town called the Javelina Club where they would sell five-point beer to minors. On weekends they had live music. I was going with this man then and we'd hit the Javelina Club nearly every weekend. He was a lot older than me and divorced but I wasn't exactly any Grace Kelly and my father had run off and we were real poor and my mother and me didn't get along and the garage apartment we lived in was real tiny and at least he got me out of there and was somebody to talk to and he must have thought I was a little pretty or why else would he take me out every weekend, 'cause I didn't let him go all the way with me for a long long time. Anyway, this story ain't about him. One weekend they were presenting a new young singer at the Javelina Club and his name was Elvis Presley. That's right, Elvis Presley, the same one, appearing at a little beer joint outside o' Crystal City, Oklahoma, but only he was real young then and just beginning. Lots of big name performers got their start in little beer joints like the Javelina Club I bet. I don't guess he was pulling down more than ten bucks a night and he only performed Friday and Saturday nights and what they called the Sunday afternoon matinee. Anyway, this story ain't about money either. Elvis was so beautiful then. I wish you could have seen him. Certainly he was one of the most tremendous talents I ever heard. He had this natural way of singing about things that was really special. I can't tell it too well but I do know I'd never heard anyone sing like that before Elvis and the things he would sing about were realer than other people, too. In some ways Elvis was better then, at the Javelina Club, than later on when he became so famous. There was a wildness then that made the audience wild, too, not like the Beatles and the way they made those little kids scream, we were older and I guess more mature, you know what I mean? and this wildness just kind of went from Elvis to the audience—just back and forth like that the whole time he was singing. That part of Elvis is kind of gone now it seems. Unless maybe it's just that he's older or I'm older or everybody's older. I don't know. *(Short pause.)* Now here's what this story's about:

Some nights this man I was going with would get really drunk and then he'd turn real surly and violent-like and he'd just be looking for a fight. The night I first heard Elvis Presley was one of those nights and next thing you know he was accusing me of staring at Elvis, you know, like I was attracted to him, and I told him to just hush and I could look at anybody I wanted to in any way I wanted to and I wasn't staring at Elvis in any special way no how and so then this man he started making these real loud sarcastic comments about how Elvis was dressed and his long sideburns and ducktails and his suede shoes and pink suede belt and how punks who wore their hair and clothes like that were no better than greasers, you know, Mexicans, and that hoods like him just better high ass it out o' town if they just knew how generally unpopular they was. Now while he was saying all this the whole place was going wild over Elvis and nobody was paying this man any heed at all. Finally he got so mad and futile-feeling he got up from the table and tried to get near Elvis who was up on this little stage sort of thing and all the while he kept making these real loud ugly comments and then he took like a swing at Elvis only he was so drunk and Elvis was so high above him that he just spun around and fell right down. Everybody noticed him then and they all started laughing, and most of all ol' El himself who kept right on singing, too, so that the whole Javelina Club was rocking and laughing all at the same time. This man I was with got to his feet, came over and grabbed me out o' there by the arm so hard I said he was hurting me. Boy, was I mad at him! It wasn't even near closing time. I told him to go to hell and I never wanted to see him again. I guess he knew how mad I was, too, 'cause he didn't try anything with me all the way home. That Monday as soon as school let out I went to the record shop with my best friend, Roberta, and I asked if Elvis Presley had made any records yet and they looked him up in this big catalogue of every record ever made and he wasn't in there. I tried describing him to Roberta, how he sang and moved and how cute and sexy and handsome he was, only it wasn't like seeing him or hearing him for real and we both guessed we'd never hear Elvis Presley again unless he got famous and started making records 'cause there wasn't anybody in town who was about to take us to the Javelina Club that coming weekend. The next Saturday I was getting ready to go to the movies with Roberta when he pulls up, this man I was going with, just like nothing had happened and acts real surprised that I'm not ready to hit the Javelina Club, business as usual. So I called up Roberta and told her my mother was sick and changed into my best clothes. As soon as we got into the car he started sneering 'bout how he knew I couldn't resist another look at my new lover boy sensation and I just sneered right back that I didn't care if Minnie Pearl was appearing at the Javelina Club, I just wanted to go to the only place in the country where I could hear me some live music and get served some five-point beer. We was fighting about Elvis just like last week and we hadn't even got there yet! When we did, the place was packed like I'd never seen it. I guess word about how tremendous Elvis was had gotten out. It was like a football game the way everybody was pushing and shoving to get a table or a better view or closer to the stage or dancing room. I'd never been in a crowd just listening to rock and roll like that all in a group. It was strange 'cause even though it was the crowd that made being there so exciting, you also felt like you were the only person there—an audience of one, just you and Elvis and the music he was playing for you. It was like a dream but it was real, too, you know what I mean? I guess I vaguely remember this man I was with excusing himself for a while and going outside where the cars were. But I do remember that when he came back he was real sweet and didn't seem at all jealous of Elvis or anything like he was the week before. He even offered to buy Elvis a beer when he walked by our table after the first show. I didn't get to meet Elvis then but he looked at me and kind of smiled and I felt real funny. Well sir, we stayed for the second and third shows, too, and this man I was with was on his very best behavior, hardly got drunk at all, and next thing you knew it was 2 A.M. closing time and they turned on these real bright lights to hustle everybody out of there and we were all outside in the parking lot and there was this crowd gathered around this 1954 chopped-back white Cadillac Coupe de Ville convertible with Tennessee plates. It was Elvis's. The windshield had been smashed in with a brick, the tires were all slashed, the canvas roof had been tore open, the hood was up and there was distributor wires hanging out all over the place, there was red paint all over the customized white leather seats and on the door on the driver's side somebody had painted Memphis Grease Ball. People were just staring at it, like when there's been an accident. This man I was with said, "Aw gee, who'd do a thing like that?" and from the way he said it I just knew he'd messed up Elvis's car when he went outside that time. Pretty soon Elvis himself came out and he saw this crowd and then he saw what somebody had done to his car and I guess he didn't have any real friends there 'cause none of the guys said anything to him and none of the girls could and pretty soon everybody just started drifting away to their own cars without nobody saying a word and Elvis was just staring his tore-up white Caddy and I said to the man I was with couldn't we give him a ride and this man he sneered "Hell no" and I felt like yelling out "Hey Elvis, I know who messed up your car" only I was scared to 'cause this man could be violent to me and just then the owner of the Javelina Club came out and he was talking to Elvis and you could tell that he was going to give him a ride back to wherever Elvis was staying. On the way home I told this man that now I *really* never wanted to see him again, and that if I ever saw Elvis I would tell him what he'd done and then Elvis would tear him apart just like he'd done Elvis's car. He kept denying it but I wouldn't shut up and pretty soon he hit me and I slapped him right back and then he hit me again only really hard this time and now I was really scared and I didn't say anything to him the rest of the way home. I never saw that man again. The very next day I was downtown and I saw Elvis driving a Ford pickup that somebody must have loaned him until his own car got fixed. And then two days after that I was driving my mother to the hospital where she worked and there was Elvis hitchhiking and he had a suitcase so I knew he was leaving town and I wanted to stop for him but my mother said no, I couldn't pick up any hitchhiker and she would be late for her shift and besides, what was I, some kind of a whore? I practically started crying I wanted to be with him so bad. Well, sir, I dropped her off at the hospital and tore ass back to where I'd seen Elvis. He was still there! When I pulled over he looked kind of surprised that a girl had stopped for him but he asked how far I was going and I said quite a way and he said fine and he got in beside me and he was real polite and didn't act at all the way he looked which *was* hoody but in a handsome way and we drove a long time and he didn't say much and all the time I was hoping he'd touch me so bad I couldn't stand it anymore so finally I told him I knew who he was and that I'd seen him at the Javelina Club and how tremendous I thought he was and he told me he was on his way back to Memphis to cut two sides for a small company called Sun Records (these are the same records RCA Victor heard and immediately signed Elvis up to an exclusive contract and then he recorded "Heartbreak Hotel" for them and six weeks later he was nationally famous) and then I told him I knew who had tore up his Cadillac and he said he was gonna be so rich and famous some day he'd have twenty Cadillacs and he'd never have to play in a dead ass town like Crystal City, Oklahoma, again and that was why he was leaving this one there. He didn't talk for a while after saying all that but then I guess he realized how much I was hoping he would touch me 'cause he started asking why I'd stopped for him and where exactly and just how far was I going and I got confused and flustered and started blushing and he asked me if I wanted him to drive and I said yes and he took the wheel and without saying anything he just turned off the main road onto this little dirt road and we followed it a long while until finally we stopped in the shade of this mesquite tree and he kissed me and started feeling me all up and he had his hands everywhere and he was undressing me now and we were in the back seat of my mother's pink and white Ford Fairlane with the chrome dip in the door and I can tell you Elvis was the best person I've ever made love with and we did things I didn't know people *could* do and most people don't and since him it's never been like that with anyone and I never thought I would say this, I never thought I would think it even, his cock was beautiful.

It was thick. I can still feel it inside me. I can still feel it inside my mouth. After we'd come, we were just kind of lying together there in the back seat when all of a sudden a pickup truck with this colored family in it was on top of us and the man and the woman could tell what we'd been doing and they both looked at us and just started laughing and then we started laughing back at them, too, and for a minute it was a very happy and human and innocent thing between the four of us with their two children just staring wide-eyed at us like we was all crazy. Then the truck and the colored people was gone and we was alone on this dirt road and we got dressed and drove on back to the main highway and Elvis said to let him off there, he was okay, and it was getting late and I'd better head back to Crystal City, Oklahoma, with my mother's Ford Fairlane car and he would send me a postcard from Memphis and a copy of his Sun Record when it came out. He never did but that's okay, too. I followed his career, of course, couldn't help *but* he got so famous, and for a while I kept a scrapbook on him that got yay big in no time there was so much being written about him and so many pictures everywhere and all, and I'd see his chopped-back white Cadillac Coupe de Ville convertible every so often being driven around by a Mexican boy with lots of pimples and really tacky clothes which made me real mad at first. About two years later Elvis was in Norman, Oklahoma, giving a one night concert at the downtown civic auditorium and I remember the ticket prices were way high. "Not like the old days at the Javelina Club" was the standard, boring comment. I sat up in the balcony with the boy I was engaged to. Later on, when I was home again and we'd been drinking beer all night, I tried to call Elvis but the hotel wanted to know who was calling or no calls were going through and "just say an old friend who wonders if he has twenty Cadillacs yet" wasn't good enough and they just pulled the plug on me and I felt so stupid. Six months later I married the boy I was at Elvis's concert with and then my mother died and we had two girls, Jeanette and Maurine, and after a while I didn't see Elvis's white Cadillac or the Mexican boy around town anymore and then we got a divorce 'cause Billy started drinking and couldn't hold a job down anymore and everything got to be a mess and now the girls and me are living in the Chateau Normandie Apartments and I'm working part-time as a checker at the Food Fair over at the Hill N' Dale shopping center and I'm gonna marry this carbonated beverages salesman from near Tulsa as soon as his divorce is final and then I won't have to work anymore he says. He don't like me working now as a matter of fact but it's better I told him. The last time one of Elvis's movies played in town I didn't even go see it. Jeanette, my eldest, she's thirteen, Jeanette did and she said Elvis looked fat in it. (*Pause.*) Well, that's my true story. Thanks for the beer.

(*From offstage there is a shrill scream: it is Bunny Barnum.*)

WOMAN IN SUNGLASSES: Lou.

(With a nod and a wave, the Woman in Sunglasses gets off the bar stool and exits, leaving the man from the audience sitting there. Again that shrill scream of Bunny Barnum's. Tommy runs on, the American flag still around his waist.)

TOMMY: I gave her a joint. Just one little joint. I thought it would help. And bingo! Just like that, she went bonkers! It wasn't even good stuff.

BUNNY: *(Off.)* I hate you! I hate you!

TOMMY: This is terrible. Bunny, please, stop that!

BUNNY: *(Off.)* I'll kill you, Phil! I'll kill you!

TOMMY: Phil Ochs. *(To man from the audience.)* You'd better go back to your seat. Come on. I'm sorry about this.

BUNNY: *(Off.)* Let me in there! Let me in!

TOMMY: Look. She did that. With her nails. I don't know what came over her.

BUNNY: *(Off.)* I said let me in!

(Tommy is going into the audience as he takes the man back to his seat.)

TOMMY: I'm on the john!

BUNNY: *(Off.)* I'm warning you, Phil, I really mean it this time!

TOMMY: Does anybody want to take a naked seventeen-year-old nut with a body like *you*-won't-believe-what-it's-like-either-who'll-think-you're-Bob Dylan-if-you-tell-her-you-are off my hands?

BUNNY: *(Off.)* Are you going to let me in there or not?

TOMMY: No!

BUNNY: *(Off.)* Why not?

TOMMY: I don't know!

BUNNY: *(Off.)* I hate you!

TOMMY: That's one good reason!

BUNNY: *(Off.)* I'll kill you.

TOMMY: That's two!

BUNNY: *(Off.)* So let me in there!

TOMMY: Why? Why do you want to kill me?

BUNNY: *(Off.)* You know what you did! You know what you did!

TOMMY: I didn't do anything! That's when the trouble started. It's all my fault, Bunny!

BUNNY: *(Off.)* You know what you did!

TOMMY: Please, just go away! I'm sorry about the whole thing!

BUNNY: *(Off.)* You know what you did!

TOMMY: Go back to your hotel!

BUNNY: *(Off.)* No!

TOMMY: Go give your concert! "Up, America, Up!," quick, Bunny, before it sinks!

BUNNY: *(Off.)* No!

TOMMY: Then go back to Tarzana! You think I give a shit?

BUNNY: *(Off.)* Faggot!

TOMMY: I was waiting for that.

BUNNY: *(Off.)* Queer!

TOMMY: It's not the first time.

(Sounds of a car driving by.)

VARIOUS VOICES: *(Speeding by.)* Queer! Fairy! Fruit! Faggot!

TOMMY: *(Yelling after them.)* Fuck you, too, you goddamn rednecks!

BUNNY: *(Off.)* Cocksucker!

TOMMY: Got you, Bunny! That's a bad word. Now go ahead and vomit.

BUNNY: *(Off.)* I'll give you three!

TOMMY: Three what?

BUNNY: *(Off.)* One!

TOMMY: My name's not Phil Ochs!

BUNNY: *(Off.)* Two!

TOMMY: It's John Lennon!

BUNNY: *(Off.)* Three!

(Silence.)

TOMMY: Bunny? Bunny? What's she doing in there? I'm not taking any chances. This scratch hurts like hell.

(Sounds of a car driving by: in the opposite direction this time.)

VARIOUS VOICES: Fruit! Pansy! Faggot! Queer!

TOMMY: Up yours, you no-dicked mother-fuckers!

(The voices and the sound of the car have faded away.)

TOMMY: The only guy I ever went to bed with was my best friend, Gareth Linsley. I had a big crush on James Dean when I was in high school, who didn't then? but Gareth Linsley is the only guy I ever actually did it with. I mean as a grown-up. I'm not counting circle jerks, first-one-to-come everyone has to give a quarter. I mean Big League, both eyes wide open, the age of innocence is past homosexuality. I'm not ashamed I did. Things like that happen, you know? All the time. I think Gareth was already queer when I met him in college. I mean I didn't make him that way. Whenever we'd go to a whorehouse or sneak girls into the dorm I think he was screwing them just to keep me from knowing about him. Looking back, I can't imagine he ever really liked it.

(Sounds of the car driving by again.)

VARIOUS VOICES: Queer! Fruit! Faggot! Fairy!

TOMMY: *(Yelling after them.)* Fuck you, you Nazi cocksuckers!

(Sounds of the car braking to a halt.)

TOMMY: We both came to New York and went our separate ways. I thought it was strange at first, your best friend not wanting to see you anymore, but after a while stories started trickling back and I knew the reason why.

(Sounds of a car door slamming.)

TOMMY: But then one night we ran into each other and started drinking and talking and Gareth said why didn't I come over, his roommate was out of town, so we went there and drank some more and pretty soon Gareth was telling me what I'd already heard. He was a queer.

(Some men have entered.)

TOMMY: Hello. *(Continuing, to audience.)* He told me the guy he was living with was his lover. I remember how he said the word. Lover. I'd never heard a man use that word about another man before.

ONE OF THE MEN: His what?

TOMMY: His lover. *(Continuing, to audience.)* He said we couldn't pretend to be friends unless I knew about him and I could leave now if he disgusted me but he was glad he'd told me no matter what happened between us. It was something he'd wanted to tell me for years.

ONE OF THE MEN: What was?

TOMMY: That he loved me, Gareth Linsley did. *(Continuing, to audience.)* And how he'd loved me ever since he'd first met me and how really I was the only person he'd ever loved and how I'd always be his best friend even though we hardly saw each other and our lives were so different that he had never, never tried to have sex with me because it would have ruined our relationship, which was true, and certainly he would never try it now that I knew about him and how he would still think of me when he masturbated and now that I knew everything could we please change the subject. And we did.

ONE OF THE MEN: What did he think of when he did that exactly? What part?

TOMMY: He didn't say. I didn't ask him. *(Continuing, to audience.)* We didn't completely change the subject. Every so often I'd ask him if it were true if so-and-so or x, y, z were queer, like I'd heard, and he'd answer yes or no or just laugh, like I was some kind of hick for even asking, which, I guess, I was at the time. I mean everybody in New York knows about Benjamin Franklin, right?

ONE OF THE MEN: Right

ONE OF THE MEN: What about that actor, you know, what's his name?

ONE OF THE MEN: And that politician! You know who I mean.

TOMMY: Their names didn't come up. *(Continuing, to audience.)* And then I asked about one name too many and Gareth got mad at me, said I was insensitive and what did I think he was? Information Please? and told me to leave.

(The men have moved in quite close to Tommy now. There is a sinister, menacing circle closing in on him, in fact.)

TOMMY: I couldn't blame him. *(Continuing, to audience.)* About four hours later, after I'd left him and gone to another bar and gotten really drunk, I went back to his place. To this day I still don't know why.

ONE OF THE MEN: *(Giving Tommy a shove.)* Sure you do, fruit!

TOMMY: *(Standing his ground.)* No, not really. *(Continuing, to audience.)* Gareth let me in, he was half asleep, and I said could I stay there? and he mumbled yes and pointed to the sofa and staggered back to bed. I waited a little while in the dark living room and then I took all my clothes off and stood outside his bedroom door. I could hear him breathing. Gareth Linsley breathing. And after a while I went in and lay down beside him. He didn't wake up. I didn't move for a long time.

ONE OF THE MEN: *(Another shove.)* How long was that, faggot?

TOMMY: Ten, fifteen minutes, I don't know. It seemed like forever. *(Continuing, to audience.)* And then I put one arm around him.

(The first blow is struck. One of the men has pinioned Tommy's arms.)

TOMMY: And then another. I was hugging him now.

(Another blow.)

TOMMY: And then I touched his cock.

(Smack!)

TOMMY: It was soft but after a while it got hard and so did mine...

(Smack!)

TOMMY: ...and then he was awake and turning to face me...

(Smack!)

TOMMY:...and I kissed him...

(Smack!)

TOMMY:...and then all at once we were making love...!

(Smack! Tommy's voice is rising.)

TOMMY:...only I didn't know what to do...!

(Smack!)

TOMMY:...I felt so clumsy and I wanted to please him...!

(Smack!)

TOMMY:...and I took his cock...!

(Smack!)

TOMMY:...and I guided it in me...!

(Smack!)

TOMMY:...and it was hurting me...!

(Smack!)

TOMMY:...and he was going at me! Like I was just flesh! I could have been anyone! Just going at me! Going at me! Going at me!

(Smack! smack! smack!)

TOMMY: And I hated him for that!!

(The men release Tommy. His face is a bloody pulp. Hideous.)

TOMMY: When it was all over he said didn't I want to come, too? and I said no and so we just lay there on the bed in the dark not touching now and I was thinking what I'd tell him when he asked me why I'd done that when he started snoring and I realized Gareth Linsley didn't love me at all.

ONE OF THE MEN: You didn't like it, faggot?

TOMMY: No. Too messy, you know?

> *(He smiles crookedly. Much blood but unafraid. One of the men knees him and he goes down.)*

ONE OF THE MEN: What did you say, queer?

TOMMY: I said, too messy, you know?

> *(The man kicks Tommy. This time he doesn't move.)*

ONE OF THE MEN: Now, *you* know, fruit! *(He kicks him again.)* Let's go.

> *(They start moving off.)*

ONE OF THE MEN: Is he dead?

ONE OF THE MEN: *(Taking Tommy's picture with a flash camera.)* Don't he wish! Don't you, scumbag, hunh, don't you? *(He gets his final kicks in.)* Hey, wait up!

ONE OF THE MEN: Where's Lino?

ONE OF THE MEN: Where do you think, asshole!

ONE OF THE MEN: Okay, Barry, okay. Just asking.

> *(They are gone. Sounds of car doors opening, then closing and the car driving off. Tommy raises his head.)*

TOMMY: Fuck you, you slimey mother-fuckers! Fuck you once, fuck you twice, fuck you three whole times! We're gonna bury you! *(Then, resuming, to audience, sitting up.)* And so I got dressed, went out and walked around until the sun came up, which wasn't very long, had bacon and eggs at Riker's on Sheridan Square and never saw Gareth Linsley again. *(He is speaking with some difficulty.)* About three years ago and at least five years after that night, Gareth stuck a German Luger in his mouth and pulled the trigger. Awful. I would never do that. Too messy, you know? *(A crooked, broken smile.)* But Gareth did. She lost her head, Miss Linsley did. I forget who said that. Some wag. I didn't feel any responsibility at all for Gareth's self-slaughter. Enormous and profound grief but no responsibility. When I heard they were flying his body to Dayton, Ohio, for the funeral it kind of bothered me. I'd always remembered him as being from Allentown, Pennsylvania. His family must have moved. I didn't attend. About a year later I saw the lover coming out of a gay bar, the one on West 10th Street, at least somebody told me it was him, and I almost said something to him. When someone you...*knew*...yes, when someone you knew does that to himself, you wonder a lot, ask yourself all sorts of questions. But I never felt responsible. *(Again, that crooked, broken smile.)* Too messy, you know?

> *(There is a timid knocking sound.)*

TOMMY: What is it?

BUNNY: *(Off.)* Can I come in now?

TOMMY: Go away.

BUNNY: *(Off.)* I'm all right now.

TOMMY: No.

BUNNY: *(Off.)* Please, Phil.

TOMMY: My name isn't Phil.

BUNNY: *(Off.)* I don't care what your name is.

TOMMY: It's Tommy Flowers and I blow things up.

BUNNY: *(Off.)* That's okay. Please, Tommy! I promise I'm all right now.

TOMMY: It's open.

> *(Tommy starts toweling himself off, his back to Bunny who enters. She looks almost catatonic. There is a straight-edged razor in her hand.)*

BUNNY: *(Seemingly unaware of the razor in her hand.)* See how calm I am? I mean I feel really peaceful now.

TOMMY: *(Always with his back to her as he wipes and dabs at his face with the towel.)* That's nice.

BUNNY: *(Quiet exaltation.)* Wow!

TOMMY: Just go soon, hunh, Bunny, please? And I'm very sorry about the entire episode. It was all my fault: the lack of performance, the dope, everything. I don't want you thinking it was you. You're a regular knockout; I'm the dud.

BUNNY: That stuff you gave me, I don't know, it gave me a nightmare like terrible things were happening. That's why I started screaming.

TOMMY: Don't worry about it.

BUNNY: I don't hate you.

TOMMY: I'm very glad to know that.

BUNNY: And I don't want to kill you either.

TOMMY: You're making my day.

BUNNY: Wow!

TOMMY: Now why don't you start to think about leaving? I don't want to rush you. Just ponder it a little.

BUNNY: Okay.

TOMMY: Good girl.

BUNNY: They killed me.

TOMMY: You're not concentrating, Bunny.

BUNNY: They raped me, then they killed me.

TOMMY: Think about leaving.

BUNNY: All sorts of people. White and brown and yellow and red. Some were real big and some were real little.

TOMMY: And they were all leaving for somewhere, weren't they, Bunny?

BUNNY: They wanted to get at me and there was no place to be safe from them. I knew I was in New York City but at the same time I was in Tarzana, too, and there was no way to keep them out.

TOMMY: So you left. That's what you did, Bunny, you left.

(As she speaks, she is standing behind Tommy and describing imaginary circles in his back with the straight-edged razor. He doesn't see this.)

BUNNY: I was in my pretty pink bedroom with my posters and pennants talking on my pink Princess telephone to Stephanie Lawrence. She's a cheerleader and was voted Most Likely To Succeed three years in a row. I like her. She's my best friend. And then all of a sudden the line went dead and I looked up and saw a whole bunch of them looking in the window at me.

TOMMY: *(Turning.)* I'm going to have to shower, Bunny.

BUNNY: *(Concealing the razor.)* They shouldn't have been there. No one should've been there. They were standing on our pretty bushes.

TOMMY: Sure they were.

BUNNY: I screamed and ran into our living room and there were all these people.

(Tommy has gone into the shower. Sounds of water running.)

BUNNY: White and brown and yellow and red strange people walking on our nice clean rugs, sitting in our pretty new chairs, watching our color television. Like pigs they were.

TOMMY: *(Off.)* Be sure you don't run any water while I'm in here. It's an old building and the pipes are shot, okay?

BUNNY: *(She's given up trying to reach Tommy now.)* And there was my father lying on the floor and his throat was all cut and my mother was all bloody and crying over him and my little brother, they were hurting him, too, and so I ran into our kitchen and there were more strange people making a terrible mess on our tables and sink tops and they were into our refrigerator, eating our food and frying things on our stove, cooking things and spilling grease and our maid Nana was in there and I told her to stop and she just laughed and slapped me in the face and told me that she was one of them and that they belonged there as much as I did and this was how things were going to be now and I didn't live there anymore and they were going to put me in a concentration camp and feed me pig slop and let the men do things to me for the rest of my life and then she slapped me again and I ran back into our living room and there were these men holding momma down on her avocado green rug now and her skirt was up and then one of them saw me and said: What about the girl? She's a finer piece than the old bitch mother! and they started chasing me and I ran into the garage and there were all these people sitting in our cars, running the engines and working the windshield wipers and the electric windows and honking the horns and playing the 8-track stereo tape decks and the noise and the smell in there was just terrible and the people in the cars started chasing me, too, and I ran out into our yard and there were people pulling up our pretty bushes and chopping down our lovely trees and then there were all these horrible little children in our filtered swimming pool and they were swimming and splashing and peeing in it too, and the only place left I could run to was Nana our maid's little cottage and I went in there and locked all the doors and the windows and turned off all the lights and waited and prayed to God and cried and then I found this knife.

(Sounds of water being turned off.)

BUNNY: But there was no way to keep them out. The doors and the windows and the walls and the roof just started coming in. Nothing broke.

(Tommy reappears, starts drying himself off.)

BUNNY: It was more like something was pressing in on them. Squeezing them closer and closer together until I would be trapped and crushed in there and all I had was this knife and they kept pressing in on me and then the walls and the ceilings and the windows and the roof got so squeezed in on me I couldn't move anymore and then I was dead.

TOMMY: Hey, Bunny, I'm getting dressed. Time to go now.

BUNNY: And then when I was dead, they raped me, all of them did, and they threw my body into our swimming pool, the horrible little children were still playing in it, just like nothing had happened, and as I sank to the bottom I saw my father and my mother and my little brother and our color television set and our furniture and our appliances and my mommy's mink stole she wears to the country club dances and my daddy's barbecue pit and my little brother's horse books and my pink Princess telephone, nearly everything we ever owned, in fact.

TOMMY: Let's go, Bunny, let's go!

BUNNY: And there we were, my entire family and all our earthly possessions at the bottom of the deep end of our nearly Olympic size swimming pool and our faces started rotting and our fingers, the skin on them was kind of flaking off and up at the top you could still see the little white and brown and yellow and red legs of the terrible little children just kicking and splashing away as happy as could be.

TOMMY: Come on, Bunny, get your clothes. I've got to split.

BUNNY: And then the sharks and the eels and the octopuses started coming and the sharks were tearing at my daddy's and my little brother's faces, taking big bites, and they started looking like skulls and this horrible octopus had my mother in his tentacles and was squeezing her right into his fat, pulpy head and the eels were all wrapped on my arms and legs and holding me down and I couldn't even get my knife to stab at them anymore.

TOMMY: Where did you leave them? Which room? Shit! *(He goes.)*

BUNNY: And everybody was dead except for the white and brown and yellow and red people swimming in our pool and living in our house.

TOMMY: *(Off. A furious sound.)* Hey! Hey!

BUNNY: Everybody in America dead except for the white and brown and yellow and red people anymore. *(Like a child fascinated with a new toy, she is slashing at her wrists with the razor.)*

TOMMY: *(Off.)* When did you do this?

BUNNY: Everybody dead.

TOMMY: *(Off.)* You goddamn little bitch! You vicious little bitch! You even smashed her cello for Christ's sake!

BUNNY: My daddy said the reason nothing works in America anymore is because all the inferior people are making them. In Germany that wouldn't be allowed to happen. High technological achievement goes hand in hand with high technological accomplishment in Germany, my daddy said.

TOMMY: *(Entering.)* What's the matter with you? Are you crazy? You destroyed her whole apartment, everything in it, you stupid little bitch!

BUNNY: They swam in our pool. Everybody dead now.

TOMMY: Answer me!

(Tommy goes for her. Bunny slashes at him with the razor and draws some blood.)
Give me that!

(Tommy grabs her wrist, takes the razor, sees the blood on her wrists, realizes what she's doing.)
Oh my God!…When?…Oh my God!

BUNNY: Don't spank me, don't spank me. I want my daddy!

(Bunny has slipped to the floor in a sitting position. Tommy runs to the window and calls down.)

TOMMY: Hey, you, mister! Please! Get an ambulance up here! Don't keep walking! You hear me! Turn around and look at me! Don't walk away from this! You goddamn heartless bastard! May your soul rot in hell! Lady, please! An ambulance! The phone's out! *(Answering her.)* The phone's out. I didn't pay the bill. Please. Thank you. The fifth floor. God bless you. Hurry!

(He goes back to Bunny, speaks as he rips the flag in half and tries to stop the bleeding by bandaging each wrist.) What are we doing to ourselves? Bunny, Bunny Barnum from Tarzana, California, you're not going to die on me, girl. Stay awake, look at me. You've got to keep your eyes open until they come. Can you do that, Bunny? Will you do that for me, girl?

BUNNY: I can't.

TOMMY: You've got to.

BUNNY: I'm sleepy.

TOMMY: Look at me then.

BUNNY: I want my daddy.

TOMMY: He's coming.

BUNNY: When?

TOMMY: Soon, very soon, Bunny. Keep your eyes open and he'll be here.

BUNNY: Tell me a story.

TOMMY: *(Hugging her fiercely.)* Okay, okay.

BUNNY: Everybody's dead.

TOMMY: No, Bunny, nobody's dead. That's what the story's about. Everybody's alive. That's the good news today. Everybody's alive. The sun is out so bright today you can hardly stand it. Blue skies and good air just like they used to be. Green grass and flowers, a day for going barefoot.

BUNNY: I'm barefoot.

TOMMY: You should see the park today. That's where we're going. Why it's just filled with wonderful happy people on a day like today. Everybody's alive today. Open your eyes, Bunny, and see the park all filled with people.

BUNNY: White and brown and yellow and red?

TOMMY: All sorts, all sizes.

BUNNY: No, everybody's dead now. I don't believe you.

TOMMY: They're in the park, Bunny, I can see them and they're all alive.

BUNNY: What are they doing?

TOMMY: Laughing and singing and playing games and riding bicycles and having picnics and dancing.

BUNNY: Dancing?

TOMMY: Sure they are!

BUNNY: There's music?

TOMMY: Wonderful music! Free music! One old man is doing a beautiful Greek folk dance all by himself. Maybe he was born there even, in Sparta or Crete, who knows? But there he is in our park now, Bunny, and he's dancing for us. Can you see him?

BUNNY: No.

TOMMY: I see him.

BUNNY: You do?

TOMMY: You have to want to see him!

BUNNY: I do.

TOMMY: All right, then there's a middle-aged couple dancing a tango under the copperwood trees. And right nearby two kids are dancing the Lindy. They're so young. Somebody must have taught them. Maybe it was the middle-aged couple. People do that.

BUNNY: The Lindy?

TOMMY: A very old dance.

BUNNY: I like the name. It's funny.

TOMMY: I like it, too.

BUNNY: Can you do it?

TOMMY: Unh-hunh.

BUNNY: How come?

TOMMY: Because I'm very old myself. I'll teach you.

BUNNY: That's nice.

TOMMY: I promise.

BUNNY: Tell me more story.

TOMMY: Okay, so everybody is alive, the park is full of very happy people, and you know what? They love one another, Bunny, all these people love one another, or anyway they're sure trying to love one another.

BUNNY: Love?

TOMMY: Sure there's love, I know there's love, I can feel there's love. See it, hear it, touch it, taste it. The love of those people in the park is so big it could swallow you up if you're not careful.

BUNNY: And nobody's dead then?

TOMMY: No, nobody. Everybody is alive and loving in that park and that's how the world is and how it's going to be or else nobody's going to want to be in it and most of all me.

BUNNY: That's not a story.

TOMMY: Then you weren't listening. It's the only story I had for you, the only one I know. Believe it, girl. I do.

BUNNY: I guess.

TOMMY: Bunny. Bunny look at me.

(There is a knock.)

TOMMY: In here! *(To Bunny.)* It was a true story, Bunny, you just didn't stick around long enough to find out how true it really is.

(Tommy kisses her very tenderly on the forehead and moves quickly away, like a fugitive, from that particular playing area. Lights down on Bunny as two ambulance attendants enter.)

TOMMY'S WALK

(During this sequence we will see and hear pictures and music indicative of the violence of the reality that is pressing in on Tommy. His actions, by contrast, are to ignore these sounds and images by literally blotting them out by everything he says or does. He seems determined to stay "loose" in the face of everything.

Pictures on the screens: muggings, knifings, murders, riots, accidents, arson and lots of hostile, angry faces. Among them and in contrast, we see an occasional face that will be familiar from earlier in the play: Greta Rapp, Ben, Nedda Lemon, Bunny Barnum, and so on. The music we hear is hard, aggressive, driving rock. The Stones' "Street Fighting Man" would be perfect.

From now until the end of the play, all the actors will double, triple, quadruple if necessary as various Pedestrians on the streets of New York. Also, the tempo of the sequence will grow faster and more breathless as Tommy draws closer to his final destination: Greenwich Avenue outside the Women's House of Detention.)

TOMMY: *(Panhandling.)* You got any spare change? Thank you, sir, thank you very much. *(To another Pedestrian.)* Hello. *(Blocks their path, offers the money.)* Here.

PEDESTRIAN: No, thank you.

TOMMY: It's money.

PEDESTRIAN: I don't want it.

TOMMY: It's not mine. It's his.

(Pedestrian sidesteps him.)

TOMMY: He doesn't want your rotten money either!

(He throws the coin in the air and walks on. Two people scramble for it.)

Excuse me, sir, but I think you're a very handsome man and I just thought that you might like to know that's what I thought. *(Gives the man a big kiss on the cheek.)* Trick or treat, lady. No, I mean that! I need bus fare. I'm desperate for bus fare. I'll do anything for bus fare except leave you alone. I'll follow you home, sit on your doorstep and you won't be able to go out for months. Thank *you! (Tommy is on a crowded bus.)* Excuse me, do you have the time?

PASSENGER: It's ten after four.

TOMMY: It's later than I thought. *(To another Passenger.)* Hello. Guess what? It's ten after four. It's later than you think. Pass it on. *(In a very loud voice.)* The new flic at the 8th Street Playhouse is a real stinker! Don't say nobody told you! Getting off! *(He jumps off the bus.)* Doesn't anybody want to take in a down-and-out anarchist and his lovable mutt for the night? I do dishes but I don't do no woodwork! *(Darting towards a woman.)* Miss Taylor! Miss Taylor! Could I have your autograph, Miss Taylor? You're not Elizabeth Taylor? Oh go on, you are, too! I'm terribly sorry. You look just like her.

(He dances wildly. People look at him.)

I love the world! I love the world! It's what you've done with it I can't stand! *(Dashing off.)* Mr. President! Wait for me, Mr. President!

LAST SCENE

(The music grows gentler. On the screens we see pictures of Nedda and Arnold at each side and the Women's House of Detention in the center.)

TOMMY: Arnold? Arnold!

(There is no sign of Arnold or his leash even around the parking meter.)

Hey, did you see a dog? A big scruffy dog? I left him tied up here just a little while ago. Arnold, Arnold! Did anybody see my dog? Here, boy, here! *(Sighs, stands hands on hips, looking up and down the avenue, then shrugs.)* He'll be back. *(Calling up to the Women's House of Detention now.)* Nedda! Nedda!!

VOICE: Fuck you!

TOMMY: No, you don't mean that!

VOICE: Fuck you, I don't mean that!

TOMMY: Tell her it's me, lady. Tommy, Tommy Flowers.

VOICE: Fuck you, too, Tommy Flowers!

TOMMY: Where is she? Where's Nedda?

VOICE: Fuck Nedda!

TOMMY: I've got to talk to her!

VOICE: Fuck talking to her!

TOMMY: I've got to tell her what happened!

VOICE: Fuck what happened!

TOMMY: Tell her I'm sorry!

VOICE: Fuck being sorry!

TOMMY: Tell her I think maybe I love her.

VOICE: Love!

TOMMY: Yes, love! That's what it's all about, lady!

VOICE: Fuck love! Fuck everything! Fuck you!

TOMMY: Nedda!!! *(Silence.)* Arnold!!! *(Silence. The streets are empty now.)* That's one thing about Arnold. He'll come back. He always comes back if you just wait for him.

(The stage lights come down very fast and suddenly it is night. There is a pin spot on Tommy who sits, waits and rummages in his red paper shopping bag. The rest of the stage is quite dark and deserted except for the pictures of Nedda, Arnold, and the Women's House of Detention on the screens above.)

I can wait. It doesn't end here. Tomorrow's another day. I'll meet another girl if I want to, get another dog if I have to. Sometimes they're the same thing. People like me, we just go on. Actually, I wouldn't mind calling home collect tonight and seeing how everybody is. *(Finds a magazine in the shopping bag.)* The June 1954 issue of *Photoplay*. A picture of Debra Paget on the cover. Anybody interested? *(He sails it into the audience.)* Travel light, brother. Read it in good health and then pass it right on.

(One other, and one only, light has begun to come up in the theatre. It is another pin spot. This time on a man seated in the middle of the audience. He is very elegantly dressed in theatre clothes, maybe even an opera cape and top hat. We should not be able to take our eyes off him or what he is doing: assembling a rifle in full view of the audience.)

TOMMY: All this talk about America being on the eve of some revolution, I don't understand it. The revolution is now. I mean it's already started. Do all of you know how to make your own bomb? It's easy. *(As he takes the necessary materials out of his red shopping bag.)* You start with something to put the bomb in. A cigar box will do. And then you need dynamite. And ordinary flashlight batteries. And some wire. And an alarm clock. That's all. Now watch how I do this. *(As he works on the bomb.)* It's a remarkably safe avocation. You'd be surprised. They don't have a clue who we are. Did you see the paper yesterday? That projected profile of a revolutionary? It was supposed to be me. A lot of psychological garbage about how screwed up my glorious childhood was and how rotten my parents were, them, those two sainted angels! And how I had feelings of inferiority that were now manifesting themselves in antisocial aggression, which is both untrue and rhetorically redundant. And my politics, it said, were probably influenced by a left-wing professor under whose tutelage my impressionable mind was easily swayed. Tutelage. That's a *New York Times* word if ever I heard one. Tutelage your own horn, Mr. Sulzberger. My politics! I have no politics. I am my politics. *(He waves at the man in the audience assembling the rifle.)* Hello. I said hello. *(No response. Tommy puts his new bomb in his shopping bag.)* One thing I was really looking forward to was going to a concert sometime and hearing Nedda play. I had it all planned how I would get a seat where she could see me and all during the concert I would try to get her to laugh. It wouldn't have been difficult. She's easy to make laugh. I could just tell her to look me in the eye, even when she was mad at me, and try to count to ten without breaking up. Ten? She couldn't even get to three! *(Suddenly and from the gut.)* Nedda! *(It is increasingly apparent that Tommy knows what is going to happen.)* And I had another great plan for her. Even better. Nedda hated birds. I mean she'd see a pigeon in the park and get hysterical. Well she was going to be playing with a group in Central Park this summer and I was going to throw birdseed on the stage. That way the birds would come. Lots of them. I guess I could still do it, only I don't guess she'd think it was funny now. *(Another cry from the gut.)* Arnold! *(To audience.)* Well, like I said, there's more girls, more Arnolds. The only reason that dog wouldn't come back to me would be if someone had done something terrible to him. I've actually heard about people who go around dog-napping. Can you imagine stealing someone's dog? Even worse, there are people who walk around feeding stray dogs poisoned meat. *(To the man in the audience assembling the rifle.)* It's true! They caught one two weeks ago on Avenue C. An old Armenian woman. And did you know it's against the law for a waitress in a New York City restaurant to serve you if she's not wearing a hair net? That's another plan on my Free Eats Program. Well who wants somebody's hair in their food? You see? You and me, maybe we're friends after all! *(Tommy starts slapping on black face.)* I start my new job tonight. Another one night stand. *(He pats the shopping bag.)* Louise T. Coxe. Yassuh, boss, yassuh, that's me, ol' Louise T. A maid on the night shift at the General Motors Building. $1.10 an hour and carfare. Yassuh!

(The man in the audience has finished assembling the rifle and is beginning to take aim.)

You don't have to do that. Hey, don't point that thing at me, man. I don't have my magic bracelets on.

(Two wild cries.) Nedda!!! Arnold!!! *(Suddenly out front, directly to audience, as he begins his coin-dropping tap dance.)* Has anybody here ever fainted on the grand staircase at Radio City Music Hall with a box of popcorn in their hand? That's something else I wanted to show you. *(Coins fall.)* Thank you, sir, thank you! *(He keeps on dancing.)* It's a terrific sensation. If you get enough momentum going, you can start on the balcony level and make it all the way down to the main floor. *(More coins.)* God bless you, madame! *(He dances.)* And then when there's a big crowd around you, you pretend to come to and say it was the movie and half of them start looking for the manager to get their money back before they've even seen the flic. *(More coins.)* Thank you! Thank you!

(BANG! BANG! BANG! BANG! BANG! BANG! Six shots. Tommy's body jerks with each of them in the dance of death. The man in the audience with the rifle is on his way out of the theatre.)

You didn't have to do that. No sir, you didn't have to do that at all.

(The man is walking up the aisle now.)

Don't you even want to talk about it even?

(The man keeps right on walking.)

Walk out backwards and they'll think you're coming in!

(The man is gone. No trace of him.)

Hey, Nedda!

(Tommy's voice is very weak now. The picture of Nedda is extinguished.)

Come on, Arnold, come on, boy!

(The picture of Arnold is extinguished.)

Hey, no fair. I didn't have my magic bracelets on. *(He slumps a final time.)*

VOICE: Fuck you! Fuck everybody!

(With a final gesture, Tommy gives back her finger and dies. And at once there is another explosion and the three screens above the stage are filled with a huge photograph of the American flag. Peter, Paul, and Mary singing "Where Have All the Flowers Gone?" would be ideal. Pedestrians are crossing the stage. Back and forth, back and forth. A man in a raincoat takes pictures of Tommy with his flash camera. It starts to rain. People put up umbrellas. Arnold enters on the leash of a stranger. He licks Tommy's face until he is pulled away. Nedda walks on by and doesn't notice. So does Greta Rapp. Soon the stage is empty. It continues to rain. Thunder and lightning. The Showgirl enters in a raincoat and carrying an umbrella. She is obviously in a hurry.)

SHOWGIRL: God forbid we should ever be twenty years without a rebellion. Thomas Jefferson, 1787. Thank you and good night. *(She exits rapidly through the audience.)*

ANNOUNCER'S VOICE: The management of this theatre has asked me to remind you that flowers for the artists will be accepted at the stage door only and must not be thrown onto the stage. Thank you.

VOICE: Marilyn? Marilyn, honey!

(The special light comes up but there is no Marilyn this time.)

CUBAN ACCENT: She's beezy! She's very, very beezy!

MARILYN'S VOICE: Oh wow! I sure am! Later, honey, much, much later!

(We hear her giggle and the special light is gone. The Black Stagehand has entered and stands looking down at Tommy.)

BLACK STAGEHAND: Where Has Tommy Flowers Gone? The end. *(He picks up the red shopping bag with the bomb in it and smiles hugely at us.)* Shee-it!

(He shuffles off. The bag and the bomb are his. The stage is bare. Special spot on Tommy. Three loud explosions. With each blast, a portion of the flag is extinguished. Smoke. Darkness. The play is over.)

END OF THE PLAY